T0330221

Liberty and Equality in Political Economy

NEW THINKING IN POLITICAL ECONOMY

Series Editor: Peter J. Boettke, *George Mason University, USA*

New Thinking in Political Economy aims to encourage scholarship in the intersection of the disciplines of politics, philosophy and economics. It has the ambitious purpose of reinvigorating political economy as a progressive force for understanding social and economic change.

The series is an important forum for the publication of new work analysing the social world from a multidisciplinary perspective. With increased specialization (and professionalization) within universities, interdisciplinary work has become increasingly uncommon. Indeed, during the 20th century, the process of disciplinary specialization reduced the intersection between economics, philosophy and politics and impoverished our understanding of society. Modern economics in particular has become increasingly mathematical and largely ignores the role of institutions and the contribution of moral philosophy and politics.

New Thinking in Political Economy will stimulate new work that combines technical knowledge provided by the 'dismal science' and the wisdom gleaned from the serious study of the 'worldly philosophy'. The series will reinvigorate our understanding of the social world by encouraging a multidisciplinary approach to the challenges confronting society in the new century.

Titles in the series include:

Liberty and Equality in Political Economy

From Locke versus Rousseau to the Present

Nicholas Capaldi

Legendre-Soulé Distinguished Chair in Business Ethics, Loyola University, New Orleans, USA

Gordon Lloyd

Senior Fellow, Ashbrook Center, and Dockson Emeritus Professor of Public Policy, Pepperdine University, USA

NEW THINKING IN POLITICAL ECONOMY

 Edward Elgar
PUBLISHING

Cheltenham, UK • Northampton, MA, USA

Published by
Edward Elgar Publishing Limited
The Lypiatts
15 Lansdown Road
Cheltenham
Glos GL50 2JA
UK

Edward Elgar Publishing, Inc.
William Pratt House
9 Dewey Court
Northampton
Massachusetts 01060
USA

A catalogue record for this book
is available from the British Library

Library of Congress Control Number: 2015959649

This book is available electronically in the **Elgar**online
Economics subject collection
DOI 10.4337/9781784712532

ISBN 978 1 78471 252 5 (cased)
ISBN 978 1 78471 253 2 (eBook)

Typeset by Columns Design XML Ltd, Reading

Printed and bound in Great Britain by
TJ International Ltd, Padstow, Cornwall

Contents

Acknowledgments

We begin by thanking Steven Ealy, Liberty Fund Fellow, who brought us together at a Liberty Fund colloquium. Steve recognized long ago the parallel nature, and we hope the complementary nature, of our thinking.

We owe Liberty Fund an enormous debt in that we have been able to participate in several hundred colloquia over several decades where we have had an opportunity to meet, learn from, and at times politely disagree with an extraordinary range of thinkers in many disciplines (the arts, classics, economics, history, literature, philosophy, political theory, religion, science, and so on). In retrospect, we realize that we have been part of an invisible university, a university in the true sense of the term. All this has been made possible by Charles King, William Dennis, Roseda D. Decker, Richard W. Duesenberg, Giancarlo Ibárgüen S., Joseph F. Johnston, Jr., Leonard P. Liggio, Mary A. O'Grady, Emilio J. Pacheco, Ben A. Rast, T. Alan Russell, Dane Starbuck, Chris L. Talley, Richard A. Ware, Douglas J. Den Uyl, Manuel Ayau, James F. Cote, G.M. Curtis, Hans L. Eicholz, Frederick J. Fransen, David M. Hart, G. Patrick Lynch, William P. Ruger, Sarah Skwire, Amy Willis, Mark Yellin, and Leonidas Zelmanovitz.

In 2011, we published *The Two Narratives of Political Economy* with Scrivener Press and Wiley. It was an anthology based on the same theme, namely, that Locke and Rousseau represent the two dominant and competing narratives in political economy. The anthology, with extensive introductions, ended with Marx and Engels. We were pleasantly surprised both by the success of the book and by the calls from scholarly users to expand the theme into the twentieth century and beyond. The present volume is an attempt to do so as a full length book and not as an anthology. We take this opportunity to thank Martin Scrivener not only for supporting the original publication but for giving us his blessing in incorporating those ideas into the present book.

We also want to thank APEE for holding a symposium on the original anthology, a symposium at which Jane Shaw, Randy Simmons, and Art Carden offered a highly gratifying and constructive critique. Roberta Herzberg and others who used the material in an early draft version provided us with additional useful comments.

During the Fall of 2015, Nicholas Capaldi conducted a small seminar using a draft version. Two students, Harrison Lempriere and John L. Rose gave him valuable feedback.

Last but not least we wish to thank our spouses, Nadia Nedzel and Angela Edwards, both because they have been our most severe critics and for the many hours of fruitful conversation on these topics.

Nicholas Capaldi and Gordon Lloyd

Introduction

RETRIEVING THE PAST IN LIGHT OF THE PRESENT

It will be useful to begin by telling you what this book is not.

1. This is not a history of political theory; this is not a history of economics; and this is not a history of political economy.
2. This is not a comprehensive summary of the main ideas of some main thinkers.
3. Nor is this a scorecard or ledger of prominent thinkers on an old debate.

What this aspires to be is a history, an evolutionary account of an ongoing *conversation* between two narratives or meta-narratives. To see this as a conversation is to dignify both narratives and not to prejudge them; it allows for the recognition of nuances. To see some of these authors and some of their works as part of a conversation is to bring a fresh perspective to the texts.

We are all aware that authors respond to their predecessors and contemporaries, and no account of a specific author can fail to ignore that. Just as important is the fact that some authors become seminal figures. We look back on their work in the light of how later authors have adopted and transformed what the earlier author has done. This enriches our understanding of the earlier author to the point where it is no longer possible to read the author in quite the same way. Original texts and their authors can become part of a larger conversation wherein the 'conversation' takes on a life of its own. We think the conversations are worthy of serious attention. We do not contend that these conversations have a teleology such that earlier authors are reduced to being seen as groping toward our favorite present formulation. Different elements in the conversation will wax and wane. We also wish to avoid the temptation to ignore intellectual dissonance. The dissonance may capture something about the human predicament that cannot be camouflaged by smug partisanship.

The other thing upon which we wish to insist is the importance of interdisciplinary work, hence the focus on 'political economy'. The academic world rewards those who know more and more about less and less. This says much about academics and academic institutions, but less about the world. All of the authors we discuss were exemplary multi-faceted individuals whose background, work, and engagement with the world of policy spanned a variety of disciplines.

NARRATIVES RATHER THAN ARGUMENTS

We call these narratives for several reasons:

It brings together things that frequently are treated by scholars in isolation, but for the canonical thinkers these elements were seen in relationships: philosophy, economics, political theory, religion, law, and culture.

Narratives tell a story, hence the requisite historical dimension. Narratives are also like paradigms in that they connect the dots, hopefully in a coherent and consistent way, and they structure our thought: what we regard as a serious issue, what constitutes evidence for and against, and how we respond to what does not fit. Narratives, like paradigms, also contain appeals to facts and arguments, but they are both more and less than an argument. They are less by not being as a whole themselves an argument. They are more by reflecting fundamental choices about how we engage the world, and they function rhetorically to try to persuade others to see and interact with the world in a new or different way. As such, they are not subject to routine refutation; they can only be countered or rebutted by a rival narrative.

We maintain that narratives are more important than arguments. However, in the world of scholarship, arguments have assumed a position of prominence. One of the results of that prominence is an endless stream of literature delegitimizing canonical authors. One begins to wonder how these authors achieved such prominence when they committed so many seemingly elementary mistakes. Nor is it clear why they have to be refuted repeatedly. Successful narratives get us to 'see' and engage the world in a new way.

Behind the prominence of arguments are several philosophical assumptions. The first is that a rational argument must eschew rhetoric because rhetoric appeals only to emotion. The second is that the structure of a good argument is a deduction from first principles, as in a geometrical proof. Once these principles are discovered and articulated it is further presumed that practice should adhere to the articulated structure. However important conceptual clarification is, such clarification never leads by itself to practical agreement.

This is not how either the human mind or the world works. In the real world, practice always precedes theory, and theory is the attempt to articulate or rearticulate what we take the practice to be in order to improve the practice or to replace one practice with another. Moreover, no one has ever successfully given us a theory of how practice and theory are related so that the final and definitively correct theory dictates all future practice. Admittedly, narratives frequently function as either *the* first principles, so to speak, or as side-constraints. But this still misses the function of narratives which is to get us to see the world in a new way. What rhetoric appeals to in a narrative is our imagination.

When dealing with canonical authors, arguments are important but of secondary importance to the narratives. Many authors we presume to be canonical were not primarily scholars. Scholars have 'academized' the writings of these authors. Many were, and saw themselves as, agents in the world. As such, they often sought to provide a rationale for what they believed or for the policies they were recommending or supporting. In short, they sought to 'rationalize' their engagement with the world. The term 'rationalize' is not being used here in a pejorative sense. As individuals, we often spend a great deal of time trying to articulate our intuitive grasp of the world. We may even reject or refine our own earlier articulations not because we lack the capacity for self-criticism but because self-criticism takes the form of trying to state self-consciously what we have been doing out of habit. We adjust, modify, or reject a previous conclusion but only because we are holding fast to other conclusions. In retrospect, we would applaud these authors for holding fast to their respective intuitions because they believe that they had fastened onto something very important.

An argument is an expression of an insight. It is not the insight itself. If a particular argument is inadequate, even in the eyes of the author, the author will look for or hope others will find a better argument. This is not necessarily a sign of intransigence but the sense that authors have that they are on to something important. This is a common experience outside of narrow intellectual circles.

Another feature worth noting is that successful narratives evolve. The Lockean Liberty Narrative, for example, evolved – Locke's articulation and defense of the narrative could not possibly have anticipated all the later responses and permutations. Rousseau's challenge to Locke became the basis for an ongoing conversation/debate. Hume and Smith responded to Rousseau. We see Smith as restating the original Lockean narrative in response to Rousseau – that is part of the evolution of the conversation. Smith's articulation differs from Locke's precisely because he was responding to Rousseau. We think it is important to note how each side uses the material from the other side, for example, how Marx utilizes material from Locke. We are not surprised that Hegel's work can give rise to both a 'left' and a 'right' wing.

Another instance of this evolution is the work of J.S. Mill. Mill has been interpreted, mistakenly we believe, by many as a socialist. This is an error in our view because Mill was trying to incorporate the discussion of the 'social question' (the issue of distribution) that the nineteenth century French Socialists had raised. What Mill offered was a new defense of the Liberty Narrative that incorporated both recognition of the criticisms and a new ('Kantian') understanding of freedom. Competition was defended not simply on grounds of efficiency (as in Locke and Smith) but because liberty was a means to freedom (Kantian autonomy). This is precisely the kind of thing that is likely to be missed by narrowly focused economists or even political theorists not versed in philosophy.

We do not claim that participation in this conversation is the only important thing in any particular thinker; nor do we deny that there are other authors involved in the conversation – our aim is not to be comprehensive but nuanced – we always ask: "Who adds what to the conversation?" This work is to be a history of the conversation between the two narratives and the contributions made by various thinkers in various disciplines. The focus is on the evolving conversation. As such it will focus on pertinent and relevant contributions and will not go into detail about other works by the participants – as significant as those works may be – if they do not pertain to the topic.

We do not claim that this is the only possible conversation; our claim is that this particular conversation has a long lineage and a continuing vitality that is worth articulating. In the *Cambridge History of Twentieth Century Political Thought*, Steven Lukes entitled the epilogue "The Grand Dichotomy of the Twentieth Century," and he rightly traced it back to the French Revolution; we trace it back to Locke, Rousseau, and the American Revolution along the way.

Recognizing the role of these narratives is useful to the public trying to come to terms with public policy debates. We are reminded of the words of Keynes:

> The ideas of economists and political philosophers, both when they are right and when they are wrong are more powerful than is commonly understood. Indeed, the world is ruled by little else. Practical men, who believe themselves to be quite exempt from any intellectual influences, are usually slaves of some defunct economist. (Keynes 2007, pp. 283–84)

Contemporary discussion takes on new meaning when seen against the background of evolving and competing narratives. We believe that readers as diverse as those who read Krugman in *The New York Times* or who listen when the Pope speaks about "equality" or who read the editorial page of *The Wall Street Journal* would benefit from understanding the larger context of those remarks and not simply think they are reading or hearing mere theology or economics or ideology.

Because our intention is to focus on the conversation/debate so construed, we shall keep references to secondary sources to an absolute minimum. Clearly we have benefited from the enormous secondary literature even when we depart from it. However, we wish the focus to be on the primary thinkers, to their engagement with one another, and on our fresh approach to them. On those occasions where we touch on selected themes that have been the focus of the secondary literature (for example, Locke's position on slavery) what intrigues us is the extent to which even the secondary literature reflects a subtle commitment to one side of the conversation or the other. That is, scholars themselves often reflect a Locke-inclination or Rousseau-inclination. This is not intended to disparage other scholars but to reinforce our claim that the ongoing conversation between Lockean Liberty and Rousseau Equality has become deeply embedded in our discourse.

1. John Locke and the Three Pillars of Liberty

ANCIENTS VERSUS MODERNS

It is customary to present histories in chronological order. We do not object to chronological order. In addition, some scholars have understood and presented the history of political thought per se as a debate between ancients (primarily Plato and Aristotle) and moderns. In itself this can be very insightful. It has, however, serious limitations. To begin with, it largely ignores or downplays the importance of economics, especially in the modern period. More to the point, it tends to privilege the views of the ancients, sometimes to the point of the distortion of the views of the moderns. We think that while modern thinkers may be illuminated by contrast with classical thinkers, we also think that modern thinkers are better understood in terms of their engagement with each other. This is why we begin the conversation with Locke rather than Aristotle.

As a general point of departure, we can contrast Aristotle's world view with the Newtonian world view. Aristotle's intellectual model was teleological biology. This translated into the belief that every entity had a purpose (telos) and this is what it meant to say it had a nature; the belief that the purpose of each entity fit within a larger net of purposes terminating in one hierarchical overall purpose; that the natural state of each object (Aristotle's physics) was to be at rest and that motion or original motion had to be explained; and that time was to be understood as an endlessly repeating cycle, which is why history is either unimportant or cyclical, and most certainly not evolutionary; and the belief that when applied to human beings the preeminent function was contemplation and serving a larger social purpose. The Newtonian world view was based on modern physics, wherein motion, not rest, was the natural state, and where the ultimate units were individual objects (later atoms) in endless motion without a telos, interacting/colliding with others. When this world view is extended to human beings, it came to mean that action (work), not contemplation, was fundamental, that humans are both a product of their natural drives along with the history and evolution of their previous interactions/collisions, and that in the absence of a larger social purpose, the challenge was to manage/minimize conflict.

John Locke (1632–1704) put the economic issue at the center of politics; taking economics out of the household and into the forefront of politics. The purpose of politics, says Locke, is the preservation and regulation of private property. The major consequences of this view are (1) a restructuring of the hierarchy of values, (2) economics becomes the purpose of politics, (3) the disappearance of public political virtue as the primary human objective and character building as the central political objective, (4) the substitution of labor for land as the central concept in economic thought, and with that (5) a reconsideration of the distinction between the 'deserving' and 'undeserving' rich. Aristotle would argue that the public good is greater than the sum of its parts. Not so Locke. Is there a public good or is it somehow a by-product? Answering this question helps us to understand the ideas that emerged over the next 300 years following Locke. According to Locke, we do not see the true nature of human beings in civil society. Human beings need to be 'unmasked' because, unlike Aristotle, Locke does not believe that human nature is revealed in a fully developed social condition (telos) but in its primitive condition (analogue to Newtonian laws of motion). We discover who or what human beings are by contemplating human beings in a natural/ primitive state. The modern rejection of Aristotle's organic conception of the world and its replacement by Newtonian physics requires a derivative intellectual reconceptualization of the social world. For example, Aristotle thought that usury was morally wrong, whereas Locke brought the concept of money into the marketplace. Thus individual liberty and materialistic concerns came to the forefront of life.

LOCKEAN LIBERTY NARRATIVE

The narrative can be summarized abstractly in terms of the following diagram:

$$TP \rightarrow ME \rightarrow LG \rightarrow RL \rightarrow CPA \rightarrow TP$$

TP stands for the technological project.
ME stands for the market economy.
LG stands for limited government (restraining government on behalf of individual liberty).
RL stands for the rule of law.
CPA stands for the culture of personal autonomy.

The ancients believed that there was an external, objective, and normative order in nature. This meant two things: human beings were obliged to use reason to discover that order and then to conform their behavior to it. The moderns will argue that order is an internal human construct and that we are obliged to transform the world to conform to that internally generated vision of order. This is the philosophical revolution known as the 'technological project'. The Lockean narrative is the assertion of the claims that the technological project, that is, the transformation of the physical world of nature for human convenience, functions best in a free market economy which, in turn, requires a limited government subject to the rule of law, and all of the foregoing operate best within a culture that promotes personal autonomy. Finally, the technological project is itself an expression of personal autonomy. Each of these concepts was articulated prior to Locke. So, for example, Descartes in the *Discourse on Method* (Descartes 1637) advocated our becoming "masters and possessors of nature." What is significant about John Locke was that he was among the first, if not the first, to articulate and endorse a coherent version of the entire narrative.

Locke was educated as a physician at Oxford where he also met Anthony Ashley Cooper, 1st Earl of Shaftesbury, subsequently becoming part of his retinue. Since Shaftesbury was a founder of the Whig movement (advocating parliamentary limits on royal power), Locke was drawn into politics. Locke was interested not only in political liberty but economic liberty and religious liberty as well.

At Ashley's urging, he prepared a paper in 1668 entitled "Some of the Consequences that are likely to follow upon Lessening of Interest to Four Percent" (Ashley 1692). This paper was a response to English mercantilists, for whom prosperity was a zero-sum affair, and who attributed the superior economic prosperity of their perceived rivals, the Dutch, to Holland's low rate of interest. The mercantilist solution was to urge the English government to reduce the rate of interest until it was lower than Holland's. Locke countered that England's national wealth did not thereby increase because a lower interest rate redistributed wealth from the lender to the borrower. Locke also held that the "value of money" was determined by the plenitude or scarcity of money. This implied that the purchasing power of money fell with the amount of money in circulation, where it would undercut savings and credit, thereby making the economy worse off. National wealth was the product of thrift as well as labor. Instead, Locke advocated the "natural" or the market rate as determined by the supply and demand for money at a given time. Locke later published this argument in *Some Considerations of the Consequences of the Lowering of Interest and Raising the Value of Money*

(Locke 1692). In the latter work he expanded his comments to include a critique of debasing coinage, warning that debasement is both illusory and inflationary. Ironically, the proper role of the government is to enforce legal contracts not to itself renege on the promise to ensure sound money.

TECHNOLOGICAL PROJECT

Locke's study of medicine reflected the seventeenth century emphasis upon health, which in turn, reflected two things: a specifically Protestant cosmology and what we have identified as the Technological Project! The cosmological role of God was summarized by R.G. Collingwood in his *The Idea of Nature* (Collingwood 1945). Renaissance science took its idea of God from the Bible. God is conceived of as a transcendent Being who created the world with human beings in his own image, and that created world is both knowable and benevolently disposed to human interests. During the Middle Ages, the Chinese were more advanced than the West in scientific matters, but the scientific revolution occurred in the West and not in China. In *Science and Civilization in China* (Needham [1954] 1984) Joseph Needham's explanation for this is that the Chinese lacked "the conception of a divine celestial lawgiver imposing ordinances on non-human Nature." To be sure, there was order in Nature for the Chinese, but "it was not an order ordained by a rational personal being, and hence there was no conviction that rational personal beings would be able to spell out in their lesser earthly languages the divine code of laws which he had decreed aforetime" (Needham [1954] 1984, p. 581). What the Chinese lacked was the Christian God. The Technological Project gave a new meaning to life. Instead of this world being a temporary residence, God commanded us to develop it. Martin Luther stressed that worldly work is a duty benefiting both the individual and society. The Catholic notion of good works was transformed by Calvin into an obligation to work diligently as a sign of grace.

In England during the sixteenth and seventeenth centuries, Protestants who followed Calvin became known as Puritans. Locke was a Puritan. The Puritans venerated work. God had intended us to work, and therefore had designed us so as to take pleasure in those things that required work. Good health is required for an active and useful life. Even knowledge, it was thought, originated in work with a practical import as opposed to contemplation. As an example of this view, there was in seventeenth-century England a vigorous expansion in medical studies. John Locke was part of that expansion.

God-inspired labor created something that was not already there, namely, new resources. These new resources constitute the theoretical defense of private property. This property, therefore, is a natural right given by God and does not require legitimation by government. Precisely because new property can be created there is no theoretical limit on accumulation. The only limitation is that we do not prevent others from a like accumulation. Unlimited accumulation does not operate in a zero-sum universe but in a theologically inspired conception of *creating new wealth* through labor. Locke also presumed that God created a universe in which our personal self-interest does not ultimately conflict with the interests of others. In fact:

> when his own preservation comes not in competition, [he] ought … as much as he can … preserve the rest of Mankind, and may not unless it be to do Justice on an Offender, take away, or impair the life, or what tends to the Preservation of the Life, the Liberty, Health, Limb or Goods of another. (Locke 1689, *Second Treatise*, #6)

Note the qualification, "when his own preservation comes not in competition," for it excludes attributing to Locke any form of collectivism, that is, sacrificing the individual without his/her consent to a greater social good. More importantly, we have an obligation to improve the material circumstances of others – but not through redistribution! Rather, the improvement of others is the result of our self-improvement.

In a potentially infinitely expanding economy, inequality of property is not a problem. A day laborer in England is better off than the richest king in Africa (Locke 1689, *Second Treatise*, #40–41). What becomes a social problem is the existence of those who choose to accumulate things without working (for example, theft, begging, and so on). Although Locke's argument was inspired by theological beliefs, once the Technological Project is recognized and articulated the entire argument can be held without a specific theological commitment. Later thinkers who prefer social science to theology will maintain that animals have a natural sense of territoriality. Critics of the Lockean narrative who also prefer social science will respond that the narrative leads to "social Darwinism." Other critics who prefer physical science will worry that humanity will eventually run out of resources. Defenders of the Lockean narrative will respond that human imagination is the greatest resource, that it will always come up with an alternative precisely because the price system in the market will incentivize them to do so. And so it goes. Nevertheless, there is at the heart of Locke's narrative a spiritual quest – what will evolve in the thought of others as the spiritual quest of modernity, the improvement of the human condition.

Labor does not create value except in a theological-metaphorical sense; what labor creates is a new resource or new property, even new kinds of property. The value of that property in economic terms is given a price, but the natural price is determined by supply and demand. Labor increases the supply of goods and services; the price of such is determined by demand as well as supply. Furthermore, the TP leads to the creation of "durable" goods. Human beings can now exchange their perishable goods for goods that would last longer. The introduction of money is the culmination of this process. This is consistent with the pursuit of happiness, contrary to what the Aristotelian tradition teaches.

There are numerous appeals to Biblical texts in Locke's discussion dealing with the origin and defense of private property. How important is the religious component of Locke's argument? If we were to take away the religious dimension would Locke's argument be fundamentally altered? The answer is both 'no' and 'yes.' An important part of Locke's project, as we shall see, is religious liberty. We remind the reader of the importance of the three pillars of liberty.

There is a strong moral tone – even a God inspired biblical inclination toward "stewardship" and such higher ends as the "common good" – to Locke's defense of private property. This is particularly evident in his critique of wasting and spoiling as unjust as well as his defense of individual self-reliance, public stewardship; even his 'rights' doctrine was derived from God.

The best thing God did was to punish Adam and make him work for himself. Was this punishment actually a gift? The key to human life is self-improvement. If human beings work and acquire things, they'll be more willing to work and become self-reliant. They will learn how to govern themselves economically. And, who knows, they may learn to govern themselves in matters of politics and religion. Locke did not see labor as a punishment but as a reward. The interesting thing is that the American Founding Fathers did see Locke as a Christian. They saw a difference between Hobbes and Locke. Some try to read Locke out of the American founding. In doing so, they devalue the importance of the market, and the link between the trinity of liberty in economic, political, and religious matters.

Locke understood 'nature' from a Newtonian point of view. 'Nature' was not revealed as the terminus of an Aristotelian teleological process but as the hypothetical primitive condition (first law of motion) which is itself revealed in, and modified by, the interaction among things (second and third laws), all of which is discovered by observation of the world not the reading of texts. Humanity discovers itself through work – by interaction with the physical world. As in Newton, these basic laws of nature are ordained by God. My 'rights' are 'natural' in that they are ordained by God and revealed through the interaction with and transformation of the physical world. God has granted me the 'right' to life, to 'liberty' (freedom to pursue my natural drives unencumbered by others, that is, monarchs and aristocrats) and especially the right to pursue happiness through work.

MARKET ECONOMY: ECONOMIC LIBERTY

Locke's initial intuitive grasp of economics reflected his training as a physician. He was sympathetic to the view that the body healed itself and that the role of the physician was to subtend this natural process. This medical bias, so to speak, was shared with two earlier thinkers, Rene Descartes and Francis Bacon. In Bacon's *New Atlantis* (Bacon 1627), Solomon's House was focused on gaining control over the environment, including medical advice for prolonging life. Descartes maintained that "The preservation of health has always been the principle end of my studies" (Descartes 1991, p. 275).

With regard to the domestic economy, Locke advocated a relatively free market. Wealth is measured by gold and silver, for these command all the conveniences of life. In a country not furnished with mines, there are but two ways of growing rich, either conquest or commerce. For Locke, commerce is the only way. Gold and silver, as opposed to paper money, are the appropriate currency for international transactions because they are universally recognized by all of humanity. The value of paper money is only valid under the government which issues it.

Locke later served as Secretary of the Board of Trade and Plantations and Secretary to the Lords Proprietor of Carolina, and this seems to have influenced his ideas on international trade and economics. With regard to the international economy, Locke urged England to seek a favorable balance of trade, lest it fall behind other countries and suffer a loss in its trade. Further, he was, on occasion, prepared to recommend tariffs. Locke was certainly aware of the balance of power at that time, but he also worked with the assumption that the potential for war is an unfortunate feature of the world in which he lived, just as he thought the existence of the universal moral truths in the state of nature will inevitably be violated by a few. It will be up to Adam Smith and Immanuel Kant, in later stages of the narrative, to argue for international free market and perpetual peace, but nothing in Locke's narrative precludes that.

According to Locke, if you labor over something, that something becomes your private property. At this point the argument for private property is moral. When we shift from a barter economy to a monetary economy there is a marked difference to the whole argument for private property. With the introduction of money, we have shifted from a way of life which is primarily nomadic and agrarian to an entrepreneurial one where investment and acquisition take place. We're on the road to free enterprise and an autonomous existence. Here we see the introduction of a second factor in production, namely, capital. Labor could not be as productive without the capital. In a barter economy, labor is the only factor. With capital comes interest. No longer was usury illegal. In arguing against the government setting the rate of interest, Locke is one of the first to make a case for the market price against a church or government determined price.

Locke is not defending the property of the rich. He talks about God favoring the rational and industrious. He is arguing that the rational and industrious are the many, ready to improve their plight. If just given a chance, they will take care of themselves.

God gives the world to human beings in common. But he could never have intended for the world to be divided equally. He rewards those who help themselves rightly. The origin of private property is a mix of God's gift and human labor. Private property is not deemed to be theft. What is due to God and what is due to human? The value of X is 99 percent due to human labor and 1 percent to the land. God gave the land. Ergo what God gave is useless – unless there are humans to use it. We cannot understand Locke on private property unless we understand his stance on private religion. It is part of God's design for human beings that they become self-sufficient. This stems from Protestantism, and this never would come from Catholicism.

Locke argued that the market should decide the price. Making money off of money should be done openly and if the market supports gouged prices then so be it! When the market decides, it becomes legitimate; consequently, open markets are legitimate! Prices were decided by church fathers or philosophers for too long. Locke tries to make the case for the market price. In the 1570s, before Locke, an Ethics panel decided to shift from saying usury is always bad to sometimes being good. Locke had to demonstrate that making money from money is natural.

While serving as Secretary for the Board of the Lord Proprietors of Carolina, Locke allegedly helped draft the *Fundamental Constitutions* of 1669 which sanctioned slavery. In addition Locke invested (through his patron Shaftesbury) in the African slave trade, an institution that was systemic to the overall economy of Britain. A number of interminable and speculative scholarly debates have raged around whether Locke was an advocate of slavery, and so on. On the one hand this is relevant because Locke is an advocate of universal individual freedom. Whether Locke condoned Negro slavery or was acting prudentially in an imperfect world or whether he was a hypocrite is not something that scholars can definitively establish.

What we know, following Chapter 4 of the *Second Treatise* in which Locke discusses slavery, is that one is not free to choose to become a slave. We want to suggest that this is the first coherent case against slavery ever, and this case is relevant to the future of liberty.

Moreover, none of these possibilities vitiates the narrative from TP→ME→LG→RL→CPA. Locke advocated each and every one of these elements of the logic of modernity and clearly saw the connection between and among the elements. Nor was it necessary for Locke to foresee all of the later implications and permutations of the narrative. The real importance of the scholarly debate about slavery, although it looks like a purely scholarly debate, is that it is a reflection of what will be the Rousseauean (scholarly) critique of the Locke narrative. Part of that critique, as we shall see, is that the Lockean contract, allegedly, was an imposition of the strong upon the weak; in short, an excuse for exploitation. Somehow, Locke's alleged hypocrisy and covert support of slavery is supposed to show us the true motive behind the Lockean narrative or all those who are attracted by the narrative. Critics have also added to his list of shortcomings the claim that the argument against unenclosed property is a covert argument that permits dispossessing natives in the New World. This issue is still with us in the form of eminent domain.

LIMITED GOVERNMENT: POLITICAL LIBERTY

Locke is most famous for his advocacy of limited government. Around 1689 Locke published anonymously the *Two Treatises of Government*. The *First Treatise* had critiqued Robert Filmer's argument that monarchy was a form of Biblically justified patriarchy. Locke argued that God had given the Earth to mankind in common and not to a patriarch. The *Second Treatise* is, among other things, an account of how land, originally given in common by God, leads to inviolable private property, and thus to limited government.

Three important elements of the logic of modernity are present in the *Second Treatise*: the technological project, the market economy, and limited government. The technological project is explicitly expressed in the view that human effort is what gives entities in the world their meaning and value in a philosophical and religious sense.

God, who has given the world to men in common, has also given them reason
to make use of it to the best advantage of life, and convenience … it cannot
be supposed He meant it should always remain common and uncultivated. He
gave it to the use of the Industrious and Rational … not to the Fancy or
Covetousness of the Quarrelsome and Contentious … for it is labor indeed
that puts the difference of value on every thing … of the products of the earth
useful to the life of man nine tenths are the effects of labor. (Locke 1689,
Second Treatise, Chapter 5, The Right of Private Property, sections 26, 27, 34,
and 40)

Locke's critique of Patriarchy is more than just an attack on divine right
monarchy or a rationalization for a revolution. Patriarchy was used to
justify government control of the economy, something incompatible with
human flourishing as understood by the Puritans. The royal prerogative
also meant taxation without consent, which is wholly incompatible with
the Puritan understanding of private property. Locke was not an advocate
of the redistribution of wealth. Moreover, Patriarchy reflects the view that
society was a collective whole within which individuals subordinated
their private aims for the public good, what Hayek will call a teleocracy
and what Oakeshott will call an enterprise association. This is precisely
what Catholicism advocated in Locke's time, it is what France under the
Bourbons represented, and it was what a Catholic King of England would
adhere to. Locke rejected and revolted against this collectivist understanding of society.

It is fashionable nowadays to ignore or dismiss Locke's use of
Protestant theology to express his vision or narrative. We note only in
passing that a case can be made that there were no other available
conceptual frameworks in Locke's time, philosophical or otherwise, for
articulating Locke's insights. This is part of what is intriguing in the later
evolution of the Locke narrative.

The technological project requires a market economy for its full
expression. A free market economy is a system for the exchange of goods
and services wherein there is no central allocation of such goods and
services. The goods and services are privately owned (that is, private
property). It involves competition because innovation cannot, by definition, be planned. To the extent that property is privately owned and not
centrally controlled, and to the extent that a free market economy is
competitive, there is a greater possibility for innovation. Three things, in
Locke's mind, legitimate private property: (1) it is more productive (this
was confirmed in Locke's time by the land-enclosure acts); (2) it
exemplifies a personal relationship with God; and (3) it acknowledges the
spirituality of work. Adam Smith will elaborate the first element (efficiency) by reference to specialization, and he will elaborate the second

element in the metaphor of the "hidden hand" – a quasi-theological guarantee that the self-interest of each individual is compatible with the self-interest of everyone else. The spirituality of work will be preserved in a secular fashion, as we shall see, by Hegel.

For Locke the "great and *chief end* therefore, of Mens uniting into Commonwealths, and putting themselves under Government, is *the preservation of their property*" (Locke 1689, *Second Treatise*, paragraph 124). The formation of government requires majority consent (as apparently does revolution), but the actual form of government need not be a democracy. In fact, majoritarian consent to a policy does not legitimate that policy if it violates the law of nature. This is fundamentally different from Rousseau's view.

Locke advocates a property qualification for political participation as a safeguard against democratic (mob) rule. Again, this is a signal to advocates of the Rousseau narrative that the Lockean narrative is a way for the few strong to subordinate the many weak. As made clear later by Madison in the *Tenth Federalist Paper*, democracy is a negative blocking device – not a positive creation device. Moreover, as we shall see, Locke's argument stripped of theology and advocating that government is legitimated only by consent will be reiterated by Hume, Madison, and J.S. Mill.

RULE OF LAW: ECONOMIC, POLITICAL, AND RELIGIOUS LIBERTY INTERTWINED

We are not concerned here with Locke's controversial discussion of the relationship between natural law and natural right or the relation of natural law to civil law. However important and interesting these topics are, they do not contribute to our understanding of the narrative. The rule of law attained extraordinary prominence in seventeenth century England. This is reflected in Locke's *Second Treatise*.

> The end of law is, not to abolish or restrain, but to preserve and enlarge freedom ... where there is no law there is no freedom. For liberty is to be free from restraint and violence from others ... and is not, as we are told, a liberty for every man to do as he lists ... a liberty to dispose, and order as he lists, his person, actions, possessions, and his whole property, within the allowance of those laws under which he is, and therein not to be subject of the arbitrary will of another, but freely follow his own. (Locke 1689, *Second Treatise*, VI, paragraph 57)

The purpose of law is to minimize conflict, not to achieve a positive end. As we shall see in the later development of the narrative, it is what Oakeshott will call the 'rule of law' in a civil association. This is achieved by appeal to past practice (that is, the common law) and not to abstract first principles. Past practice is substantiated by historical experience, and that is why Locke and others appeal to their understanding of an historical tradition that stretches back to time immemorial (and the state of nature) in which the struggle of the Commons against prerogative is the major theme.

As an early advocate of the separation of powers, his main focus is on limiting "him that has the executive power" (Locke 1689, *Second Treatise*, paragraph 159). Although conceding the necessity for the executive to exercise prerogative power or discretion (Locke 1689, *Second Treatise*, paragraph 164, "*Prerogative* can be nothing, but the Peoples permitting their Rulers, to do several things of their own free choice, where the Law was silent, and sometimes against the direct Letter of the Law, for the public good; and their acquiescing in it when so done"), Locke reminded executives that such acquiescence could turn into revolution. The only thing worse than revolution is oppression; and revolution is a historically grounded practice, not a theory.

In describing law, Locke stipulated the following characteristics: (1) law cannot be arbitrary (Locke 1689, *Second Treatise*, #135); laws must be (2) general, (3) public, (4) everyone including the ones who make laws must be subject to law (Locke 1689, *Second Treatise*, #137), and (5) no legitimate act of government can appropriate property through taxation without consent.

CULTURE OF PERSONAL AUTONOMY

Following Hobbes, Locke accepts the ontological priority of the individual will. Locke's *Essay Concerning Human Understanding* (1690) is known largely for its epistemological doctrines, but it is at the same time an early expression of what Oakeshott will later identify as the modern Renaissance conception of the self and personal identity by reference to each individual's consciousness. In the *Vindication of the Reasonableness of Christianity* (1695), Locke went so far as to cite *Genesis*, specifically the biblical doctrine of *Imago Dei* specifically as a basis for individual freedom and equality, including equality of the sexes. By proclaiming political individualism Locke repudiated 500 years of hierarchical political communitarianism.

A Letter Concerning Toleration (1689) is not only a classic statement of religious toleration or liberty but an expression of Locke's emphasis on the importance of individualism. Inherent in Christianity is the recognition that salvation is only attainable by sincere inner personal belief. Hence individuals must be free to come to God each in his/her own way. Moral sovereignty over one's personal core beliefs and practices is constitutive of being an individual. This position will be subsequently elaborated in a secular manner by J.S. Mill when he writes *On Liberty* (Mill 1859). The great threat to social disorder is not individual dissenters, but those who insist that society must be a collective (an enterprise association in Oakeshott's terminology), for the latter masks personal ambition under the guise of ideology. This will be the 'Lockean' refrain against those who maintain that civil strife requires subordination to a collectivity. It is modernity's answer to the ancients and modern collectivists.

Locke does recognize the existence of the socially dysfunctional, identifying them both as those who refuse to support themselves through work and in the expression the "Fancy or Covetousness of the Quarrelsome and Contentious." In contrast with Rousseau, Locke recognizes the existence of the dysfunctional as reflecting a personal moral shortcoming and not a systemic failing. Locke thus introduces a continuing issue in the debate between the Locke narrative and the Rousseau narrative. For Locke and his followers, the dysfunctional fail to grasp or choose to disregard the liberating effects of the technological project, just as they failed in the state of nature to accept the God-guaranteed inner moral law. In Kant, the failure will be explained as the substitution of the heteronomy of the will as opposed to autonomy – an autonomous person never exploits others for that is to define oneself by one's victims. For Hegel, the recognition of our autonomy requires that we promote it in others. In Oakeshott, the dysfunctional will be identified as the anti-individuals who still cling to a pre-modern collective identity. In the Lockean narrative, the polity is defined by the successful; in the Rousseau narrative the polity is defined by the alienated.

Locke provides a quasi-historical account of the evolution from agriculture to commerce with its accompanying evolution of human personal sensibility. This evolutionary account will be extended more explicitly during the Scottish Enlightenment by Smith and further developed by Kant and Hegel.

Advocates of holism or collectivity insist that conflict can be avoided and fulfillment obtained only by participation in a substantive collective telos – this is a view shared by ultra-conservatives on the right and radicals on the extreme left. The 'Lockean' response is twofold:

(1) minimizing or eliminating conflict is best obtained by agreement on procedure (for example, toleration) not on substance; in fact, the latter fuels conflict; (2) happiness is what we pursue not necessarily what we obtain in this life; substantive fulfillment is something for the afterlife. Substantive views, whether religious or philosophical, are private.

There is a marked tendency for advocates of the Lockean Liberty Narrative to present themselves in a triumphalist fashion. Francis Fukuyama's *The End of History* (Fukuyama 1992) is among the latest such expressions. This is not to deny the existence of problems, tensions, and misunderstandings, but it does reflect a sense that somehow they speak for the inevitable and established point of view.

2. Jean Jacques Rousseau and the Three Pillars of Equality

TECHNOLOGICAL PROJECT

It is useful to understand Rousseau's work (1712–1778) as a response primarily to Locke. What Locke and Rousseau share and what makes them defining figures of the modern conversation is the recognition that the modern world was transitioning away from Feudal agrarianism into something economically novel with important social implications (a form of "creative destruction" to use Schumpeter's phrase). What they also recognized was the existence of a new persona, a new form of self-consciousness. Locke welcomed the new persona, but Rousseau argued that a further transformation was necessary.

Rousseau first gained attention and prominence with the publication of the *Discourse on the Arts and Sciences* (Rousseau 1750) (hereafter the *First Discourse*). It was in response to an essay contest designed to highlight in a positive way the contributions of science and technology to the advancement of civilization. Rousseau argued against the original purpose of the contest, but still won the prize. He argued that the arts and sciences, and therefore the entire technological project, did not respond to genuine human needs. Rather, the technological project was a reflection of pride and vanity. Rousseau asks whether these arts and sciences have improved human character or the human condition. This puts the Lockean narrative on the defensive.

The arts and sciences, according to Rousseau, are motivated by human vices: "Astronomy was born from superstition; eloquence from ambition, hate, flattery, and falsehood; geometry from avarice, physics from vain curiosity; all, even moral philosophy, from human pride" (Rousseau 1986, p. 14). The sciences distract our attention from what is humanly important, a sense of community, friendship, and concern for the less fortunate. Technical knowledge does not provide moral guidance. Worst of all, the technological project leads to idleness, the desire for luxury, and moral corruption. We become envious of what others possess and fearful of losing what we have. Reason corrupts because it is purely

15

instrumental (Hume), selfish, and encourages calculation. Rousseau questions the Lockean project at its core. The Lockean metaphor of improvement is challenged by the Rousseau metaphor of corruption. Finally, the technological project leads to a government in which the powerful crush the individual liberty of the less fortunate. The market economy, a consequence of the technological project, merely replicates the exploitative feudal hierarchy. An essential feature of the Rousseau narrative is the existence of the 'bad guys.'

Before discussing the market economy and government, we need to make clear what assumptions Rousseau made about the human condition that led him to decide it was incompatible with the technological project. In the *Discourse on Inequality* (Rousseau 1754), the so-called *Second Discourse*, Rousseau outlines his anthropological account of humanity. By analogy with Newton's first law of motion (we postulate what would be the properties of a single body in motion if it never interacted with other bodies even though the second law tells us that all bodies interact), we imagine what human beings would be like if they were not socialized, that is if they did not interact with other human beings. In place of Locke's philosophical/metaphysical/theological starting point Rousseau offers a natural history.

Rousseau identifies two characteristics of human nature: humans as free agents and as perfectible. Rousseau argues that humans realize they are free, which animals do not. By human freedom he understands that human beings have free will (Kant) in the sense that they are not governed by their physical and emotional drives. They, unlike animals, can resist the promptings of appetite. Human beings are also perfectible, unlike animals which achieve their entire adult like qualities earlier than humans, and these qualities do not change in different social and historical contexts. Human beings can choose how they want to live – they are not determined by their environment.

Rousseau rejects some of the ancient Greek, Aristotelian views: mankind is not comprised of rational animals; there is no human teleology, and human beings are not naturally political. Rousseau also rejects some modern views (Hobbes, Bacon, and Machiavelli): human beings are not fundamentally egoistic. What characterizes human beings in the natural state, according to Rousseau, is *Amour de soi*, the instinctive human desire for self-preservation (not to be confused with domination) and compassion (Hume and Smith on sympathy). Thus, human beings are naturally social (but still not political). These are traits found throughout the primates. Rousseau's two principles are "preservation of self" and "love of others (compassion)." Locke would argue that our instinctive affection for others breaks down and we therefore need government. Rousseau feels that people are naturally concerned about others.

Our 'natural' condition is thus to be understood as our 'primitive' condition, not our fully-developed and political condition. In the primitive or natural condition it makes no sense to evaluate people in moral or political terms. Locke was mistaken in his appeal to natural right, because he believed that nature only dictates self-interest. Moreover, civil society is for Rousseau a convention (Hume would agree) of historical origin (Hegel would agree). (Where useful, we shall try to tie insights from one author to how earlier and later authors in the conversation would respond.)

How then do we understand our development into social and political beings? The growth in population required human beings to associate with each other. As a consequence, humans were led to value the others' opinions as necessary for their well-being. This transformation of self-awareness, this:

> passage from the state of nature to the civil state produces a very remarkable change in man, by substituting justice for instinct in his conduct, and giving his actions the morality they had formerly lacked. Then only, when the voice of duty takes the place of physical impulses and right of appetite, does man, who so far had considered only himself, find that he is forced to act on different principles, and to consult his reason before listening to his inclinations. Although, in this state, he deprives himself of some advantages which he got from nature, he gains in return others so great, his faculties are so stimulated and developed, his ideas so extended, his feelings so ennobled, and his whole soul so uplifted, that … he would be bound to bless continually the happy moment which took him from it forever, and, instead of a stupid and unimaginative animal, made him an intelligent being and a man. (Rousseau 1762, Book I, Chapter 8, The Civil State)

This transition, however, was accompanied by another change, the transformation of *amour de soi* into *amour-propre*. The latter is a form of pride in which we compare ourselves to others in such a way as to take pleasure in the pain or weakness of others. "[T]he abuses of this new condition often degrade him below that which he left" (ibid.). Social interdependence can, therefore, also be inimical to human well-being. There is a strong sense here of how ordinary people are victims of modern market societies based on the technological project. Rousseau asks what the character of modern life is and answers that it is "hypocrisy." Rousseau answers the question of why people gave up the state of nature. The answer is that they were swindled in the market economy.

MARKET ECONOMY

Social interdependence, the development of agriculture, the division of labor, and the rise of private property all lead to economic inequality. As opposed to Locke, Rousseau maintains that the privatization of property is the source of all evil:

> The first man who, having enclosed a piece of ground, to whom it occurred to say *this is mine* ... was the true founder of civil society. How many crimes, wars, murders, how many miseries and horrors mankind would have been spared by him who, pulling up the stakes or filling the ditch, had cried out to his kind: Beware of listening to this impostor; You are lost if you forget that the fruits are everyone's and the earth no-one's. (Rousseau 1754, *Second Discourse*, Part II, paragraph 1)

Inequality leads to conflict, and out of this conflict there arises a social order in which the rich and powerful force the general population to acquiesce in a fraudulent form of social hierarchy. This is the origin of class conflict. Hereafter, an essential part of the Rousseau narrative is the postulation of the exploitation of one group by another and thereby a subsequent victimization. The interdependence of a market economy leads to institutionalized inequality and social hierarchy. The false promise of luxury, that is, unlimited economic growth, does not promote peace but undermines our integrity. We are victimized by the appeal to our appetites. We are in conflict with our true selves because at one and the same time we are dependent upon others and in competition with them.

Thus, the Rousseau Equality Narrative assumes that:

1. Improvements in the arts and sciences make society worse because the improvements increase luxurious habits and contra-communitarian conduct (anti-the technological project).
2. Private property is theft rather than the reward of labor (anti-market economy).
3. A luxurious society is one that has deception, greed, and calculation at its core. Carnival, for Rousseau, is one huge put on of the aristocracy and monarchy. You don't know whom you are seeing. The arts and the sciences have brought all of this clothing so that everyone can conceal who they really are. Rousseau sees the country bumpkin as far better than the oligarch.
4. The taking of property (by government) is just because in reality property is owned by the few rather than used in a fashion central

to the human condition. Thus takings are warranted and probably without "just compensation" (anti-limited government and the rule of law).

5. A good society is not the same as a society of free individuals. Rather a good society is one where individuals realize that their happiness is to be found in bonding together in a collective enterprise (anti-culture of personal autonomy).

The Lockean world, according to Rousseau, actually leads to inequality and hypocrisy. The remedy is a return to nature. Rousseau's version is distinguished from Locke in that in the beginning there was inherent conflict. There is a fall and the cause of the fall is knowledge. Private property arose because we acquired the knowledge to dupe others into accepting this notion of "mine" and "yours." This is the origin of inequality.

In a Lockean society, there is a commercial/market economy because humans are presumed for the most part to be capable of taking care of themselves, and they also help others. People take care of each other through negotiation and commerce. Competition is to be preferred over monopoly and that goes for economics, politics, and religion. In a Rousseauean society, there is a communitarian ethic. We are all in this together and we have to watch out for the conniving few who will put one over on us the innocent many. But we can defeat the enemy by bonding together, or avoid the enemy by dropping out. Cooperation and a collective approach to issues are to be preferred to competition and that goes for economics, politics, and religion.

GOVERNMENT: THE GENERAL WILL

There is something that differentiates human beings from animals besides speech, says Rousseau, and that is the fundamental metaphysical truth that human beings have a free will. The discovery of the capacity for free will is the awareness that we can resist temptation (not by classical reason but by an act of will), but this capacity is not a matter of following reason (the ancients were wrong). We can only appropriate our freedom through an act of will. We are free when we impose order on ourselves! We were born with this capacity (that is, born free) but subsequently have placed ourselves in bondage. The opening lines of Rousseau's article *Economie Politique* (Rousseau 1755) written for Diderot's *Encyclopédie* (1755), states "Man having been born free, is everywhere in chains. One man thinks himself the master of others, but remains more of a slave than they" (Hegel will appropriate this insight but interpret it differently). All present societies are historical artifacts that originated in force (Hume would agree) and are therefore illegitimate (Hume would disagree).

Is it possible to appropriate this freedom and make it the fundamental value of civil society? This is what Rousseau attempts to do in *The Social Contract* (Rousseau 1762). The authentic social contract requires us to abandon any claim of the natural right of private property (contra Locke). We enter this contract naked (as Rawls will later argue as well). Essential to any genuine contract, according to Rousseau, is the binding of oneself, but to what? What each of us agrees to do is to voluntarily submit to the authority of a "General Will," one in which we are not subordinated to the will of another or to the wills of others. We need not be concerned about getting people to obey this General Will because they themselves are the authors of the "General Will."

How can we identify the General Will? Negatively, the General Will is neither the will of an individual, nor of any group, not even the majority, and it is not the will of all – since the latter can be mistaken. In Rousseau's mind, since the General Will is established by an act of will (for example, the decision/choice to love or trust another person) it is not an independent and objective fact or set of facts about the world including humanity, and therefore cannot be apprehended by and con-firmed by experts. It is what we would all agree to will if we all really knew and understood the fundamental truths about the human condition (Rawls' veil of ignorance). As Rousseau said, "the general will is always right" (Rousseau 1762, *Social Contract*, II, 6). In the evolving tradition of the Rousseau narrative some will claim this special expertise (Saint-Simon, Comte, and so on), but this is not Rousseau's position even though he inspired it. Rousseau was the original advocate of liberty, equality, and fraternity – as he understood it.

It is not possible to give a positive or final and definitive account of the General Will. Hence, it is never possible to offer a clear alternative to whatever exits or to whatever flows from the Lockean narrative. This is both the strength and the weakness of the Rousseauean narrative. The Rousseauean narrative does not insist upon strict equality but inequalities must not be 'excessive'. Problematically, excessive can never be defini-tively specified. The gap must not be "too" large. It is important for Rousseau that "everyone has something and no one has too much" (Rousseau 1762, *Social Contract*, I, 9, n. 5). It is a rhetorical refrain that can be employed almost anywhere and anytime. We are not denying the intrinsic importance or the legitimacy of the concept of a 'gap'. We are concerned about the extent to which this is (a) a substantive issue that can be given some specificity, (b) an issue of perception, or (c) demagoguery. Yet, there is an important sense in which the Rousseau narrative is thereby perpetually parasitic upon the Lockean narrative. Without Lockeans, so to speak, there is nothing for Rousseaueans to be against.

The General Will is a "Platonic" regulative ideal in terms of which we evaluate existing or proposed policy. Unlike Locke, there are no natural rights, neither life (contra Hobbes, Rousseau approves of the death penalty), nor liberty (if liberty puts limits on government intervention), nor property. Again, in opposition to Locke, sovereignty in Rousseau is indivisible and inalienable. The community as a whole in the form of an assembly makes the law, and the law is carried out by the government. Rousseau's description of the General Will is largely formalistic, and the content he chose to give it is a commitment to the pre-modern community. Kant, in opposition, will maintain that the content could just as easily be to the autonomous individual in a commercial republic (hence, right-wing versus left-wing Hegelians, Rawlsians versus Nozickeans, and so on); but for Rousseau this is precluded by his initial rejection of both the technological project and the market economy.

Given his allegiance to the concept of the General Will, Rousseau is caught in, and bequeaths to posterity, a permanent and unresolvable tension. On the one hand, he is the permanent critic of any existing social/political order, and in assuming this role he is, arguably, the first modern public intellectual. This is captured in Said's expression "speaking truth to power." On the other hand, Rousseau wants to reconstruct society. In addressing the question of how to bring people to the realization of true freedom and the General Will, Rousseau invokes education. He does this both formally as in the *Emile* (Rousseau 1762) but also when he identifies the role of the legislator (who is not formally a part of government), as a charismatic figure who leads one to the point where the individual must then be independent in grasping the truth of freedom and the General Will. This 'outsider', so to speak, reflects a kind of perennially alienated intellectual critic, a modern version of Plato's philosopher (Socrates) who escapes from the cave and realizes he has not seen the truth but has been living in a world of shadows. Unlike Plato's Philosopher-King, and unlike the medieval priesthood, Rousseau's legislator will not exercise power. Identifying social dysfunction is not the same thing as having correctly diagnosed its source nor is it the same thing as proposing the right solution and a coherent program for implementing the solution.

Saddled with the presumption that the existing order is inherently corrupt because it is the inevitable product of a grand deception (the power elite so to speak), Rousseau is incapable of appreciating the case that can be made for the legitimacy of existing institutions and practices. This notion that the Lockean world is conceived in sin is reflected, rhetorically, in the expression "trickle-down economics." Rousseau is neither a revolutionary nor an outright utopian (see, for example, his *Considerations on the Government of Poland*, Rousseau 1772). However, by rooting future practice in theory, he is powerless to prevent others from turning his position into a radical revolutionary and utopian blueprint. Rousseau's death was followed by cult-like versions of his concept of the General Will, a cult reflected in Robespierre and Saint-Just, especially during the Reign of Terror. The French Revolution cannot be understood apart from this cult-like version of Rousseau's narrative, and the difference between it and the American Revolution cannot be understood in the absence of the evolution of the Lockean narrative. Denied access to a positive evolutionary account (something Marx will provide in the form of dialectic), Rousseau must offer a revolutionary account. In his case, the revolution is intellectual and mediated by the non-political Socratic "legislator." Some of his followers will not hesitate to invoke revolutionary violence, and they, in turn, will be confronted by advocates of a revolutionary return to the pre-modern.

Given his perceived role as a Socratic critic, Rousseau is understand-ably reluctant to advocate specific policies or institutional structures. Here are some examples of the tension. Rousseau maintains that the correct social contract requires unanimous approval and does not bind future generations. At the same time, there can be original unanimous approval to be bound in the future by the majority. But majority approval does not confirm that a policy is consistent with the General Will. Rousseau is especially adamant that representative democracy is a bad idea because the representatives are spokespersons for particular inter-ests. Constant characterized Rousseau's conception of liberty as the liberty of the ancients, consisting in:

> exercising collectively, but directly, several parts of the complete sovereignty; in deliberating, in the public square ... compatible with this collective freedom [is] the complete subjection of the individual to the authority of the community ... . No importance was given to individual independence, neither in relation to opinions, nor to labor, nor, above all, to religion. (Benjamin Constant [1819] 1988, *The Liberty of the Ancients Compared with that of the Moderns*)

Rousseau's conception of liberty is the "liberty *to*" participate in collect-ive decision-making (and this can take many modern forms – for example, voting in an election or agitating in a general strike). Lockean liberty, on the other hand, is a "liberty *from*." The General Will in the end embodies the ancient (and medieval) conception of a collective good, what Oakeshott will describe as an enterprise association.

Rousseau is willing to accept the existence of private property, but property rights are subordinate and therefore may be overridden. There are natural inequalities but they may not be rewarded unless they contribute to the benefit of all, most especially the least well off (something Rawls will repeat). Here is the now classic tension between wealth is bad versus it is unfair for others to have more wealth than you. Rousseau wants everyone to keep the General Will in view and to subordinate any potentially conflicting loyalties, but he recognizes that small associations can be fulfilling. Tocqueville's critique of Rousseau will not only insist that the great collective will crush individuals and their smaller voluntary associations, but echo Rousseau's recognition of the fulfilling nature of such associations.

RULE OF LAW

Rousseau's treatment of law per se is abstract and formal. Law does not or should not evolve from prior custom as in the Anglo-American case law tradition (which, again, is inherently corrupt). Law must be the fresh product of legislation and it must reflect the General Will. As such, law must be universal and not applicable to single persons or groups (that is, equality before the law). The government (presumably Philosopher-King-like judges) and not the Assembly decides the application of law, and the law must be enforced without discretion in order to make sure that citizens are forced to be free, that is, to act consistently with what they have chosen or should have chosen in the form of the General Will. There is no a priori limit to the scope of the law.

In this conception of law, Rousseau shows himself to be the inheritor of the Greco-Roman Continental tradition in which laws are deductions from first principles, but where such first principles now reflect the General Will (as opposed to natural law or Justinian's *Digest*). The best modern example of this is Hans Kelsen's (1881–1973) assertion of the existence of a *Grundnorm* in his *Pure Theory of Law* (Kelsen 1934). The legal system is self-sufficient, and its legitimacy rests upon internal formal validity rather than conformity to external standards. There is no distinction between the law and the state. Nor is there a distinction between public and private law.

COMMUNITY

Rousseau's essay *Economie Politique*, written for Diderot's *Encyclopédie* in 1755, uses the expression "political economy." Locke never uses this phrase. So what is the content of Rousseau's political economy? And what is the objective? How can you tell a good political economy from a bad one? A good 'political economy' is an economy that works for the benefit of the entire polity, rather than Locke's version in which a good political economy is an economy which leaves people alone to make their own decisions. So we have two different understandings of what politicians should be doing. If we follow the Locke narrative, the less politicians do the better. The role of the government is to serve the economic interests of its citizens as they define those interests individually and to prevent the domination of one interest over another (e.g., Madison's *Tenth Federalist* [Hamilton et al. 1787–88]). This is precisely what would alarm Rousseau – he would fear that the government would become the puppet of the oligarchs (Marx). In the Rousseau narrative it seems the polity itself is a place where people grow and come together and become one. Therefore, the overall condition of the community becomes an important variable for Rousseau. The economy should be, in Rousseau's eyes, an instrument for achieving community. It is difficult to imagine how this would operate without the presumption of an objective collective goal to which all individual goals are subordinate. Moreover, the collective goal would not be exclusively economic.

Rousseau suggests two possibilities to deal with modernity:

1. Drop out (solitary walker). Radical anarchy. If we drop out, what we're doing is living like the animals. And government is necessary only because we have quit following the model of the innocent animal.
2. Drop in. Become full-fledged citizens. This requires corrupt humans to shed their social existence and start all over and, in effect, to re-acquire their angelic or innocent nature which was lost not in an initial human fall, but through the development of the enlightenment. If we cannot do this for the whole of society, we can seek to become members of an agrarian commune.

True freedom, for Rousseau, is not individual autonomy but requires membership in and identification with a community. For Rousseau, there is a fundamental contradiction "between our situation and our desire, between our duties and our inclinations, between nature and social institutions, between man and citizen." Mankind can only achieve harmony and fulfillment by giving itself "entirely to the state" (Rousseau 1762, *Le bonheur public*). That membership is reinforced by a political theology. But this sense of freedom that Rousseau articulates is not an end in itself; rather it is the start of something bigger and better where you can be "forced to be free." In other words, you can be forced – by the society and the government – to abandon a Lockean sense of false individual liberty and acquire a new true persona, one that fuses freedom and bonding rather than see them as opposites.

Both Locke and Rousseau paid particular attention to the purpose and content of education in considering these issues. What kind of education would Rousseau suggest if the simple life is the best life? Perhaps an agrarian Israeli kibbutz or a Maoist re-education by peasants? What kind of education would Locke suggest if the improved life is the better life? Is education in the arts and sciences the way to corruption or improvement? Rousseau in the end would argue that insensitivity to others is the greatest sin. Rousseau would have no problem with sensitivity training.

Rousseau identified but rejected three traditional conceptions of religion: (1) the "religion of the priests" which led to a divided loyalty and contradictory standards for piety and citizenship; (2) the "religion of man" (no rituals) which undercuts loyalty, encourages meekness and mitigates opposition to internal and external tyranny; and (3) the "religion of the citizen" (God = State) in which citizens become superstitious, sanguinary, intolerant, and engage in perpetual war with neighbors (French Revolution?). In its place he proposed a tolerant "Civil Profession of Faith" (anticipating Kant), encompassing (a) the existence of God; (b) a belief in immortality; (c) a belief in the future happiness of the just and the punishment of the wicked; and (d) the sanctity of the Social Contract and of the Laws. Despite making room for toleration of individual religious belief, the civil faith makes loyalty to the General Will a substantive commitment. The voice of the people is the voice of God.

SUMMARY

Both Locke and Rousseau believed in liberty and equality. For Locke, liberty meant restraint on government in the name of natural rights understood to be absolute, do not conflict, and possessed only by individual human beings. Rights are morally absolute or fundamental because they are derived from God (or later the categorical imperative), and as such cannot be overridden. These 'rights' do not conflict in the sense that one does not choose between or among them. "Life, liberty, and property" are expressions of religious liberty, political liberty, and economic liberty. The role of these rights is to protect the individual human capacity to choose. Finally, such rights impose only duties of non-interference. For Rousseau, so-called Lockean rights are at best *prima facie*, may be overridden, and may be possessed by any entity, not just individual human beings. More importantly, Rousseauean liberty entails welfare rights, that is, they may be such that others have a positive obligation to provide goods, benefits or means. For Locke, equality is equality before the law and equality of opportunity; for Rousseau, equality entails the addition of equality of outcome. Rousseau also believes in fraternity (community) understood as the General Will. We shall see as it evolves in later supporters that the Rousseau narrative puts equality before liberty, nature before civilization, and it romanticizes aboriginal societies as living in the Garden of Eden before the fall.

ROUSSEAU NARRATIVE VERSUS LOCKE NARRATIVE

Both Locke and Rousseau offer modern narratives. What is meant by 'modern' is that ultimate standards are internal as opposed to external. The ancients believed in an external objective truth (Plato's 'forms' or Aristotle's organic/teleological metaphysics or God's word in Scripture). For the ancients, reason enabled us to grasp the external truths and to educate or subordinate our feelings to those truths.

For Locke, the internal standards are expressions of the personal relationship with God unfiltered by institutional structures of any kind. As Locke understood it, our obligation is to transform the world to reflect those inner-apprehended standards, specifically after the "Fall" to work and thereby create private property. It is in our interaction with and transformation of the world that we preserve our lives, achieve freedom, and find meaning in the *pursuit* of happiness. The ancients somehow got it wrong when they thought we could find fulfillment through contemplation, and the medievals got it wrong when they thought finding one's role in a static agrarian feudalism led to fulfillment. Private property, limited government, and individual conscience are better than a collectivist understanding of the human condition; the individual pursuit of happiness is more important than the collectivist achievement of happiness. Locke's state of nature is peaceful, though it is poor. At the core of Locke's agenda is improvement. Locke's God encourages individuals to be self-reliant. Material improvement properly understood is a means to moral improvement. And, just as God created physical harmony not as the ancient cosmic static cyclical motion seeking rest but as in 'Newtonian' perpetually restless linear motion in concert with interaction among individual atoms, so there is a social harmony properly understood among private individuals each working to subdue the physical world.

Rousseau also rejected external standards in favor of internal standards. For him, however, we apprehend those standards through our feelings, the most important of which is sympathy for others. The ancients were correct in advocating a 'republic' (Spartan as opposed to Athenian) but wrong in excluding whole classes from citizenship. Medieval writers were correct in construing the social world as an agrarian community living in harmony with nature, but again erred in making it hierarchical. For Rousseau, however, the modern Lockean commercial republic is a complete sham. Whereas Locke originated the Liberty Narrative in response to forms of social control that disturbed him, so Rousseau is the originator of the Equality Narrative because when he looks around and sees inequality he becomes disturbed. The Equality Narrative wants to take a lunge toward perfection rather than settling for a step toward improvement.

There is in the Lockean narrative a presumption that life is an endless quest for self-expression (Newtonian and Hobbesian), a constant creation and re-creation. It is easy to see how this might degenerate into a destructive ambition. This presumption is viewed within the Rousseau narrative as a dysfunctional condition (Marx's alienation). The socialist critique of capitalism is that it is not just inefficient but immoral. Rousseau emphasizes society and its discontents. On the other hand, the insatiable demand for holistic fulfillment will be viewed by Lockeans as a pathological inability to come to terms with reality, which is why Locke emphasizes nature and its discontents. Rousseau would be, for Locke, one of the malcontents. Is Rousseau a pre-Marx collectivist or actually a supporter of radical independence in the form of the social drop out or the solitary walker? Or both? Is it reasonable to consider Rousseau's personal life of vice as evidence of personal dysfunction (something Lockean critics are apt to do) when analyzing his public remarks about virtue? Or can articulated ideas stand apart from personal life?

3.   Adam Smith and the System of Natural Liberty

INTRODUCTION: HUME AND SMITH

Adam Smith was part of a remarkable period of intellectual ferment now known as the Scottish Enlightenment. His closest friend both personally and intellectually was David Hume, arguably the greatest philosopher to write in the English language. We shall focus on Smith both because from the point of view of the Two Narratives there is no significant difference and because Smith's *Wealth of Nations* (1776), over 1000 pages long, has been the most or certainly one of the most influential works in political economy.

Before moving to that work we pause to note some important philosophical preconceptions shared by Hume and Smith. Both are quintessentially modern thinkers. Epistemologically and metaphysically, Hume anticipated the Copernican Revolution in philosophy, as Kant himself acknowledged. Despite his reputation as an alleged empiricist and skeptic, the whole point of Hume's epistemology is that knowledge is not a matter of reproducing in our mind external structures but in structuring our experience both psychologically in terms of the association of ideas and in terms of customary social practice. And, while reason may be the slave of the passions, our greatest mental asset is the imagination. For the first time in Western thought, the imagination in Hume and Kant becomes a positive force – not a disorienting liability. It is our capacity to imagine (even "feel" within), the perspective of others or of some abstract social perspective, that allows us to share the social world even beyond the narrow range of a natural benevolence.

Likewise, Hume and Smith were both enamored of the Newtonian World View in which nature is the primitive condition not the teleological end state. Whatever ultimate principles of explanation we formulate, we are finally confronted, philosophically, with the question why there is that order in either physical nature or the social world (a vital question in a non-teleological universe); and the answer to which Newton, Hume, and Smith subscribed is to attribute it to God (who bears some remote analogy to the human mind but remains a mystery without endorsing a particular theology). Newton, Hume, and Smith took the philosophical issue seriously whatever their orthodox religious detractors or atheistic friends alleged. Hume's and Smith's overall philosophical framework may be summarized as follows:

1. Human action, not contemplation, is primordial, hence the adoption of the technological project.
2. Reflection is always ultimately reflection on prior practice, hence thought is fundamentally 'conservative' and not radical. Explanation is not the grasping of an external structure but the subject's imposition or projection of structure.
3. Social practice is the pre-theoretical ground of all theoretical activity. How we understand ourselves is fundamental, and how we understand the non-human world is derivative. We cannot, ultimately, understand ourselves by reference to physical structures.
4. Physical world: Newtonian (atoms already in motion); science is not the observation of nature but experimentation on and with nature. It is technological.
5. The social world is the interaction of self-directed individuals. Social knowledge and understanding do not consist of the discovery through reason of absolute (timeless and context less) standards external to humanity but involve, instead, the clarification of standards implicit within the human mind and/or social practice/interaction. Our ability to sympathize with others through imaginatively generated sympathy and the consequent ability to adopt a social perspective by means of sympathy accounts for human sociability.
6. Ethics is the clarification of individual autonomy and responsibility (that is, natural liberty).
7. Politics is focused on limiting (not eliminating) the power of the state in the interest of expanding human autonomy (natural liberty). The primary function of government is managing and minimizing, not eliminating, potential collisions. The sum-total of all of the interactions ('collisions') does not point to a collective good.
8. Since the pre-theoretical ground is not itself capable of being conceptualized, and since there is no collective good, there can be no intellectual elite, either clerical or secular.
9. Philosophy is both (a) the explication of the logic (procedural norms) of each and every human activity and (b) the articulation of the larger vision of how these activities relate to each other. It is both analytic (conceptual clarification) and synthetic (larger vision);

it is neither the accession of an independent cosmic order nor a form of advocacy.

HUME, SMITH, AND ROUSSEAU

It is our contention that Hume and Smith refashioned the Lockean narrative. Nevertheless, there are several factors that link Hume and Smith together with Rousseau. All three were modern in the philosophical sense of rejecting key features of classical thought; all three were deeply influenced by and believed in a natural history account of the human world; all three recognized sympathy as the basis of the social world. More importantly, all three recognized and grappled with the immense social and political challenges created by the transition from a feudal agrarian economy to a commercial and industrial one.

Rousseau published his *Discourses* in 1750 and 1754, both wholly critical of the transition. Hume published "On Commerce" in 1752, wholly supportive of the transition. Nevertheless, Hume was so impressed with Rousseau that he not only exchanged mutually flattering letters but finally met with Rousseau in Paris in 1765 and helped him find refuge in England. Unfortunately the mutual admiration faded and ended in a now famous quarrel.

Before leaving Hume, it is useful to quote him on why equality cannot be the basis of public policy:

> these ideas of perfect equality ... are really, at bottom, impracticable; and ... extremely pernicious to human society. Render possessions ever so equal, men's different degrees of art, care, and industry will immediately break that equality. Or if you check these virtues, you reduce society to the most extreme indigence; and instead of preventing want and beggary in a few, render it unavoidable to the whole community. The most rigorous inquisition too is requisite to watch every inequality on its first appearance; and the most severe jurisdiction, to punish and redress it. But besides, so much authority must soon degenerate into tyranny. (Hume 1751, *An Enquiry Concerning the Principles of Morals*, III, ii, # 155)

When Smith read Rousseau's *Discourses*, he took a more balanced approach as seen in his letters to the *Edinburgh Review* in 1756. Smith acknowledged the legitimacy and timeliness of some of Rousseau's concerns. Smith began to respond to those concerns, without naming Rousseau directly as he had in the letters, both in the *Theory of Moral Sentiments* (Smith 1759), and in the *Wealth of Nations* which he started in the early 1760s and published in 1776. It is fair to say that the *Wealth of Nations* in particular is in part a restatement of the Lockean narrative in response to Rousseau.

TECHNOLOGICAL PROJECT

There are four themes in Adam Smith's *Wealth of Nations*: (1) in Book I, Smith presents his version of the technological project amid what he calls the System of Natural Liberty where he asks the reader to first imagine and second to understand what would happen to an economy if left to its own "natural" devices; (2) Book III provides a non-Marxist account of what we might call a natural theory of economic growth; (3) Book IV looks at the competing theories of political economy with special emphasis on the Mercantilists and their vast range of public policy tools which they used to intervene in the economy both at home and abroad; and (4) Book V examines the legitimate role of government, namely, those activities that are consistent with the natural system described in the earlier books.

Echoing Locke, Smith maintains that wealth and growth are the result of the labor that human beings put into nature. Specifically, the division of labor leads to the invention of labor-saving devices: "the invention of a great number of machines which facilitate and abridge labor, and enable one man to do the work of many" (Smith 1776, *Wealth of Nations*, I, i, 5). This is manifest in his famous example of the pin factory (now represented on the present UK £10 note). Moreover, like Locke and Hume, Smith thinks that technology and growth are on the whole better than living in a primitive agricultural society.

Smith is interested in some real measure of the wealth of nations. He pays more attention to how the wealth of a nation changes over time. Smith argues that the wealth of a nation ought to be measured by the total amount of the necessities and conveniences of life produced divided by the total population. Today, we might call this the per capita Gross National Product. Smith contrasts this natural measure with the balance of trade and accumulation of gold measures of the Mercantilists. And he focuses exclusively on increasing the numerator, or production of wealth, rather than decreasing the denominator or size of the population to be fed, clothed, and housed by the wealth (anti-Malthusian, the opposite of China's former policy of limiting family size). The cause of the wealth of nations thus depends on increasing the output of the nation and this depends on the productivity of labor, which depends on the division of labor and which, in turn, depends on the extent of the market. Both here and later, Smith claims that natural inclinations and accidental geographical discoveries (spontaneous order) are more important in the story of human liberty than "human wisdom."

The reason to move toward some sort of objective measure of well-being is because Smith is arguing against mercantilism, which loosely speaking means the doctrine of the nation state as the unit of analysis and its wealth is to be measured by how successful an international merchant it has been. Thus the balance of trade and the balance of payments and the flow of bullion become the proper measures for the well-being of the nation. Mercantilism then and now takes a variety of forms, but the core is that it has a special view of political economy. The political is the governmental and the governmental involves the well-being of the nation state as determined by governmental and economic leaders. This phenomenon can be associated with the extent of the market made possible by the discoveries of the new world, but the activities that take place are not left to the natural working of the markets both domestic and international. Rather certain industries are protected through tariffs and others subsidized.

MARKET ECONOMY

One of the main points is a parsing of the title of the *Wealth of Nations*. There is an assumption in Smith, as there is in Locke, that the well-being of the nation is closely linked to the wealth of the nation. There is the old nursery rhyme about Solomon Grundy: born on Monday, christened on Tuesday, married on Wednesday, took ill on Thursday, got worse on Friday, died on Saturday, buried on Sunday. That is the life of Solomon Grundy. But is that the inevitable lot of the vast bulk of mankind for the rest of eternity? The assumption here, as in Locke, is that in the beginning life was poor and short, but it need not be solitary and brutal. With the help of the arts and sciences we can replace the presumption of inevitable poverty with the hope of human improvement. The further presumption is that human beings both want to respond to that challenge and have the ability to improve their condition (economic development). Thus, the full title of Smith's book is *An Inquiry Into The Nature And Causes Of The Wealth Of Nations*. Interestingly, he does not ask what is the nature and causes of the poverty of nations. Poverty is the original condition of man, but it does not have to be the permanent condition. So how do we get out of poverty?

To anticipate, the socialists of the nineteenth century and beyond are much more interested in asking about the poverty of nations; they think that wealth is concentrated in the hands of the few and thus talking about the wealth of a nation is actually a misguided effort. Why people are unequal – is the central question. And the cause of this unequal nature is the greed of the few.

In a manner of speaking, the central claim of Smith is that the market economy allows the technological project to raise the living standard of everyone. Echoing Locke, Smith reminds his readers that "the accommodation of an European prince does not always so much exceed that of an industrious and frugal peasant, as the accommodation of the latter exceeds that of many an African king, the absolute master of the lives and liberties of ten thousand naked savages" (Smith 1776, *Wealth of Nations*, I, I, ii).

Just as important is the claim, echoing Hume, that commercial society fosters positive human interaction and the moral character needed to sustain it:

> The woolen coat … which covers the day laborer … is the produce of the joint labor of a great multitude … without the assistance and cooperation of many thousands, the very meanest person in a civilized country could not be provided … the easy and simple manner in which he is commonly accommodated. (Smith 1776, *Wealth of Nations*, I, I, ii)

Also central to the productivity of the process of wealth creation is the natural capacity of human beings to "truck, barter, and exchange" with the butcher, baker, and brewer for their daily beef, bread, and beer. Like Locke, Smith argues that the process of exchange is facilitated by the invention of money which, properly understood, is a medium of exchange rather than wealth itself. It is instructive that both Locke and Smith only introduce money into the discussion after they have talked about what is *real* in the process.

Book III supports a natural theory of economic growth against a planned theory of economic growth. There is a natural pattern to progress: food, then clothing, and then shelter. The domestic market first and then exchange internationally.

There are a number of positive features to a market society. It encourages participants to take others seriously, for example, your potential customers or employers, or employees. It leads to a meritocracy based on ability and achievement rather than an aristocracy which encourages flattery, obsequiousness, and connections. One of the advantages of a commercial society is that it leads to the abolition of slavery because wage laborers are more economical. Slaves have no incentive to produce more than what they need for their own subsistence, whereas free wage laborers have a motive to maximize production to increase their personal income above subsistence, and this, in turn, maximizes the profits of capitalists.

INVISIBLE HAND

Adam Smith's *Wealth of Nations* is over 1000 pages in length yet the moral and intellectual foundation of the work turns on one critical page in Book IV, where Smith refers to an "invisible hand." Moreover this crucial reference is buried in a chapter that criticizes the first of six public policy instruments, the use of tariffs that constitute the political economy of the mercantilist school. This concept is present as well in the *Theory of Moral Sentiments* (Smith 1759: Smith has a further reference in the *Astronomy* where he is dismissive of "the invisible hand of Jupiter"):

> Every individual is continually exerting himself to find out the most advantageous employment for whatever capital he can command ... . He generally ... neither intends to promote the public interest, nor knows how much he is promoting it ... he intends only his own gain, and he is in this ... led by an invisible hand to promote an end which was no part of his intention ... . By pursing his own interest he frequently promotes that of the society more effectually than when he really intends to promote it. (Smith 1776, *Wealth of Nations*, IV, ii, iv)

What does this concept mean and how central are these couple of pages to Smith's overall project? Can we dismiss these pages and not lose anything in Smith? Is it a metaphor or does it have a supernatural quality? Is he articulating an early version of the doctrine of unintended consequences? Does it make any difference if we read the passage to be saying "led *as if* by an invisible hand," rather than "led by *an* invisible hand?" Is this proto-cybernetics or just a mystical explanation? And does the use of the indefinite article, "an," rather than the definite article, "the," make a difference? We are thinking of references in the Smith literature to his apparent reliance on "*the* invisible hand of the market."

There is an obvious explanation of what the "invisible hand" expresses. Newton, Locke, and Hume all believed that there were discoverable regularities both in the physical world and in the social world. The ultimate explanation of why there are these regularities is God. Among the regularities is the discovery that the pursuit of economic self-interest by myriad individuals within the framework of the technological project and the market economy enhances the interests of all. The world is not zero-sum. The labor saving device that I invent contributes not only to my fortune but to yours as well. The invisible hand is a disciplining device, it is information providing, and it helps us to make rational decisions. It accounts for, justifies, and defuses the issue of inequality for those who subscribe to it. And, it precludes central planning.

In the eyes of some later defenders of the Lockean narrative the concept of the "invisible hand" is an embarrassment. Economists inclined to positivism do not want to rest their defense of the market economy upon empirically unverifiable theology, preferring instead that the invisible hand is portrayed as an automatic self-correcting mechanism, a deterministic activity governed by unchanging laws of social order. They portray it as a metaphor. According to them, Smith did not really mean that there was literally an invisible hand. People were led "as if by an invisible hand." Several lovers of the market – Friedrich von Hayek, Milton Friedman and George Stigler – are embarrassed by the phrase because it suggests an interventionist God rather than a spontaneous and evolutionary mechanism that produces order. These defenders of the market argue that it is the coordinating device of the price system that guides. There isn't anything mysterious about the invisible hand at all. The "invisible hand" is simply a metaphor for the phenomenon of unintended consequences. Thankfully, in their eyes, we don't have to deal with moral arguments, individual character, ethical concerns and the public good. Smith is a realist, rather than a normativist, who describes how the market process or mechanism really works. His genius is that he explained how individuals pursuing their own gains respond to incentives that lead to equilibrium outcomes whereas government interferences will be injurious to economic growth. We appeal to what others want and in doing so Smith relies on the competitive system of exchange rather than the benevolence of others or the wisdom of statesmen to improve the human condition.

Nevertheless the positivists are missing something important in Smith, something that becomes increasingly important in the evolution of the Lockean narrative. There are three issues that need to be distinguished. First, is the self-interest of each individual compatible with the self-interest of every other individual? With regard to the first issue, the Rousseau challenge to the Lockean narrative is not just that it leads to inequality but that inequality reflects a fundamental social disequilibrium, one in which the success of some is bought at the expense of others. Another way of putting this challenge is to ask how we know that the ultimate interest of each (both economically and otherwise) is compatible with the ultimate interest of all. Advocates of a collectivist or communal conception of humanity believe that they have the obvious logical answer

– the ultimate good of each individual is to be part of the collective. Smith's answer, like Locke, is that in the light of the technological project and the market economy we are better off economically by cooperating.

Second, how do individuals come to take each other's interests seriously? With regard to the second issue, Smith's answer is (a) that we have a natural inclination to engage in commerce and (b) that through imagination we are able to sympathize with others and with a larger social perspective.

Third, am I always better off taking the interests of others seriously or should I merely pay lip service to it? Another way of asking the last question is: are we, as individuals (Hume's sensible knave), best served by cooperating with, seeming to cooperate with, or on occasion cheating and exploiting others. With regard to the third issue, it does not matter how often Lockeans embarrass Rousseaueans by exposing the inadequacy of the collectivist model. Are we doomed to individual greed, avarice, and opportunism? The successes of the technological project and the market economy exacerbate the problem. One of the most important things about Smith is that he acknowledges and grapples with this problem. It does not seem that either Hume or Smith has an adequate or satisfying answer to this third issue. It is Kant who will address this issue in his version of the Lockean narrative.

A final note on the 'invisible hand' concerns the meaning of the expression "public interest." It cannot mean the 'collective interest' because this is what moderns who deny teleology would say, namely, that the concept of the 'collective interest' has no meaning. This is what Hayek will later maintain. Could it mean the 'common interest'? The 'common interest' might mean the sum total of the economic interests of all the individuals in society. If this is what Smith meant then he is on firm ground and consistent with what he said earlier about how a market economy improves the living standard of everyone. Finally, the 'common interest' might mean the procedural norms (rules of the game) on which we all agree in order to pursue our private substantive interests. We do not think this is what Smith meant, but it is what later expositors of the Lockean narrative, specifically Hayek and Oakeshott, will understand the 'common interest' to mean. For the latter two, the common interest is the rule of law in a civil association that only recognizes individual interests; and this is compatible with what Smith was saying. In any case, for Lockeans the "public interest" is never a collective interest.

Are there limits to markets? Is it market or government failure then to make up for deficiencies in markets? It is neither; it is human nature because the enemy of the good is the perfect. Smith's System of Natural

Liberty maintains that the market essentially does not fail because people make incorrect decisions; people are inclined by nature to trade, and we aren't beggars. Beggars depend upon the benevolence of others. The premise is if people are left to themselves they will work problems out without bringing harm or danger. If this is true then a crisis involves the outside forces of government because of external effects that can't be controlled. Smith writes that market failure is not a natural part of the system. If government has a big role, then cause and effect goes in the opposite direction – then the law of unintended consequences goes into effect. Therefore, the solution is less government and a deregulation of ownership with the means of production as a catalyst.

Some scholars are quick to point out that Smith does allow for a role for government in the economy, most especially with regard to infrastructure. Was Smith or wasn't he a libertarian? If by "libertarian (anarchist variety)" is meant the complete absence of government, Smith was not a libertarian. But that is to miss the point. Smith is not an ideologue. He believes that government can help the economy if there are no private players with the resources to carry out certain economically useful projects. On the other hand, if there were such players, there would be less of a role for government. Smith would no doubt welcome many contemporary libertarian proposals for privatization. He would also point out the law of unintended consequences – government bureaucracies as feudal fiefdoms, sovereign debt associated with unfunded public pensions, and so on. Smith was not doctrinaire but saw himself as a natural historian of the social world.

Smith thought the government needed to provide education to help workers cope with the changing economy. But, he insisted that teachers not be paid exclusively by the government lest it lead to government control and mismanagement.

ECONOMICS

Smith's view of economics is Newtonian. Just as Newton imagines inertia, Smith believes it is possible to conceive an economic way of perfect competition, which is the heart of microeconomics. Smith believes in this economic state of nature, not just individuals (Locke), that individuals come together, and cooperate with each other because they are inclined to trade, truck, and barter with one another. It is a natural economic system because people need to cooperate with each other – a division of labor helps people to work with one another – a natural inclination. The haggling of the market helps people reach agreements and equilibrium. The heart of mercantilism was that human beings need a certain kind of knowledge to fix a market that won't work by itself. Smith also embraces the division of labor for improvement, whereas later Marx will see it as dehumanizing.

Smith makes the reader ask if the system grows over time. Yes, and is there a natural way to make it grow? Yes, but what is emphasized? The basic point of departure is food, shelter, and clothing. Yet Smith shows agriculture is not the end, but the beginning. His world has made us graduate from food, shelter, and clothing to beer, bangles, and beads – Ha! We move from a primitive society (Third World) to First World (where there are choices of bread: sourdough, rye, light brown, wheat rolls, and so on – a civilized world gives more choices of everything within the market). Butter is no longer a luxury, and the list is endless. Smith – you don't really grow unless you do something with the land (very Lockean) and do something to make labor more productive (which is done by introducing machinery).

According to Smith, there are three factors crucial to the production of wealth: natural resources (land), capital, and labor. Corresponding to these three factors there were three kinds of income: rent, interest, and wages. A consequence of the three sources of income was three social classes: landlords, capitalists, and laborers. Wealth is maximized to the extent that all parties in the process engage in postponed gratification: landlords should charge minimal rents, capitalists reinvest their profits and laborers accept subsistence wages and only modest increases. Anything beyond subsistence wages leads to a decrease in the amount of capital and a subsequent decrease in the amount of potential wealth. Ultimately, equilibrium will be attained among a stationary population, wages, and profits. Smith worried about the idea of a stationary economic state. On the whole Smith presented a harmonious growth model.

What Ricardo added to this analysis was a critique of landlords. The landlords were identified with Tory aristocratic landowners who had not acquired that land through labor but originally through conquest and later through inheritance. Landlords tended to think in feudal terms, rather than industrial terms, and seemed more interested in maintaining their position of social preeminence and political control than in increasing national or international wealth. Landlords tended to favor mercantilist policies, including monopolistic privileges and tariffs. Tariffs on the importation of grain (corn) led to a corresponding increase in the cost of subsistence. This in turn leads to an increase in wages. The increase in wages leads to a decrease in profits. This will be followed by less incentive to save and form capital, and so growth will come to an end sooner. The weak link in this chain is the rapacious and profligate landlords bent on conspicuous consumption. In a curious sort of way, Ricardo would agree with Rousseau but see this as an historical accident and not a necessary feature of market economies.

LIMITED GOVERNMENT (POLITICAL ECONOMY)

Smith was arguing against everyone of influence during his time. The mercantilists were the specific target of his wrath. Mercantilism is the doctrine where the state becomes the merchant. The state decides how much is produced and for what price. Mercantilism replaced church fathers or agrarian life, and emerged before Columbus discovered the new world. Mercantilism believes the nation state is more important than the individual consumer. Why is the nation state more important in their eyes? It is because the world is zero-sum and nations must aggressively compete for a stationary or shrinking pie.

Today's mercantilists say saving a factory in Pittsburgh is more important than a consumer receiving a lower price. They believe putting a tariff on Chinese-made toys would help promote our domestic toy industry in the US. The slippery slope of mercantilism could also mean the State is not only the merchant, but sets prices and uses slogans such as, "Buy British beef, because her Majesty the Queen demands it!" What's important to understand is that what is good for the consumer, the individual, the producer, and the country or nation state are all different economic values. This is very important to understand when discussing or studying Smith.

Smith was very interested in trade but disliked merchants – because thcy sought to restrict trade by having the government create licenses and so on, and brought about permanent monopolies. Merchants are prone to monopolize and collaborate to restrict trade – they are interested in market share, not competition. He associated merchants with mercantilism – restricting free trade at home and abroad in the name of something abstract – national safety, too big to fail, whatever. Smith was pro-market not pro-business people. He understood crony capitalism.

Herein we have Smith's answer to Rousseau. Mercantilism is a continuation or an extension of feudal political organization in the rising market economy. Mired in its belief that wealth is zero-sum, mercantilism is the source of the social dysfunction that Rousseau attributes to market economies. What Smith sought was to free market economies from its vestigial feudalism. Just as the ancients did not understand physics, so they did not understand economics.

Smith contrasts natural liberty with mercantilism. "This division of labor, from which so many advantages are derived, is not originally the effect of any human wisdom, which foresees and intends that general opulence to which it gives occasion." As if human wisdom has the ability to foresee. Smith never sees much good occur from those who "intend" to do the public good – the appeal to a substantive and collectivist public good is a myth that camouflaged private ambition. Smith advocates a "natural" wisdom over and against human wisdom. Smith wants the economy to work on its own and not have the government set fair prices or even regular prices. Underlying this model is that competition between producers, rather than government protection of producers, will advance the well-being of the consumer and thus the working class in general:

> The statesman who should attempt to direct private people in what manner they ought to employ their capitals, would not only load himself with a most unnecessary attention, but assume an authority which could safely be trusted, not only to no single person, but to no council or senate whatever, and which would nowhere be so dangerous as in the hands of a man who had folly and presumption enough to fancy himself fit to exercise it. (Smith 1776, *Wealth of Nations*, IV, ii, 10)

It is important to keep in mind that since there is no social collective goal, the good statesman is not one who is focused on civic virtue in pursuit of that goal, but is one who does not violate public trust for motives of personal gain. Given his understanding of the role of government, and given his opposition to crony capitalism it is not surprising that Smith opposed colonial empires, especially those that exploited the colonists or natives.

Smith gives us a new understanding of the phrase, "a rising tide lifts all boats," when we acknowledge that the tide is raised by productive workers in a productive society. This has taken the classics to a modern-era understanding that is still relevant in an interwoven twenty-first century world. Smith has given a framework to navigate the various frameworks of political economy, which thus far have included the fundamentally different approaches of Locke and Rousseau.

A nation state should divide the labor tasks among people and not have a nation where everyone is a Jack of all trades the way an agrarian society forces farmers to know everything about their farm for survival. That stifles economic activity and GNP according to Smith. The increase in productivity of labor is a result of an increase in the division of labor that leads to an increase in the extent of the overall market. The extent of the market means that degrees of specialization can take place. If someone is truly interested in human improvement they would focus on the higher productivity of labor, and not social justice or the causes of inequality (Rousseau and Marx).

Smith and Locke look at the well-being of nations, not the source of poverty. The rising tide metaphor applies internationally as well. Smith understands comparative advantage, namely, that a nation is better off by specializing and trading. There is an immediate global outreach into the causes and nature of the wealth of nations.

RULE OF LAW

Like Locke, Smith believes in natural rights divorced from any medieval theory of natural law. As in Locke this is a Protestant view, not a Catholic one. Unlike Locke, Smith does not offer a direct theological account of the origin of natural rights. He begins with the presumption that God created a certain order in nature, that order is discovered empirically, and we can identify what is natural in that sense. At the same time, Smith subscribed to an evolutionary (natural history) account (first suggested by Montesquieu) of human society that involved four economic stages: hunters and fishermen, shepherds, agriculture, and commercial societies. In the first, there is no permanent property and hence no magistracies or positive laws.

The moral theory of natural rights is logically independent of the economic evolution of law. What are the natural rights? Each person has a natural right to "do what he has a mind when it does not prove detrimental to any other person" (Smith 1762–3, *Lectures on Jurisprudence* (A), i, 13). This statement takes on huge significance when we come to J.S. Mill. In addition, according to Smith, we have the natural right to our labor, to engage in commerce, and to marry, among other things. The natural right to labor is "the original foundation of all other property" and therefore "the most sacred and inviolable" (Smith 1776, *Wealth of Nations*, IV, v, b.43).

There is, however, no natural right to property. In societies that recognize private property and inequality of possessions, there are both natural rights and laws. Because inequality breeds envy and resentment by the poor, the rich need to secure their possessions against the danger of invasions, violence, and assaults on reputation. "Till there be property there can be no government, the very end of which is to secure wealth and to defend the rich from the poor" (Smith 1776, *Wealth of Nations*, IV, v, b.43). It will be interesting to see what Marx does with this conception of government. In feudal societies, according to Smith, laws develop to suppress and exploit; in commercial societies, laws develop to protect private property. In any case, laws must be consistent with our natural rights, understood negatively. The rule of law exists then when individuals can pursue their private goals without involuntary subordination to the goals of others or to an alleged collective social goal. This is quite consistent with what Hayek and Oakeshott say later.

PERSONAL AUTONOMY

The ancients had a world view in which everything both in physical nature and in the social world was teleological, and, therefore there was no conflict between the individual and society and nature as they understood it. In practice it never prevented conflict. In theory, all of that was swept aside by modern physics. Smith and Hume followed Newton and consciously distanced themselves from the ancients. The physical world is mechanical, and in the social world they do not see a teleological moral harmony between the individual and the social order. Thus there is a need for a moral philosophy that addresses the relationship between the individual and the society.

The task of the philosopher says Smith is to imagine the "concealed connections" that produce harmony, order, and justice. In his *Astronomy* he defined a system as "an imaginary machine invented to connect together in the fancy those different movements and effect which are already in reality preferred." The invisible hand is invisible to human eyes but it is visible to the human imagination. And "philosophy, by representing the invisible chains which join together all the disjointed objects, endeavors to introduce order into the chaos of jarring and discordant appearances, and to all, this turnout of the imagination" (Smith 1982, p. 45).

In addition to a limited benevolence, Hume and Smith replace classical reason with "imagination" and thus elevate sympathy to a place of prominence in which society is a construct of individuals capable of change. The self is not egoistic. This is the view Smith expressed in the Theory of Moral Sentiments. This view is expanded in *Wealth of Nations* wherein the phenomenon of the division of labor and specialization pervades the life of civilized men. Not only do we accept that as the road to human improvement; rather it is the road to cooperation between individuals. We realize that we have a fundamental need for each other and therefore we exchange with each other. It is the distinctive quality of humans, says Smith, to make contracts. No other animal does this. Failure to see this interaction led to the endless and pointless debates that German scholars had dubbed the "Adam Smith Problem" (namely, trying to reconcile sympathy in the *Theory of Moral Sentiments* with the pursuit of individual gain in the *Wealth of Nations*).

Smith's view of 'natural' is similar to, but different from, Locke's view. It is similar in the sense that it is possible to conceive or imagine nature as different from what exists around us. So Locke can imagine – it is not necessary that it exist in fact – a state of nature where individuals are free of custom and convention in order then to remake custom and convention in accordance with the ideal of nature. Smith imagines an economic system free from the customs and conventions of the past and present. And if you leave people alone, they have natural instincts prior to knowledge that inclines them to cooperation. Smith says that humans, unlike dogs, are inclined to truck, barter, and exchange. "Nobody ever saw one animal by its gestures and natural cries signify to another, this is mine, that is yours; I am willing to give this for that" (Smith 1776, *Wealth of Nations*, I, ii, 4–5). Interestingly, he uses the same language as Rousseau to arrive at a different conclusion: humans understand that this is mine, and that is yours, so let's trade. Rousseau turns the "this is mine" idea into the teaching that private property is theft rather than private property is to be exchanged.

If there are dysfunctional selves, it is the result of dysfunctional institutions in feudal societies, or it is the result of ignorance about what our self-interest is when properly understood (Tocqueville). The *Wealth of Nations* is written in part to explain how to become a fit participant in a market society. So part of Smith's correction of both Hobbes and Locke is to suggest that the state of nature is more peaceful, and nature has a way of bringing about plenty rather than breaking down because of the inclination of humans to war. Perhaps this is the reason why Smith can entertain an even more limited government than Locke.

In Book V, Smith outlines three major areas where government has an important part to play in a market orientated system: defense, justice, and public works, which last mentioned is broken down into the facilitation of commerce, the education of youth, and the instruction of all ages especially in the area of religion. Among other things, Smith encourages the government to be involved in overcoming the negative effects to the individual of a life defined by the division of labor. So we have a paradox: the division of labor is central to the well-being of the nation but also contributes to the degradation of the individual.

Unlike Rousseau, Smith believes that civil society can be viewed separately from religion. There is nothing comparable in Smith to Rousseau's advocacy of a civil faith that makes loyalty to the General Will a substantive commitment. There isn't a need for an established church because it is a bad idea, but what the citizen needs is free enterprise religion. Let people go shopping for religion, and if they are dissatisfied with one church they go find another church. Smith would advocate for a citizen not to become an atheist but instead have religious competition match political and economic competition. Locke would agree, whereas Rousseau does not believe in private religion because it takes away from the state's social contract.

Given the absence of a universal and all-encompassing teleology, there is no way to prove to, or to persuade a specific individual that he/she is better off cooperating with others in good faith. Given human fallibility, humanity needs moral structure, rules, and constraints to have the opportunity for a great life. For Smith, Locke, and others, without some type of morality usually expressed as a religious narrative, humanity is doomed. But the narrative must be freely chosen by the individual or it loses its effect. Smith advocated religious liberty by encouraging competition among religious sects. Neither classical reason, nor a Rousseauean act of will, can eradicate my radical sense of individuality or self.

We remain interested in the invisible hand for both practical and intellectual reasons. With the collapse of state socialism, the single most important criticism of the commercial republic has withered away. But the need to grasp the moral and intellectual foundations of the commercial republic has not gone away but has become even more important than before. The end of the history of socialist economics is not the end of all history. This is not the time to be complacent about the relationship between economic liberty and political freedom. Winning the Cold War is an insufficient defense of the commercial republic.

We still hear from people of civility that a market economy is pathological, that it treats humans as means and not ends, it is destructive of culture and tradition, especially the religious tradition of sacrifice and benevolence, it promotes greed and inequality and the satisfaction of immediate desires. As the head bishop of the Los Angeles Episcopalian Diocese sarcastically put it, one of the wonderful things about faith in the invisible hand is that is absolves humans of the responsibility of doing the work of hard thinking and cooperative planning. If the public sector isn't doing well, just turn it over to the hand. Efficiency is not a good enough defense.

4. The Arrival of the Liberty Narrative in America

JOHN LOCKE AND THE COMMERCIAL REPUBLIC

What joins commerce or trade with republic and law is the centrality of consent and contracts as normal parts of living in society. People have been exchanging goods and services for centuries, but it is only when money replaced barter and money-making became defensible that commerce emerges as a way of life. Similarly, the word 'republic' has been used by philosophers and the statesmen of Rome for centuries, but it is only when we grasp what a republic *is not* that the word becomes clearer. The attachment to public things inherent in the word republic is best understood in terms of its opposite, namely an attachment to private things. By the seventeenth century, republicanism was seen as an improvement over monarchy or absolute rule by one person for his or her own private interest. The rallying cry for republics was that the rule of law should replace the rule of man.

But it is not obvious that commerce and republic should be joined together. After all, the People's Republic, Socialist Republic, Islamic Republic, and Protestant Republic have all existed and they are all suspicious of the commercial way of life. And one can at least imagine widespread commercial activity taking place in nineteenth century Victorian England and twenty-first century Communist China.

We could begin our study of the commercial republic with Plato's *Republic* where he remarks that a commercial regime would create a city fit for pigs while a philosopher-run regime would create a civilized city. Or we could turn to Aristotle's *Politics* where we learn that the management of the household (*oikos-nomos*) is inferior to governing the polis and that certain economic activities are more in line with the natural order than others. In particular, making money from money (for example, finance) is an unnatural act whereas self-sufficient farming is praise worthy. We could then work our way through Aquinas and beyond and discuss such concepts as the just price, the just wage, and other criticisms of the deadly sins that emerge from devoting too much attention to the life of the body and the secular world. Such a study would reveal two important points: (1) the case had to be made in favor of a commercial republic, and (2) there is something unsatisfying about the modern commercial republic whether from attachment to ancient virtues or attachment to post-modern values.

Instead of focusing on the ancients, we begin our coverage of the commercial republic with the late seventeenth century work of John Locke. The dominant theme in Locke's work is that improvement in mankind's material condition is both possible and desirable. With the help of the discoveries of modern science generally and Rene Descartes, Newton, and Francis Bacon particularly, Locke presented a view of human progress and the transformation of nature (the technological project) that was unknown to the ancients. And he argued this could best be achieved both by challenging the then existing mixed economic system of mercantilism and feudalism, and the notion of the divine right of kings and absolute monarchy and endorsing the view that the church should be separated from the state. Unlike the classicists and the post-moderns, Locke envisioned the essential unit of analysis to be the autonomous individual in a state of nature free from social restraints and governmental regulations. Locke portrayed this fundamental natural position of humans to be one of abject poverty. Nevertheless, since God gave the world to man to enjoy and improve rather than to simply suffer and to starve, to those who are rational and industrious and care for themselves by ploughing the land and investing in the useful arts and sciences, and they are to be held in the highest esteem. Private property is the source of human improvement, and although God gave the world to man in common, it is through the privatization of this property that the overall well-being is advanced. Accordingly, the acquisition of private property is natural and neither suspect, as the ancients would claim, nor theft, as the post-moderns would challenge.

Locke did not stop with a defense of private property. He went beyond offering an alternative to the mercantilist theory of production and the aristocratic distribution of property according to the law of primogeniture. He even went beyond a defense of commerce broadly understood and actually challenged the traditional answer to the political question of who should rule. Locke seriously undermined not only primogeniture in the economic world but also the divine right of kings in the political world by arguing that legitimate government came into existence by the consent of autonomous individuals who willingly surrendered the right to adjudicate disputes and reluctantly gave up the power to make laws that were necessary and proper for the well-being of the community. He rejected the idea that the rights of the people came from the government; rather the powers of the government were a limited grant by the people out of necessity. It's better to separate the powers of government and limit its reach to specified objects so that people retain control over vast areas of their lives.

The standard Rousseauean-derived critique of commercial society is that the very expression is an oxymoron. How can monetary economies based on exchange for profit and investment for profit produce an outcome where the public good is served? It rests on the fallacious assumption that competition actually exists in both spheres and produces a fair outcome, while experience proves that the economy does not work in this imaginary way and thus a government can't be limited to enforcing the rule of laws against the theft of property and the abuse of power. The government, particularly a democratically inclined government – according to the critics – must control commerce so that it works on behalf of the people rather than the advancement of the interests of the few. The new case for government is not the classical claim of molding (re)public(an) virtue, but the claim that the purpose of government is to secure the equal claim to happiness.

ADAM SMITH AND THE AMERICAN FOUNDING

Smith built on the Lockean foundation that the human condition was capable of improvement by individual initiative. Smith focused on improving the human condition by increasing the wealth of the nation. Poverty was to be solved by increasing production which in turn depended on the productivity of labor which was strongly influenced by the division or specialization of labor that depended on the extent of the market. But Smith's building on Locke's theory gave commerce an even greater moral support. Human beings' natural inclination to self-preservation gives them the right to the means to self-preservation. The butcher, the baker, and the brewer all have a natural inclination to "truck, barter, and exchange" beef, bread, and beer with other human beings. No "human wisdom" was needed to create this situation; the "propensity" to cooperate with others (Hayek's spontaneous order) is a vital part of a commercial or civilized society. In seeking the cooperation of others, however, we do not appeal to their generosity, but to their self-love, and never talk to them of our own necessities but of their advantages. Nobody but a beggar chooses to depend chiefly upon the benevolence of his fellow-citizens.

In the *Wealth of Nations*, Smith presents his System of Natural Liberty where a commercial society, if left to its own devices, produces both improvement and equilibrium. In contrast to Rousseau's belief that the technological project leads to the degradation of society, Smith wrote that the practical arts and sciences actually lead to the improvement of society and that there is a natural progress from a primitive agricultural community to an advanced, or "civilized and thriving country." In the final two books of the *Wealth of Nations*, Smith addressed the question of what should government do that is consistent with the System of Natural Liberty. He distinguishes, on the one hand, between a Mercantile system of political economy, where the government is extensively involved in the day to day operations of production and the granting of special privileges to a few companies, and, on the other, a commercial society where the government is limited to a few yet essential operations and the market operates in the area of production, distribution, and exchange. This defense of an active market against an active government was called the system of laissez-faire by John Stuart Mill in 1848 and the system of free enterprise by Hayek in the twentieth century. The presumption through the subsequent centuries is that individuals know what is best for themselves and that the market system works favorably for society in general. The government should resist the urge to interfere against the contrary defense of government action which points to market failure as justification for involvement.

There is a common thread that runs through both the defense and the critique of commercial society. That thread is the role of human wisdom. From Smith to Hayek and Friedman there is the suspicion that human wisdom is incapable of planning and anticipating what should be produced. On the other hand, there is a strong presumption from the Mercantilists through the Progressives – heirs of the philosopher kings if you will – that selfless administrators can be educated in how to determine the level and kind of production necessary for an efficiently run economy.

The other problem that needs to be considered is whether a commercial society promotes personal greed at the expense of a concern for the public welfare? And how is it possible that a concern with self-interest in fact leads to desirable outcomes? And how scientific is it to say that an invisible hand somehow works to turn unintended actions into favorable outcomes? To Rousseaueans this sounds like flashing mirrors economics. The defense from Locke through Smith to Hayek and Friedman is that a concern with self-interest is not the same as personal greed or self-indulgence. A commercial society requires its habitants to learn the values of hard work, thrift, and moderation. On the contrary says Smith "I have never known much good done by those who affected to trade for the public good" (Smith 1776, *Wealth of Nations*, IV, ii, 9). And to borrow from Tocqueville, the heavy hand of government involvement in the day to day lives of the people is likely to turn self-reliant citizens into obedient sheep or permanently dependent children.

THE AMERICAN FOUNDING AND THE COMMERCIAL REPUBLIC

The American authors of the *Federalist Papers* (Hamilton et al. 1787–88) followed the Smith model in their efforts to manage rather than eliminate faction. The well-being of the nation depended on the presence of economic, political, and religious liberty. These liberties in turn required and encouraged the growth of a variety of opinions, passions, and interests, which in turn depended greatly on the encouragement of a commercial society across an extended territory. Commerce and faction are not just tolerated, they are embraced.

This leads us to emphasize what is critical in the origin and development of the commercial republic. Commerce is vital for the preservation of economic, political, and religious liberty. At the heart of commerce is not only the idea of trade and exchange, but also competition. It is through the competition of firms and industries for the support of the consumer that economic liberty is secured. Similarly, the competition of the separate branches of government and different levels of government, augmented by frequent and fair elections helps secure political freedom. Linked to this is the notion that religious liberty is strongly influenced by the competition between a vast number and variety of religious sects for the support of the "religious consumer."

Perhaps the greatest contribution of the *Federalist Papers* was the claim that republicanism could be – in fact must be – built on a larger scale than had ever been previously imagined. The 'oracle' Montesquieu, for example, argued that republics could only thrive in small and homogeneous communities where people knew each other and had a sufficient range of experiences in common to care for the public things. To be sure, Montesquieu had supported federalism and the separation of powers, but he saw these republican institutions as auxiliaries to the social infrastructure of a small and homogeneous society such as Athens in ancient Greece where the inhabitants were involved as citizens and thus their public virtue was vital. But such small communities were not conducive to the encouragement of a variety of interests. The *Federalist Papers* 'corrected' Montesquieu by arguing that republican institutions will also work, even better in a large republic than in a small one. That is the whole point to *Federalists 10* and *51*.

Madison put it this way in *Federalist 51*: "if men were angels, no government would be necessary." We add, if men were beasts, free government would be impossible. Thus free government presupposes a sufficient degree of virtue in the people such that when supported by institutional and economic competition, the republican principle of "the deliberate sense of the community" will prevail. Contrary to Rousseau, Madison had no intention of trying to transform men into angels or to eliminate the causes of faction.

We have said that the very idea of republicanism in the modern world is to replace the arbitrary distribution of economic and political power with a reasonable criterion, the evidence for the truthfulness of which appears so obvious to the reasonable person. The conventional law of primogeniture and monarchical rule were deemed to be self-evidently false by the standard of nature. The rule of law is better than the rule of man. That is the key to the modern case for republicanism. One might add that the rule of markets – the law of supply and demand – is better than the rule of men in the economic realm. So it is not as unnatural as might first appear that commerce and republicanism belong together. A modern republic is designed to protect the rights of individuals and not just the rights of the few or the many, even the majority. Nor does modern republicanism stress the pre-existence and importance of a common good. Nor is it willing to rely simply on the voice of the people as the expression of a common good. Modern republicanism has a constitution which specifies the powers of government, the rights of individuals, and the powers and limitations of the majority of the people. To be sure, this institutional arrangement receives its continued legitimacy from frequent and fair popular elections as well as the super majoritarian amendment process.

Inspired by the political essays of David Hume, James Madison wrote, in *Federalist 10*, that "the most common and durable sources of faction" are the "various and unequal distribution of property." As we shall see, Karl Marx also considers the distribution of property as the great divide in modern society. But Madison and Marx differ over whether the Madisonian distinction between the "various" distribution of property and the "unequal" distribution of property is relevant. Madison does not deny Marx's claim that the battle between the few who are rich and the many who are poor – the unequal distribution of wealth issue – is at the core of class war and factious politics, and thus the "mortal disease" of every regime. He does, however, take seriously the possibility that economic disagreements can be framed in terms of the more manageable differences of degree, or variety, of property ownership. These differences of degree, in turn, are linked to an income or flow distribution of property concept rather than the more dangerous distinctions of wealth distribution or ownership of the means of production concept of property. Thus, an important distinction between the Liberty Narrative and the Equality Narrative turns on whether we are discussing wealth or income distribution.

It is better for free governments to tolerate unequal distribution of income because it is a by-product of a system of human improvement whose core value is individual liberty and the pursuit of happiness. By increasing the overall quantity and variety of the necessities and conveniences of life we can increase the size of the pie and avoid the nasty politics of redistributing the slices of a fixed size pie. The improvement in the human condition, which includes the preservation of liberty, requires an increase in the wealth of the nation so that we can avoid the negative impact on liberty and justice of a zero-sum-game condition.

Madison's adaptation of Smith can be expressed as follows: the well-being of the nation depends on controlling faction, and this depends on encouraging the productivity of labor, which in turn depends on generating a division of labor and a multiplicity of interests which, finally, depends on "the enlargement of the orbit," or what Smith called the extent of the market. Hence, a large republic is better if it is commercial. Competition, as opposed to monopoly, is at the core of Madison's solution to the problems of faction that emerge out of necessity in every civilized society. With competition comes prosperity which is vital for the enhancement of political liberty.

Madison continues his theme of controlling the effects of faction in *Federalist 51*. We know from *Federalist 10* that faction is sown in human nature. But it is impossible and undesirable to eliminate faction by (1) transforming humans into angels and (2) eliminating the very liberty that leads to the division of opinions, passions, interests and productivity in the community. Madison says experience has taught us to supplement a dependence of the government on the people with "auxiliary precautions," or "inventions of prudence." Thus, the separation of powers is an auxiliary to aid regular elections in the effort to oblige the government to control itself. He supplements this competition between the three branches of the federal government with the advantages of a "compound republic" where competition between the different levels of government makes the formation of a tyrannical majority unlikely.

"Let ambition counteract ambition," in a system of "opposite and rival interests." That seems to be Madison's theory of political economy. Madison, consistent with the teachings of Smith in the *Wealth of Nations*, adds one last word in favor of competition facilitated by the extended orbit or extended market: it provides the infrastructure for the development of a multiplicity of religious sects which is the prerequisite for the preservation of religious liberty. And thus, like Smith, he underscores the interrelationship between political liberty, economic liberty, and religious liberty.

Like Locke, Madison was aware of the interrelationship between the three pillars of liberty. With regard to the US *Declaration of Independence*, it is important to note in the emphasis on the natural right of the individual to life, liberty, and the pursuit of happiness, (natural) equality is the point of departure rather than a social outcome to be secured. And, by liberty, the *Declaration* means economic liberty – the right to the fruits of one's labor in the form of private property – political liberty – the right to choose the form of government under which one shall live – and religious liberty – the right to worship God according to one's conscience.

The *Constitution* and the Bill of Rights also demonstrate the interconnection between the three pillars. Note that (a) all the representatives of the federal government are to be paid an income for their services, (b) the powers of Congress extend to the regulation of (regularizing of) international and interstate commerce and the promotion of "the sciences and useful arts," (c) private property is protected by due process of law, (d) Congress shall pass no law with respect to the establishment of religion or abridging the free exercise of religion, and that (e) the powers not granted to the general government are reserved to the states or to the people.

Madison in 1787 explains why they were at the Constitutional Convention: because state legislatures habitually pass too many laws which means, in effect, too many rules for conduct. This proliferation of rules undermines the rule of law because we have no idea what these rules are. Madison, like Locke, wants the rule of law in order to support a free society. The law of rules undermines the notion of a free society. The rule of law, in contrast, presupposes that somehow if left to our own devices, for the most part, we can govern ourselves. The second reason for the Convention is that not only are rules so many but they change all the time. So it undermines the rule of law since you never know what's going on. Third, these rules have a way of violating the rights to property and religion. Two centuries later, Hayek made the same point about the growth of bureaucracy and the proliferation of rules in *The Road to Serfdom* (Hayek 1944) and Hernando de Soto proved it empirically in *The Mystery of Capital: Why Capitalism Succeeds in the West and Fails Everywhere Else* (de Soto 2000).

The Rule of Law means arriving at a situation where those in power must exercise their power in a reasonable fashion. It is defined in terms of the regulating and the preservation of property and the common defense of the country rather than for the benefit of the ruler per se. It is for the benefit of the public. In that regard there is a connection between the rule of law and the public good.

THE US *CONSTITUTION* AND THE COMMERCIAL REPUBLIC

Let's take a look at the constitutional support for a commercial republic. Let's take the language seriously. And let's ponder two central questions: (1) what does the *Constitution* have to say about republicanism, and (2) what is commercial about the *Constitution* and the republic it establishes?

It is far easier to answer the first question than the second. According to the Framers, a republican form of government is where (a) a scheme of representation takes place in contrast to both a monarch and a (pure) democracy, (b) there is a separation of powers between the legislature and executive branches, (c) the judicial branch is independent from the political branches, and (d) the legislative branch is bicameral rather than unicameral. There is also (e) a provision for frequent elections by the people, but there is room for debate about the mode of election, the length of term of office, whether the terms should be staggered, who can vote and who can run for office. There is also (f) provision for the removal of governmental officials.

Article 1, Section 6 of the *Constitution* indicates that "senators and representatives shall receive a compensation for their services, to be ascertained by law, and paid out of the Treasury of the United States." We think this underscores the commercial nature of the republic. As Ben Franklin reminded the delegates at the Philadelphia Convention, and political thinkers from Aristotle to Montesquieu argued, a republic required a deep attachment to public service by both the citizens and statesmen. The thought of paying someone to serve the public was certainly untraditional. But that is what the Framers proposed. Now that did not mean that the electorate and the elected were to be motivated simply by money; rather it meant that it is appropriate to pay someone for services rendered and we can always refuse to hire them again by means of frequent elections. Besides, paying a House member or senator for their service certainly broadens the pool of who can run for election. We would no longer be limited to those who are independently wealthy.

The Framers also realized that paying the representatives could itself lead to abuse. Thus in Article 2, Section 1, the President shall not receive a pay increase until after the next Presidential election. This move was an attempt to check the potentiality for corruption in the executive branch. Similarly in Article 3, Section 1, the judges shall be compensated for their services, but their pay shall not be reduced while in office. This is an attempt to secure the independence of the judiciary.

Article 1, Section 7 states that "all bills for raising revenue shall originate in the House of Representatives." This clause is grounded in an American axiom of republican liberty: no taxation without representation.

Among the 18 clauses of Article 1, Section 8 outlining the powers of Congress, there are at least six that deal directly with a commercial society. There was close to unanimous consent at the Constitutional Convention that Congressional action under the Articles of Confederation was impeded by the unavailability of a regular source of funding and borrowing. Thus the delegates agreed to grant the power to tax and borrow to Congress under the new *Constitution*. See Article 1, Section 8, clauses 1 and 2.

But what if Congress abused this power? One answer is that the power is limited to public policy that supports the general welfare and common defense. But what if these two clauses are used as invitations to expand the role of government rather than to limit the role of government? What policy can't be justified in the name of the general welfare or common defense? The Framers' answer is that ultimately the people themselves initially through regular elections and ultimately through the amendment process must express their "deliberate sense" on the issue. Whether one interprets these clauses loosely or strictly has had a huge impact on the kind of commercial society and republican government that has unfolded in the United States. For example, the New Deal and Great Society programs in the twentieth century and Obamacare in the twenty-first century owe much to a broad constitutional interpretation of these clauses.

One of the most famous clauses granting power to Congress is Article 1, Section 8, clause 3, known popularly as the interstate commerce clause. The clause granting Congress the power to "regulate commerce … among the several states" is vital to the creation and preservation of an interstate commercial republic over an extended territory. But what exactly does this clause mean and has its meaning changed over time? Is it possible to draw a clear line between intrastate and interstate commerce as the Supreme Court in the New Deal era attempted to do? What exactly is commerce? Does Chief Justice John Marshall's decision in *McCulloch v Maryland* settle the issue for good? Again, the New Deal, the Great Society and Obamacare programs relied on a very expansive rather than a restrictive interpretation of the meaning of this clause.

The Progressives in the late nineteenth and early twentieth centuries relied on this clause to regulate the relationship between capital and labor and support the development of labor union activity. The Progressives also provided a significant challenge to the traditional understanding of the role of government in a commercial republic. They introduced three new cabinet departments that were directly responsible for regulating the three sectors of the economy: the Agriculture Department, the Labor Department, and the Commerce Department. The roles of these departments have expanded exponentially over the last hundred years in an effort to control rather than encourage the operation of a commercially based republic.

THE AMERICAN FOUNDING AND THE TWO NARRATIVES

There is a paradox in Locke and Madison: our nature is at once peaceful and combative. Locke argues that government is necessary because people cannot live by themselves without a regulator. But if people are not sufficiently virtuous, then free government is not possible. We argue that this is exactly what *Federalist 51* is claiming. Government steps in to protect and preserve property that has been naturally acquired. And that private property is to be widely understood as having a private right to conscience and consenting to the government to which obedience is owed.

What kind of government does Locke envision? He advocates a limited government. Locke gives this limited government to the majority (of property owners). Madison corrects this by warning about the tyranny of the majority while still supporting majority rule, though that majority rule is tempered by a bicameral Congress and other mechanisms of a federalist system.

Locke feels that the greatest problem we faced was the actions of the people that the majority elected, not the majority itself. He therefore justified the right of revolution against those in power. Madison never denied the right to revolution but certain "inventions of prudence" could constrain both the Locke problem of the tyranny of the few in power and the new issue of the tyranny of the electorate. The right to revolution is similar to the right of self-defense. It is not an invitation to revolt all of the time.

Autonomy, or the notion of self-reliance and the ability to govern oneself, is not the right to do whatever one wants, without limits. Locke is making the case for human autonomy, and private ownership of property helps him make the case. An autonomous individual is better off than a slave or a serf. God did not intend us to be slaves. There is an end to serfdom (Hayek). It is nature's wish that we govern ourselves. The right to conscience is not central in Catholic teachings – but it is among Protestants, and most of the early settlers and founders belonged to dissenting (non-Anglican) Protestant sects.

The fusion of Locke and Smith is seen most visibly in Madison's *Federalist 51*. Here we learn that competition between the branches of government is critical for political liberty and the competition between religions is vital for religious liberty. And the *Constitution* adds the economic dimension by encouraging economic competition by limiting the length of patents and creating a free trade area with Congress having the power to regulate interstate commerce.

The controversy over the establishment of the national bank between 1791 and 1831 – and the whole issue of money and credit generally – are a case study in the emerging American version of the two narratives. The retrieval of this original conversation shows the extent to which the expression of the two narratives is shaped by the debates over the *Declaration of Independence*, the *Constitution*, and the Bill of Rights. And lurking in the wings of the conversation, as it were, is the whole issue of what should the government do if, and when, we are faced with a national emergency. Hamilton's strong message, on the contrary, was that we live in a mercantilist world, and the whole idea of a system of natural or perfect liberty advocated by Smith and his American followers is tantamount to sleep walking. Is a constitution, then, along with the separation of powers, and the notion of free markets, only defensible in an era of peace or in the tranquility of an ivory tower mind?

Raising the question of the proper role of government in the American context leads to three other questions: which level of government, which branch of which level, and to what clause of the *Constitution* or to what concept in the *Declaration* are we appealing in validating or in rejecting a certain political economy initiative? We see this initial controversy over the establishment of the national bank and the role of government in the credit markets and the manufacturing sector setting the tone for the later debates in political economy in the Progressive, the New Deal, and the Great Society eras. These debates, moreover, are not just over the latest theory in how to control inflation or solve unemployment. These debates raise the question of the relationship between limited government and good government and between a free society and a fair society.

We do not mean to suggest that Hamilton in the 1790s and Justice Marshall in 1819 are initiators and defenders respectively of the Equality Narrative. Rather, their greater willingness to envision a broader and deeper role for government, especially the federal government, via a loose construction of the *Constitution* in the day to day operations of the economy prepares the way for the general acceptance of the proposition that an activist and protectionist government is important for the well-being of the nation taken as a whole. That is why Madison was so upset with both Hamilton and Marshall: once their opinions made their way into the mainstream of American life, it would be even more difficult to make the case for the Liberty Narrative.

One major unintended consequence of the original mercantilist and Hamiltonian neo-mercantilist approach to political economy is that this approach sets the foundation for the centralized administrative state and a collectivist disposition in the citizenry which are the necessary conditions for advancing the Equality Narrative. We also see the extent to which money and banking on the one hand and the well-being of the manufacturing and commercial sectors of the economy play a very big role in the formation of the first political parties in America. We will see later how questions of political economy were central to the emergence of the Progressives and the transformation of the Democratic Party in the twentieth century.

5. The French Revolution and the Socialist Alternative

INTRODUCTION: THE AMERICAN VERSUS THE FRENCH REVOLUTION

Scholars have long noted the differences between the American Founding and the outcome of the French Revolution. Those differences reflect the evolving tension between the two narratives. The French Revolution was the decisive event for the next stage in the development of the Equality Narrative just as the American Revolution provided the next step in the Liberty Narrative. Compared with the American scene, which emerged in a fairly smooth fashion from the *Declaration of Independence* through the *Constitution* and beyond, the French situation went far less smoothly.

While Locke, Smith, and the American Revolution brought the economic question out of the household and made it a political question – and thus gave birth to political economy – Rousseau, the French Revolution, and European authors of the early nineteenth century brought the economic question out of the polity and made it a social question. They gave birth to the Equality Narrative of socialism that understands itself in opposition to the Liberty Narrative of political economy.

The Equality Narrative challenges political economy on behalf of "social economy." Poverty replaces profit as the central category of the scope and method of economic inquiry. What do "we" do with the poor? What do "we" do with the marginalized? Where is "our" social conscience? What is the cause of the poverty of a nation rather than what is the cause of the wealth of a nation becomes the focus of attention. Besides, isn't there something greater than the individual? How about the national good or the common good or the class good or the social good? Should we replace the profit-seeking entrepreneur with the scientifically trained administrative expert?

There are a number of similarities between the 1776 American *Declaration of Independence* and the 1789 French *Declaration of the Rights of Man and the Citizen*. We are struck, however, by the following three differences. The French Declaration:

1. Is far shorter and less particular than the American Declaration, confining itself to 22 abstract principles and omitting even a brief list of particular grievances against the French monarchy and aristocracy. (Tocqueville thinks that liberty is preserved by an appeal to particulars, whereas the passion for equality is revealed in the attachment to general principles.)
2. Announces, in the fashion of Rousseau's *Social Contract*, that "Men are born free and equal in rights. Social distinctions may be based only on common utility." The point of departure is liberty and the goal is equality. The American *Declaration*, by contrast, announces that all "Men are created equal," and proceeds to state that the purpose of government is to protect the individual right to the pursuit of life, liberty, and happiness. The American point of departure is equality and the goal is liberty. How important is the difference between "born" and "created" as a point of departure?
3. States, again in Rousseauean *Social Contract* fashion, that "the law is the expression of the General Will." How "sacred" are individual natural rights, if the "General Will" of the citizen becomes the voice of God?

Equally revealing are the similarities and differences between the American of 1787, as amended in 1791 with the addition of a Bill of Rights, with the three French Constitutions of 1791, 1793, and 1795. We are struck, once again by the potentiality of the differences for the future of political economy.

Suffice it to note that the 1791 French *Constitution* attempts to restrain, but not abolish, the monarchy. And the 1795 French *Constitution* attempts to restrain, but not abolish, the republic created in 1793. The 1791 *Constitution* contains within its very Preamble a confrontation between the past and the present rather than, as in the Preamble to the United States *Constitution*, a promise between the present and the future. What are we to make of the "guarantee" of the right to "public relief" and the institutions of "national festivals?" The word "guarantee," is absent from the American *Constitution*, but very present in twenty-first century America. We note that the monarch is referred to as "King of the French." Also interesting is that the 1795 *Constitution* leads off not with the Legislative powers or a statement of purposes but the construction of the Executive Power in the form of an Executive Directory. Does this move toward a Directory, and the restrictions on intermediate institutions, anticipate or confirm the arrival of the administrative state?

It is the 1793 *Constitution*, also known as the "Montagnard *Constitution*," that is the central contribution of the French Revolution to the

Equality Narrative. It repeats the tension between the "sanctity of property" and the "right to subsistence." But it removes the monarchy entirely from the picture much to the delight of the Jacobins. The Rousseau inspired Jacobin, Maximilien Robespierre, born in 1758 and executed in 1794, offered an explanation of the virtues. In his Justification of the Reign of Terror speech in February 1794, officially called, "On the Principles of Political Morality," he says that the "fundamental principle of the democratic or popular government ... is virtue which is nothing other than the love of country and ... the love of country necessarily includes the love of equality." Moreover, "terror is nothing other than justice ... it is an emanation of virtue."

1789 *CONSTITUTION*

The 1789 French document contains 17 provisions of which 15 are at least arguably compatible with the individualistically inclined *Declaration of Independence* and the US State constitutions of 1776–80. But numbers 3 and 6 raise some interesting possibilities of divergence. According to number 3, the principle of all sovereignty rests essentially in the nation. "No body and no individual may exercise authority which does not emanate expressly from the nation." The key here is that sovereignty does not reside in the individual, so all the other items in the Declaration addressing the autonomy of the individual are at least compromised by number 3. So there is really no way in which the support for the individualistic inclinations of 15/17 items can prevail against number 3.

Number 6 adds a further complication: "The law is the expression of the General Will." This Rousseauean clause is clearly in violation of the partially inclined 'Lockean' clauses 15/17. The question cannot be avoided: Will numbers 3 and 6 prevail over 15/17 or will they be defeated by 15/17? Will the French Revolution mark an important departure in political economy from individual liberty to collective equality? The French did not settle this ambiguity between an attachment to individual rights and a collective good in 1789.

1791 *CONSTITUTION*

The French *Constitution* of 1791 reiterates the American concerns for individual liberty of speech and rights of conscience as well as "the inviolability of property." In fact, it claims that these rights can be secured by means of a constitutional monarchy. Unlike the Americans there is no thought of substituting a republican form of government for a monarchy; the French still hope that the monarchy can be constitutionalized while at the same time appealing to the natural rights of man. But the 1791 French *Constitution* contains some warning signs precisely because it addresses the rights of the citizen as well as the rights of man. It unequivocally spells out the underlying claim of Rousseau: "Sovereignty is one, indivisible, inalienable, and imprescriptible. It appertains to the nation; no section of the people nor any individual may assume the exercise thereof."

Something else is important about the 1791 French *Constitution*. If it wasn't fighting against monarchy per se – that is if it wasn't a republican political revolution – just what kind of republican revolution was present or anticipated? What the 1791 French *Constitution* put in motion was to introduce the social question as a primary feature of republicanism. As Tocqueville would point out later with great clarity, what was going on in France was a clash between the decaying era of aristocracy and the emerging era of democracy. So the 1791 *Constitution* is quite prepared to constitutionalize the monarchy because its main aim was to abolish aristocracy. Thus the first paragraph declares that, in the name of "the principles it recognized" in 1789, the 1791 *Constitution* "abolishes irrevocably the institutions which were injurious to liberty and equality of rights." Apparently the monarchy was not one of those institutions that was to be capitated. Not yet anyway. What took the American founders four words – no titles of nobility – took the French four paragraphs to declare, namely, independence from feudal "distinctions."

There are also three items to which we call attention in *Title I: Fundamental Provisions Guaranteed by the Constitution*. The *Constitution* specifically calls for the "guarantee" of "a general establishment of public relief" and for "public instruction free of charge." In addition, all the better to "preserve the memory of the French Revolution," national festivals shall be instituted.

1793 *CONSTITUTION*

This *Constitution* contains 124 sections thus setting the tone for constitutions to become more like statutes of law that try to cover every possible contingency. This 1793 *Constitution* takes citizenship seriously including 11 sub-provisions concerning the definition, the suspension and the loss of French citizenship. But for our purposes, Sections 122–124 are the most interesting. According to Section 122: "The constitution guarantees to all Frenchmen equality, liberty, security, property, the

public debt, free exercise of religion, general instruction, public assistance, absolute liberty of the press, the right of petition, the right to hold
popular assemblies, and the enjoyment of all the rights of man." Sections
123 and 124 "guarantee" these purposes by the promotion of public
virtue in "public places."

1795 *CONSTITUTION*

We turn, finally, to the French *Constitution* of 1795. The monarch has
been beheaded and the effort to create a non-aristocratic constitutional
monarchy has also been abandoned. The French now face directly the
issue of what it means to be a democratic republic. The answer is an
executive "Directory of five members appointed by the Legislative Body
which for such purpose performs the functions of an electoral body, in
the name of the nation." And that is just the first paragraph. The
Constitution details just how powerful this Directory is supposed to be.
The Directory is empowered to provide for the "internal and external
safety of the Republic." It has the authority to investigate conspiracies
against the Republic, of course "according to law."

What is also important is the bold change in the calendar. There is a
specific reference to the day of the establishment of the new order: "the
French era shall date from 22 September 1792," when the "Republic was
established." If we take Robespierre as our guide, this French Revolution
is "the dawn of the bright day of universal happiness." What does this
require? "Virtue and terror; terror without virtue is disastrous, virtue
without terror is powerless. Terror is nothing but prompt, severe, and
inflexible justice" (Robespierre 1794, "On the Principles of Political
Morality").

That leaves us pondering the question whether or not the reign of terror
was central to the French Revolution or was it a temporary aberration?
Also important for our purposes is whether or not terror is an acceptable
portion of the argument for equality. Which leads to another question: is
deliberative or representative government essential in making the case for
liberty? Terror is the most obvious face of control over the individual, but
as Tocqueville explains, there is soft terror as well as harsh terror. The
former, he claims, is what lovers of liberty have to watch out for. Not too
far behind the policy of soft terror lies the specter of harsh terror that is
justified in the name of public virtue and perfect justice. At a certain
point lovers of liberty have to recognize that the difference between
coercion and terror is a matter of degree. Both forms of action reject the
principle of consent.

THE ENLIGHTENMENT PROJECT: THE FRENCH EGALITARIAN EMBRACE OF SCIENTISM

The Enlightenment Project is the attempt to define, explain, and control the human predicament through the use of scientific technology. As Carl Becker put it in his book *The Heavenly City of the Eighteenth Century Philosophers* (Becker 1962, Chapter 4), the dream of a technological utopia is the common inheritance of liberals, socialists, and Marxists. This project originated among the French 'philosophes' during the eighteenth century, among whom the most influential were Diderot, d'Alembert, La Mettrie, Condillac, Helvetius, d'Holbach, Turgot, and Condorcet, many of whom interacted with Rousseau.

It is generally said that the Enlightenment replaced authority, faith, and tradition with reason. It is also said that the Enlightenment identified reason with physical science. Philosophically, this amounts to the following contentions or what we shall call 'scientism':

1. Physical science is the whole truth about everything.
2. Physical science is self-explanatory.
3. Human beings are to be understood in the same way the physical world is understood.
4. There is a social science, modeled after physical science, and such a social science will lead to a social technology. The social sciences, including economics and politics, can be reduced to sociology, which is reducible to psychology, which is reducible to physiology, which is reducible to biology, and so on, all the way to physics.

Proponents of this program, like d'Alembert, point back to the inspiration of Bacon, Descartes, and Hobbes. It is tempting to suggest that the program was already present in much earlier thinkers. However, science must not be confused with scientism. To advocate the importance of science for helping us to understand the physical world and to advocate the practical importance of a scientifically based technology is not to believe that physical science is intellectually autonomous or self-explanatory. Bacon, Descartes, Hobbes, all defend the importance of physical science, but none of them advocates scientism. On the contrary, there is an explicit rejection in each of what we here call 'scientism'. Moreover, even among some of the philosophes there is an explicit awareness of the limits of science. As d'Alembert expressed it, "the supreme Intelligence has drawn a veil before our feeble vision which we try in vain to remove." (d'Alembert 1759, *Melanges de Philosophie*, vol. iv, pp. 63–64). It is specifically amongst a subset of the members of the philosophes that we find the advocacy of scientism, specifically in Condillac, d'Holbach, and La Mettrie.

In advocating 'scientism', the French philosophes responded to their critics by offering a historicist rhetoric and a methodological pose. Whenever challenged, the first line of defense was the claim that scientific progress would in some unspecified manner meet these objections. In an ironic sort of way, a providential history without God became a substitute for argument. One of the first theorists in the eighteenth century to suggest historicized-teleology was Turgot. His thesis was later to be refined into attempts to formulate laws of development. The most important figures to continue Turgot's work into the nineteenth century were Fourier, Saint-Simon, Comte, and Marx.

It is during the Enlightenment that we see the equating of the history of philosophy with the history of science and the rhetoric of progressive scientific histories. It is important to recognize that this is a narrative and not an argument. This progressive historicism is a crucial part of intellectual history. While it is certainly clear that the philosophes inherited from Bacon and Descartes the notion of progress through physical technology, it was the philosophes who openly proclaimed that physical science could define and totally explain humanity as well. Whereas their predecessors had recognized the limits of scientific explanation, the philosophes sought to overcome those limits through the notion of the historical progress of science. Ironically, Descartes himself had wisely refrained from applying this super-rationalism to the human and social world and had even insisted that the use of this kind of reason presupposed the acceptance of common sense traditional moral and social practices. But by the end of the eighteenth century this super-rationalism was adopted without any restraints and applied to every facet of human endeavor. This is reflected in Condorcet's statement that "all errors in politics and morals are based on philosophic errors, which, again, are allied to physical errors. There exists neither a religious system, nor a supernatural extravagance, which is not founded on ignorance of the laws of nature" (Condorcet [1795] 1955, *Sketch for a Historical Picture of The Progress of the Human Mind*, n.p.).

What we see in Condorcet's remark is the view that scientism entails the existence of a special kind of social knowledge, modeled after physical science, such that the first result of that social science will be an explanation of why individuals oppose scientism. What we are promised is a scientific delegitimation of the opposition to scientism. Advocates of the Enlightenment Project respond to these criticisms with a plea for scientific tolerance coupled with the claim that traditional views of human nature are idols or obstacles to accepting the new scientific view. We are told such things as people could not previously imagine standing at the antipodes or we are reminded of such episodes as those who refused to look through Galileo's telescope. In short, there is a story about scientific progress with a special kind of rhetoric that is supposed to establish the legitimacy of turning subjects into objects, and an important component of that story is an allegedly 'scientific' account of why people oppose scientism. The history of ideas comes gradually to be construed as an historical progression in which earlier ideas are only worthwhile to the extent that they reflect the current 'mature' intellectual agenda. Condorcet's *History* is just such a work.

One consideration is that the naturalistic-mechanistic world view allows for a social technology that could in principle solve all human problems. Mechanistic views of human nature are attractive because they are compatible with the idea that human beings are either a *tabula rasa* or fundamentally good. Hence, human beings could be either caused to be good or obstacles to their natural goodness could be removed. This fits perfectly with the conception of 'liberty' as the absence of arbitrary external constraints. In an analogous way, rationality could seemingly be promoted either mechanically or by removing constraints such as the belief in religion, authority, custom, or tradition. This has the added benefit of reinforcing the progressive-scientific story by seemingly providing a naturalistic account of why it has taken so long to arrive at the super-rationalism of the Enlightenment.

Another consideration is that given the economic and social challenges of the modern world, it seemed to many of those impatient to alter the status quo that a wholesale rejection of authority, tradition, and the religious institutions that seemed to support the status quo was the quickest way to achieve reform; hence, the enthusiasm for a seemingly liberated reason. Since traditional institutions had justified themselves on the grounds that they embody wisdom about innate human shortcomings, mechanistic theories about the natural goodness of human nature will seem doubly attractive to critics of the status quo.

It is not immediately clear what constitutes 'progress'. The advocates of the Enlightenment Project not only believe that such standards are available, but they also believe that knowledge of them is itself progressive. The standards will be defined, apparently, as we advance towards them and their validity can be verified only in the process of attaining them. In the end, what science declares to be 'progress' will become the definition of 'progress'.

What advocates of the Enlightenment Project do is to adopt two complementary discourses. On the one hand, they speak from within our common heritage by invoking intellectual and political norms when needed, and, on the other hand, they reserve the right seemingly to step outside the common heritage into the atmosphere of a context-less reason in order to amend or reject the common heritage when they deem it is necessary. We are told at one and the same time that science is the whole truth about everything and that we can never be sure that we have the whole truth. Both the speech 'within' and the speech 'without' are billed as provisional, but what is not provisional is the assumption that scientific progress will show that the two speeches are ultimately coherent and that there is some kind of historical progression from one to the other. The historicization of the two kinds of speech serves to deflect counter-argument.

Going back to Rousseau's ambivalence about whether he is alienated from his society or a reformer of his society, we can combine that ambivalence with the intellectual program of the Enlightenment Project. There are two new but overlapping personae: the Rousseauean public intellectual and the intellectual who subsequently serves in the new social technology bureaucracy. The public intellectual usually expresses the well documented hostility of intellectuals to modern commercial society. This expression derives partly from their identity, and partly from their anomalous position in a democratic society. Such intellectuals often give their allegiance to a popular democracy. At the same time, they share some characteristics of the traditional clergy and aristocracy. Like the aristocracy, they are a self-proclaimed elite minority with tastes that are very different from, and disdainful of, the desires of common people in a mass commercial society. As Tocqueville puts it, an aristocratic body is composed of a certain number of citizens who, without being elevated very far above the mass of the citizens, are nevertheless permanently stationed above them.

Intellectuals both share and reject the economic consequences of equality, namely, that all people must work and that all work is equal. Intellectuals work hard, and they consider work a virtue. But not all work. They have the aristocratic contempt for work whose chief motivation is profit, though they exempt the poor from their contempt as people who have no choice. As Tocqueville notes, in "aristocracies it is not exactly work itself which is despised, but work with an idea to profit. Work is glorious when inspired by ambition or pure virtue ... the notion of profit remains distinct from that of work" (Tocqueville Volume II, Part II, *Democracy in America*, p. 970 of Liberty Fund edition, 2010).

THE SOCIALIST APPLICATION OF ROUSSEAU AND THE ENLIGHTENMENT PROJECT

The term 'socialism' can easily give rise to pointless semantic debates. We suggest that the term captures two important historical features: (1) opposition to the Lockean narrative of political economy (socialists assert that we are to be understood as social beings and not autonomous individuals) and (2) strong support for the Rousseau inspired emphasis on the *social* question – namely, how are we to understand and how are we going to deal with the social problems associated with poverty, specifically those who do not seem to be benefiting from the demise of feudalism and the apparent successes of the technological project. In the early nineteenth century, 'socialism' did not connote government owner-ship and/or control of the means of production. Rather, it was a broad term for social theorists and reformers who believed that laborers were victims of the market economy not just those who failed to be beneficiar-ies. While advocates of the Lockean narrative also recognized and conceded the existence of those who failed to benefit, they did not attribute that failure to inherent features of the market economy. To this day, the term 'capitalism' connotes to many, especially outside the Anglosphere, not just a market economy but what they consider to be a dysfunctional and exploitative social and political system.

Robert Owen (1771–1858) is an interesting case in point. Owen was a successful British 'capitalist', but in his essay *New View of Society* (Owen 1816), dedicated to William Wilberforce, Owen critiqued the Liberty Narrative as individualistic and selfish and advocated what he portrays as the more humanitarian Equality Narrative. Like Rousseau, he believed that the individual is not responsible for his miserable condition. Unlike Rousseau, he did not attribute this to innocence and ignorance. Owen agrees with Rousseau that human nature is malleable and thus if we transform society, we can change human nature. Where they differ is in the identification of the cause of the misery. Rousseau saw the cause as the result of the development of the useful arts and practical sciences. For Owen, the cause is ignorance about what education can achieve and a lack of Christian conscience. For both, there is a collective responsibil-ity to apply the General Will to removing the blight of poverty from the body politic. Owen urged reform of the Child Labor Laws and Poor Laws in Britain as well as setting up agrarian reform communities in Scotland and America. Religion, education, and philanthropy all played a role in Owen's analysis of, and solution to, the poverty problem. He ultimately advocated a national government plan to deal with the problem of poverty. He maintained that poverty is the cause of crime, and that public policy is better off fighting poverty through education than punishing crime through incarceration. Owen suggested that fighting poverty is the moral equivalent of fighting slavery. His associates included Andrew Bell and Joseph Lancaster, Christians active in the late eighteenth and early nineteenth centuries who opened schools for the poor in India and London respectively.

Owen, although English, was the first in a long line of subsequent mostly French so-called 'utopian' socialists. When used in a positive sense, they were 'utopian' in believing that through a collective sense of identity (Christian heritage) all social problems could be solved or greatly ameliorated within the framework of the technological project and a market economy. Notable members of this group included Saint-Simon, Proudhon, Fourier, and Louis Blanc. They advocated a wide diversity of planned (utopian) communities.

Marx and Engels would later use the expression 'utopian' in a pejorative sense precisely because these early socialists allegedly did not understand that it would take radical reform requiring collective government ownership and control of the entire economy or society to solve the social problem. For Marx, socialism is a transitional stage characterized by common (but still private) and/or state ownership of the means of production under democratic workers' control and management. Distribution was still to be based on individual contribution. Under full-fledged communism, distribution is based on need, hence, "from each according to his ability, to each according to his needs!" There will be no classes or class warfare.

Claude-Henri Saint-Simon (1760–1825) had fought with Lafayette in America, had been imprisoned during the Reign of Terror in France, and, among his many accomplishments had formulated a plan for a Panama Canal.

What was especially important in the works of Saint-Simon was his view of history. The Saint-Simonians, including Comte, saw history as a teleological process developing toward a final phase. He is best known for his account of historical progress. Every society, he alleged, is based on a set of fundamental beliefs, both philosophical and economic. Those beliefs evolve and the social order erected upon them either collapses or transforms itself into another system.

According to Saint-Simon, the conditions of one's own time might not be universal. For example, the Enlightenment attack on religious belief was one of the things that led to the collapse of feudalism. Institutions which played a positive role at one point in history could become counter-productive at another, as witnessed by the Catholic Church, which in the Saint-Simonian scheme of things was a constructive force in the Middle Ages but a reactionary one in the rise of the new industrialism.

Post-feudal society is based on what we have identified as the technological project. One of the consequences is the end of the domination by the old ruling class of aristocracy and clergy and their replacement by a kind of new technocracy composed of the rising middle class of entrepreneurs and technicians. According to Saint-Simon's economic theory, the virtues of the new entrepreneurial class included the idea that merit accrues to one from thrift, postponed gratification, ingenuity, and hard work. This left no room for a traditional philanthropic relationship with workers. At the same time, workers emerging out of a feudal context were not always ready to adopt the habits of responsible and autonomous individuals. Two things were needed: (a) an economic theory that recognized historical context and transitional policies for turning workers with feudal thought patterns into independent individuals, and (b) a new kind of leadership that was neither hierarchical-feudal nor indifferent to and ignorant of the nature of the new potential class conflict.

Saint-Simon was among the first to critique the emerging economic leadership because of the disposition to sacrifice everything to accumulation, and the exclusive and engrossing selfishness which accompanies it, and he recognized the existence of poverty and economic class conflict. In his 1825 work *Nouveau Christianisme*, Saint-Simon foresaw a new harmony in which leadership would pass to a technocracy composed of intellectuals and industrialists. In addition, the Saint-Simonians advocated the equality of women. Although Saint-Simon's own views were hospitable to private property, some of his followers transformed his movement after his death into a kind of religious collectivism. One of his more influential followers was Auguste Comte. Comte's own writings served as the inspiration for the later French embrace of a technocracy, rule by enlightened administrators.

Saint-Simon is often referred to as the "Father of French Socialism," or the "Father of Christian Socialism." His work, like Owens's work, raises an interesting paradox in the Equality Narrative: the main focus is on alleviating poverty, but this is to be accomplished by a managerial class of (scientific) experts infused by a renewed attachment to a "true" religion. In his *Geneva Letters* (Saint-Simon 1803), cited favorably by Engels in *Socialism: Utopian and Scientific* (Engels 1880), Saint-Simon attempts to persuade the three classes of society – he actually addresses the lower or third class as "my friends" – to adopt his project, namely, to select "men of genius" who will make decisions in the "collective interest." On the surface, this seems more of a call for elitism than it does for egalitarianism. But is he not suggesting that there is an important alliance, even community of interests, between the intellectual and scientist (technocrats) on the one hand and the mass of the people on the other hand? This reliance on well-trained neutral experts, men of science is a 'correction' of Rousseau and marks the importance of planning in an administrative state for the accomplishment of the Equality Narrative.

This detached expertise is also infused with a religious zeal! In *Nouveau Christianisme* (1825), Saint-Simon proclaims "that it is the duty of religion to direct society to the great end of ameliorating as rapidly as possible the lot of the poorest class" (Guyot 2013, pp. 76–77). The market can't accomplish this amelioration. Most of the argument is replete with accusations. "J'accuse," he says "les papes," and "les Lutherans" of being "heritiques." But he claims to have discovered the true meaning of Christianity: social justice implemented by caring officials. We are seeing here the emergence of Christian Socialism. Saint-Simon is anticipating a new direction in political economy where the government takes an active role in eliminating poverty in the name of divine justice or secular fairness. In other words, political economy is becoming social economy. He also reflects the joining of the Equality Narrative with the nationalist narrative in the form of state socialism.

Like Rousseau before him, P.J. Proudhon proclaimed in the opening paragraph of *What is Property? Or an Inquiry into the Principle of Right and of Government* (also called his *First Memoir*, Proudhon 1840) that "Property is Robbery." Proudhon's point is that the pursuit of the equality of condition ought to be the principle of right and the project of government. This equation of property and robbery is also significant because he refers to "Property is Robbery ... [as] ... the war cry of '93" thus suggesting a remarkable continuity to the Equality Narrative beginning with Rousseau in the mid eighteenth century to the French Revolution and beyond. And that the purpose of the French Revolution, as expressed in the *Constitution* of '93, is to establish the "equality of condition." Proudhon sees a different relationship among economics, politics, and religion. He calls for "science" to replace religion. He clearly suggests that justice and property are in an antagonistic relationship. Proudhon begins *The Philosophy of Poverty* with an affirmation: "I affirm the reality of an economic science." He contrasts this with the non-science of "political economy." Proudhon anticipates the claim of Marx and Engels that socialism can be scientific, as well as fair, but political economy (that is, the Lockean narrative) is "the glorification of selfishness."

Also interesting is that he quickly tempers his opening remarks in the *First Memoir* with the comment that "I am no agent of discord." It is as if he anticipated a critical response to his bold challenge to the established order. Suffice it to note, that this *First Memoir*, originally published in 1840, caused considerable controversy. Proudhon, in a prefatory dedication, praised the Academy of Besancon which, in turn, distanced itself from the "bold defender of the principle of equality of conditions." He was defended in this confrontation by Louis Auguste Blanqui (1805–81). Blanqui advocated state socialism whereas Proudhon was an anarchist socialist and responded to Blanqui in a second memoir entitled *The Philosophy of Poverty* (Proudhon 1847). Marx critiqued the *Second Memoir* as insufficiently scientific in a work which Marx entitled *The Poverty of Philosophy* (Marx 1847).

6. The Evolution of the Liberty Narrative in Nineteenth Century Continental Thought: Tocqueville, Kant, and Hegel

INTRODUCTION: THE 'CORRECTION' OF THE LIBERTY NARRATIVE

With some serious qualification it can be maintained that the Lockean Liberty Narrative has remained most vibrant in the Anglo-American world and that the Rousseau Equality Narrative has remained most vibrant on the Continent of Europe. The element of truth in this observation deserves a separate book of its own. There is also a sometimes neglected tradition in which Continental thinkers enamored of the British Lockean narrative have attempted to import it to the Continent – we are thinking of Montesquieu, Voltaire, and Constant. What we want to focus upon here are two things: first, in the hands of several Continental thinkers, namely, Tocqueville, Kant, and Hegel writing under the influence of Smith and in response to the issues raised by Rousseau and the French Revolution, we have for the first time a self-conscious recognition of the clash of the two narratives. Second, we note how the Liberty Narrative underwent a serious evolution that culminates in J.S. Mill.

TOCQUEVILLE'S RESPONSE TO ROUSSEAU'S CHALLENGE

Alexis de Tocqueville (1805–59) insists upon distinguishing between the American Revolution and the French Revolution. Tocqueville proclaims two theses: first, even though the French Revolutionaries attempted to completely abolish all the institutions of the Old Regime, they reverted to many of its foundations. Most importantly, they attempted to dismantle the powerful state that was the monarchy, but ended up creating an even stronger, more centralized state themselves. Second, if people want freedom not for its own sake but for some other goal, to further their material interest, it will turn into a despotic form of rule, where everyone may be free to further their material interest but without political freedom. He thus argues that if material, self-interested behavior is the offspring for action, people may vote for a government that gives them economic stability, even if the price to pay for this is political freedom.

Tocqueville perceived France to be the opposite of the United States in terms of revolutionary achievement and the manipulation of the idea of 'freedom'. In France, before and after the revolution, people relied on a central authority instead of becoming economically or politically active themselves. By contrast, in the United States, political action permeated to even the lower levels of society. There, private individuals formed the basis of economic and political life, but, in France, this center of gravity was taken up by the bureaucratic machine.

Tocqueville was an unabashed supporter of the Liberty Narrative: "I have a passionate love for liberty, law, and respect for rights … . I am neither of the revolutionary party nor of the conservative … . Liberty is my foremost passion." He was also firmly and self-consciously opposed to the Rousseau Equality Narrative: "one also finds in the human heart a depraved taste for equality, which impels the weak to want to bring the strong down to their level, and which reduces men to preferring equality in servitude to inequality in freedom." What is problematic for Tocqueville is that love of equality rather than love of liberty is the ruling passion of modernity. Tocqueville wrote a scathing critique of Rousseau's *Second Discourse* in his own *Memoir on Pauperism: Does Public Charity Produce an Idle and Dependent Class of Society?* (Tocqueville 1835). That passion for equality manifested itself in the violent unfolding of the French Revolution where "the economic question" not only came out of the household and into the polity, but made its way into the society at large. Humans in modernity prefer equality in slavery to inequality in liberty. In short, equality and not liberty is the default position of modernity. Thus, liberty is in constant need of being defended and equality is in constant need of being moderated. He thought he saw this defense in America as opposed to Great Britain, and hence his magisterial two volume work *Democracy in America* (Tocqueville 1835 and 1840). Mill reviewed both volumes of this work positively and insightfully and acknowledged its influence on his own work.

Briefly, Tocqueville argues, in the light of Smith (Tocqueville's the "Creator's hand" echoes Smith's "invisible hand"), that modern commerce (technological project and the market economy) not only undermines the economic, social and political structure of feudalism but economic growth narrows and changes the gap between rich and poor. There are two consequences of economic growth: politically we see the rise of democracy (the inevitability of majority rule) and socially we witness the growth of the passion for equality in an anti-aristocratic culture. This constitutes the great challenge to liberty, the need for individual freedom and achievement. Some of the features of a commercial society include a focus on the newly emerging possibility of material prosperity, a narrowing of the orbit of concern to petty pleasures, and, as Constant warned, a disregard for participating in the discussion of, and resolution of, the great issues of public concern. We retreat into our private lives and leave the big questions to elected representatives. We are under the illusion that because the representatives are democratically elected they will respect and protect our private interests including liberty. In this, we are sadly mistaken. Political democracy gives way to new forms of tyranny, a soft despotism. We become isolated individuals subject to the growing power of a centralized government that focuses on preventing rather than encouraging creativity, an allegedly protective power that renders us child-like and reduces us to a flock of sheep.

There are dangers associated with the progress of the division of labor. Adam Smith had already noted the negative impact of the division of labor on the character of the individual. Tocqueville echoes Smith's recommendation that statesmen be alert to this phenomenon. He warns that if ever aristocracy were to return to the modern world it would be in the form of an industrial aristocracy (Saint-Simon). He thinks that statesmen should be on the alert to the corrosive effects of this development. He also warns about what happens to those who are workers in this system. The task of statesmen and educators in modernity then, says Tocqueville, is not to do battle with the inevitable march of equality and democracy by longing for the good old days of inequality and aristocracy. Rather, the task is first to discover, and then keep, the mores and institutions of liberty alive and well. Again, he thought he saw the answers in the aftermath of the American Revolution in the new world.

Central to Tocqueville's project is the distinction between self-interest rightly understood and self-interest wrongly understood. This, in turn, is linked to what we call the distinction between liberty properly understood and liberty improperly understood. His understanding seems to be this: what we need is a prudent attachment to intermediate institutions, such as civic associations and religious sects, and the defense of the non-sublime morality that being virtuous and helpful to others can be useful to the advancement of one's own interests. This is what Smith was getting at in the butcher, the baker, and the brewer story; it is what Madison means by a system of rival and opposite interests. What Smith and Madison and Tocqueville were suggesting was that (a) by helping myself I help others, and (b) by helping others or working with others I help myself. This is self-interest rightly understood. This is our ability to take control over our own lives and to participate in the larger community.

The critics of the Liberty Narrative were correct to point out the dangers of a modern commercial society. But they were wrong to advocate a materialist approach to history and the reliance of revolutionaries or the centralization of administration. A defense of liberty recognizes non-commercial spiritual values that are equally important to who we are, and the need for institutions in which the interests of the individual coalesces with those of a larger social context. In pointing out the need for religion that supports a commercial society, Tocqueville explicitly warns, what Locke, Smith, and Madison implicitly recognized, that the alternatives are either the despotic bureaucratic option or an atheism that ends up doubting the centrality of all values of restraint or an unreasonable religion that fills the soul with an extreme rejection of the secular world. Tocqueville understood that you can't have liberty without some form of restraint and that's where religion teaches not just restraint, but tolerance, self-reliance, and the undergirding of the bourgeois virtue of moderation.

An appeal to self-interest doesn't seem to be high minded. Rather, it seems to appeal to what is wrong, namely, an appeal to self rather than others. But, according to Tocqueville, if we are in the age of democracy then an appeal to self is necessary. What can the 'common man' understand? We need to answer an additional question: how do we remain free or autonomous individuals? This requires that we accept the arrival of democracy and the fundamental point of departure in the equality of the human condition. This leads us to a critical point: what things are inevitable or more generously no longer relevant or interesting and what can and must we change to keep the human spirit alive. Tocqueville believed that self-interest was the inevitable point of departure in modernity consistent with the preservation of liberty. The issue is whether we have self-interest rightly or wrongly understood. Wrongly understood is what he calls individualism or egoism or withdrawal or alienation from society. So that is a false understanding of liberty. But we need to remind ourselves that Tocqueville is not suggesting that we abandon the self and become absorbed in a larger collectivity. This is precisely where self-interest wrongly understood leads us on the road to serfdom where we become 'sheep' or one of Smith's 'beggars'. He leaves us thinking whether a condition of dependency is actually worse than a condition of alienation.

It was Tocqueville who suggested that the arrival of the equality of condition is inevitable or even providential but the consequences of liberty or servitude is a matter of choice. Is the doctrine of self-interest rightly understood, which Tocqueville admits is not sublime, good enough to save liberty? Does the existence of these intermediate institutions imply that there is not yet a mass society? If we are, Ortega argues, already a mass society then it is a society that cannot self-actualize or self-motivate. What does this do to the existence of liberty?

In the twentieth century, one of the great voices of the Liberty Narrative will be Hayek. At the 1947 inaugural meeting of the Mont Pelerin Society, Hayek proposed, unsuccessfully, that the organization be called the Tocqueville Society.

KANT: PERSONAL AUTONOMY BEYOND THE STATE OF NATURE

Immanuel Kant's (1724–1804) moral theory begins with a fundamental insight about human beings: human beings are agents, not objects, and as agents they are both free and responsible for their action. This insight into human nature is something Kant learned from Jean Jacques Rousseau along with the idea that our freedom is not something immediately obvious to us but something we come to discover in history, through time, as befits an agent. Instead of seeing man as an observer set against an objective world and engaged in a theoretical task, Kant saw man as an agent whose primary tasks were practical. It is within action, and therefore history, that we come to learn who we are, and it is in further action dictated by our choices that we add to what we are. In saying that human beings are not objects, Kant rejected the traditional Aristotelian and natural law theories that claim (a) that we can understand ourselves in the same way that we understand the objects in this world, and (b) that we had built-in objectives. On the contrary, the way we understand the world is dependent upon how we understand ourselves, and the way in which we understand ourselves cannot be replaced or translated into a form of theoretical knowledge. Kant would have wisely rejected the whole notion that there could be such a thing as social science. In addition, human beings do not have fixed natures and fixed objectives such as the pursuit of life, liberty, and property or liberty, equality, and fraternity, and so on. Our fundamental condition is one of freedom. This will lead to a further "correction" of the Liberty Narrative. What is important is the dawning recognition of that freedom and what that freedom entails.

Taking Rousseau seriously, Kant understood freedom as autonomy. Unlike Rousseau, he will see liberty as a means to freedom. Taking Locke seriously, Kant embraces liberty. Unlike Locke, Kant distinguishes between 'freedom' and 'liberty'. 'Freedom' is an internal condition or human capacity and constitutive of who we are; 'liberty' is an external condition that can aid in the recognition of, embrace of, and exercise of the capacity of freedom.

What does it mean to be 'free'? The free individual or the individual who is self-conscious of his freedom lives a life of self-imposed rules. This is what it means to be a self-defining animal. An undisciplined life degenerates into slavery to one's passions, whims, and glands. A life that is disciplined only externally is the life of a slave, a child, or the life of someone who is mentally or morally retarded. A life is free when it disciplines itself. There is an important insight here that stretches back through Rousseau to Luther, and to Augustinian Christianity. A free being seeks out the company of other free beings, for it is only in such company that his own freedom is respected and can be exercised. Most important of all, a free being does not oppress others. In the act of oppression I define myself in terms of others, that is, I define myself by my victims. To the extent that I need victims, I am not autonomous. This is the point behind one of Kant's formulations of the categorical imperative in which he says that we should treat others as ends and not only as means. An existence given over to tutelage and domination diminishes our sense of our own freedom.

The idea that freedom involves the lack of restraint, says Kant, is a fundamental error. Lack of restraint characterizes the state of nature. Even those philosophers who laud the state of nature try to extricate us from it as soon as possible by means of a social contract. What Kant stressed was that the social contract itself has to be legitimated by the appeal to human autonomy. The law of freedom is that each of us has the right to restrain others consistent with that freedom.

Kant's discussion of freedom requires a certain understanding of history. By its internal necessity, the human consciousness has created time in order to represent its objects and, though itself dominating time in a way that they do not, must live in and through time to the extent that its goals are not fulfilled. Our historicity is a consequence of the way we know ourselves. Freedom is an interiorized fact in the historical world that draws us toward a future for which we will be responsible. For the sake of man's undoubted moral career, history needs to be seen as a plan whereby certain obvious and disagreeable facets of human nature can be regarded as paradoxically contributing to the goals of pure practical reason. Within those parameters are traced a progress of society, a formal valuation of political institutions, and a rhythm of human development.

Kant asserted two key historical theses. First, according to Kant, there are two sources of history: one is nature and the other is the capacity for human freedom. Historical progress is a form of spontaneous order which is twofold in a way that reflects history's two sources. On the phenomenal level there is a kind of Smithean invisible hand at work in nature in which order emerges from conflict, peace from war and public benefit from private vice. On the noumenal level, there is the development of the sense of duty. History, thus, cannot be understood simply in terms of impersonal forces. Moreover, the sense of duty is a temporal achievement not an immediate and obvious fact. Freedom springs from nature and progressively emancipates itself from it in history.

Kant maintained a second historical thesis: nations with market economies and republican forms of government are less likely to go to war. This is an expansion of Smith's point that a nation's competitive advantage promotes world trade. There is a close connection in Kant's theory between freedom and property, for violations of the duty to respect human beings as ends in themselves are most conspicuous in attacks on both personal liberty and private property. How insightful a view of history since the end of the eighteenth century is this? How many wars have there been in the last 200 years in which all the combatants on both sides were commercial republics?

THE MARKET ECONOMY, LIMITED GOVERNMENT, AND THE RULE OF LAW

Every human being has free will, or in Kantian terms, enjoys 'transcendental' freedom (that is, it is a basic assumption we must all make in order to think and speak intelligibly). Such freedom must be respected and promoted, even if we do not approve of the manner in which it is exercised. Liberty, or in Kantian terms 'political freedom', is "independence from being constrained by another's choice ... insofar as it can coexist with the freedom [liberty] of every other" (Kant 1991, *Collected Works*, 6:237). This is what legitimates government, not the alleged happiness of citizens. The government should not impose any particular conception of happiness upon its citizens, otherwise it is treating citizens like children who do not understand their true self-interest (telos?). Kant held that every rational being had both an innate right to freedom and a duty to enter into a civil condition governed by a social contract in order to realize and preserve that freedom. In this way, limited government is a means to freedom. The government may legitimately limit your liberty when that liberty conflicts with the freedom of others. This kind of limitation on liberty provides the framework within which individuals may exercise their freedom. You have a right to demand that the government enforce the laws on your behalf. What Kant has done is take Rousseau's notion of the "General Will" and interpret it to mean that it is what everyone would want, namely liberty, a market economy, and limited government, if they truly understood their ultimate good, namely, autonomous freedom.

Kant endorses the importance of private property and hence a market economy and the possibility of inequality of outcome. However, he rejects the Lockean notion that we have a natural right to property because we have invested our labor into it (Kant does not reject the technological project only one of the ways in which Locke uses it). Instead, he maintains that property is a means to the realization (and expression) of freedom. Our possession of property becomes legal when there is recognition that another's use of my possessions without my consent harms me even when I am not physically affected directly and even when I am not currently using the object. What the latter harms is the expression and realization of my freedom. Keep this conception of 'harm' in mind when we get to Mill.

In opposition to Rousseau, Kant endorses the idea that equality means equality before the law and not equality of outcome:

> [U]niform equality of human beings as subjects of a state is ... perfectly consistent with the utmost inequality of the mass in the degree of its possessions, whether these take the form of physical or mental superiority over others, or of fortuitous external property ... they are all equal as subjects before the law, which, as the pronouncement of the general will ... concerns the form of right and not the material or object in relation to which I possess rights. (*"On the Common Saying: 'This May be True in Theory, but It does not Apply in Practice'"*) (Kant AA8: 291)

The state or government is based on the abstract (rational not historical) notion of a social contract. The existence of the state is a means to protecting my property in order to realize my freedom. Kant endorses the concept of a republic, not a democracy. In a 'republic' the executive power is separated from and subordinate to the legislative power. Despotism occurs when a private will imposes on the public will. Only autonomous people have the right to vote, which means only those who have property or can support themselves independently are voting citizens. Pure democracy allows the majority, who may not be autono-mous, to appropriate the property of others.

PERPETUAL PEACE: AUTONOMY WRIT LARGE

In his essay, *Perpetual Peace* (1795), Kant's discussion of peace takes the literary form of a peace treaty signed by several nations at the end of a war. The treaty consists of six preliminary articles, three definitive articles, two supplements, and two appendices. The preliminary articles specify in logical terms what peace is:

1. No conclusion of peace shall be considered valid as such if it was made with a secret reservation of the material for a future war.
2. No independently existing state, whether it be large or small, may be acquired by another state by inheritance, exchange, purchase or gift.
3. Standing armies will gradually be abolished altogether.
4. No national debt will be contracted in connection with the external affairs of the state.
5. No state shall forcibly interfere in the constitution and government of another state.
6. No state at war with another shall permit such acts of hostility as would make mutual confidence impossible during a future time of peace. Such acts include the employment of assassins or poisoners, breach of agreements, the instigation of treason within the enemy state, and so on. (Terrorism?)

Kant insists that Articles 1, 5, and 6 must be adhered to immediately. Article 1 makes clear that a truce or a 'cold war' is not a peace. The state of peace must be formally instituted, for "a suspension of hostilities is not yet a guarantee of peace."

The most important of these articles is Article 5. In order to achieve harmony in international affairs there must be a mutual recognition of autonomy. Kant is here suggesting that states must relate to each other in the same way that individuals within a civil society relate to each other, that is, by reference to the categorical imperative which entails that we treat each other as ends and never as means only. Independent states must be permitted to develop in their own way. Kant qualifies this remark by pointing out that in a civil war there is no recognizable state.

The serious issue raised by Article 5 is when do the acts of states concern others? Granted that the answer to this question in specific cases is always going to involve judgment and discretion, Kant's concept of freedom as autonomy provides considerable guidance. Clearly, when the internal policies of a state have international implications and when those international implications threaten the autonomy of other states, then interference is more than warranted. For example, if the official and publicly stated political policy of a state or its regime is to foment world revolution, then such a state or regime is a threat to the autonomy of all others. Tolerance extends only to states that accept the principle of tolerance. This is a point of logic.

Suppose one were to argue, in opposition to Kant, that it is wrong for us to impose our ideas of freedom as autonomy on others. Instead, we should allow others to decide for themselves how they want to understand freedom. In defense of Kant, we point out that merely stating this objection shows that the objector already accepts the Kantian notion of freedom as autonomy. To let others decide for themselves is exactly to treat them as ends and not as means.

In addition, when we talk about others deciding for themselves we most certainly do not mean that a self-appointed elite decides for all. "Deciding for themselves" means allowing each autonomous individual to decide for himself/herself, and when applied to a state this has to mean a public and free election. That is, it means a republican form of government. Is it possible that a collection of individuals would in an un-coerced fashion freely choose a despotic form of government? To the best of our knowledge no political party which rejects the republican form of government has ever won a majority in a national election. By the time states have arrived at the point where free elections are held the majority of its citizens already implicitly accept the Kantian principle of autonomy. In this sense, Kant seems to be articulating a moral insight that itself reflects an important stage of development in Western Civilization.

The philosophical answer then to the question when does the action of a state constitute illegitimate interference in the affairs of other states is that interference is illegitimate when it threatens autonomy. If interference promotes autonomy then it is indeed legitimate. There are still practical questions to be raised and answered about the most judicious means for promoting autonomy, but the philosophical grounds remain clear. Even if one is justified in interfering in the affairs of another state there may be prudential grounds for not doing so. That is, sometimes the cure may be worse than the disease. No matter how just our cause it is not always wise to advance it in every given context.

With regard to Articles 2, 3, and 4, Kant recognizes the obvious extenuating circumstances. Article 3 calls for disbanding standing armies. Nevertheless, Kant advocates "some subjective latitude according to the circumstances in which they are applied." So, for example, Kant recommends that professional mercenary armies be replaced by citizen armies. Kant's plan for perpetual peace is not a plan for ending all conflict among states but is, rather, a plan which envisages such conflict as taking place in a progressively less destructive and unjust way. Perpetual peace is a task and not a foregone conclusion.

Having specified in the preliminary articles in what peace consists, in the section entitled the "Definitive articles" Kant explains how we are to achieve peace. The first definitive article is that "the Civil *Constitution* of every state shall be republican." The ultimate purpose of a republican constitution is to make a nation genuinely self-determining. A republican constitution rests on the assumption that each citizen gives his or her consent .by being directly or indirectly represented in the legislature. The citizen can in a moral sense, therefore, regard all laws as emanating from his or her will. Equally, he can regard the actions of the executive as susceptible to his control because it can only act within the confines of laws framed by the citizen's representatives. This, in Kant's view, furnishes a powerful lever of control over governments and curbs their aggressive instincts. Under a republican constitution those who have to bear the brunt of the financial and human costs of war have the power to decide whether or not they wish to prosecute the war. Although the problem of peace is on the surface an international problem, it is also a serious issue of domestic politics. Even after a national state is formed the state of nature still exists among states. Hence the problem cannot be solved by a legal analogy, that is, by appeal to a social contract. And, it requires going beyond military and political solutions to economic and moral solutions. That is why the discussion of a commercial Republic is grounded in Kant within his theory of moral autonomy.

In his discussion of perpetual peace Kant offers one of the most powerful arguments ever offered for freedom of speech. Kant maintained that freedom of speech follows from the categorical imperative. The bond of mutual respect that holds a society together requires that there be no principles which cannot be universalized. The test of universalizability is that policy be publicly discussable. Only in a Republic is this achievable, and hence only in a Republic is the categorical imperative realized. A Republic is the only consistent form of a moral commonwealth.

The second definitive article is that "the laws of nations should be founded on a federation of free states." Kant is clear that this federation is not itself a world state. A world state is, according to Kant, a contradiction in terms, for it implies domination by a superior. Such domination is inconsistent with autonomy.

Kant opposes a universal state on three grounds:

1.   A universal state becomes despotic.
2.   A universal state performs no function beyond what federated states can perform.
3.   A universal state is inconsistent with Kant's theory of property.

More important, the purpose of the federation is to serve both as a defensive alliance and as a vehicle by way of example of how international law may be established. "This federation does not aim to acquire any power like that of a state, but merely to preserve and secure the freedom of each state in itself" (Kant 1795, *Perpetual Peace*, Article II, paragraph 356). In a highly prescient remark, Kant expresses the following hope:

> For if by good fortune one powerful and enlightened nation can form a republic (which is by its very nature inclined to seek perpetual peace), this will provide a focal point for federal association among other states. These will join up with the first one, thus securing the freedom of each state in accordance with the idea of international right, and the whole will gradually spread further and further by a series of alliances of this kind. (Kant 1795, *Perpetual Peace*, Article II, paragraph 356)

This makes clear why the UN is largely dysfunctional, namely, that it is made up of states which are for the most part not republican or eschew the principles of republican government and is therefore structurally incapable of being a vehicle for perpetual peace.

We come now to the third and final issue of importance to Kant's treatment of the possibilities of peace, and that is the role of the military. Kant addressed this issue in his discussion of International Right in the *Metaphysics of Morals* (Kant 1797).

The right to make war, according to Kant, arises because the relationship among sovereign states is that of a state of nature, namely, there is no common superior or mutually agreed upon legal proceeding to settle disputes. World courts do not have meaningful jurisdiction over sovereign entities that do not accept the court's jurisdiction. In the absence of a consensual agreement on how to settle disputes, states have the right to enter into hostilities. Kant further specifies that in addition to inflicted injury:

> a state may be subject to *threats*. Such threats may arise either if another state is the first to make *military preparations*, on which the right of *anticipatory attack* [i.e., a preemptive strike] is based, or simply if there is an alarming increase of power … . This is an injury to the less powerful state by the mere fact that the other state, even without offering any active offence, is *more powerful*; and any attack upon it is legitimate in the state of nature. On this is

based the right to maintain a balance of power. (Kant 1797, *Metaphysics of Morals*, paragraph 56)

The right to go to war can only be justified by two things: the right conduct of the war and the establishment of right after the war. This means that the guiding policy of carrying out a war must have as its ultimate aim the creation of a confederation of Republics. What does this mean about the conduct of war: it means that (a) a war cannot be punitive, since every peace treaty contains an amnesty; (b) it cannot be a war of extermination, or involve the dismemberment of the offending state and dividing it up among the victors; (c) it cannot be a war of expansion; and (d) the methods used cannot frustrate the ultimate end. Here Kant is alluding to the previously discussed sixth preliminary article of perpetual peace (assassination, instigating treason, and so on).

It is also within this context that Kant raises the prospect of an unjust enemy. Notice that Kant does not try to formulate the idea of a just war, rather he focuses on the notion of an unjust enemy. An unjust enemy is defined as:

> someone whose publicly expressed will, whether expressed in word or in deed, displays a maxim which would make peace among nations impossible and would lead to a perpetual state of nature if it were made a general rule. Under this heading would come violations of public contracts, which can be assumed to affect the interests of all nations. (Kant 1797, *Metaphysics of Morals*, paragraph 56)

With regard to unjust enemies, Kant asserts that:

> the rights of a state against an unjust enemy are unlimited in quantity or degree, although they do have limits in relation to quality. In other words, while the threatened state may not employ *every* means to assert its own rights, it may employ any intrinsically permissible means to whatever degree its own strength allows. (Kant 1797, *Metaphysics of Morals*, paragraph 60)

What then is the role of the military? The use of force is a necessary evil in a morally immature world. The military is a transitional institution designed to lead to perpetual peace through its capacity to conduct war justly. The transitional nature of the institution reflects the assumption that some states including our own have reached a stage of moral maturity, as reflected in their republican forms of government, but we still live in a world where not all states have arrived at this point. Without this sense of our own moral maturity the military either becomes an instrument of personal and national aggrandizement in which case citizens are being used as means and are not being treated as ends or its own morale and effectiveness is undermined by lack of confidence in the intrinsic worth of its role. With regard to perpetual peace it is much easier to think of the right conduct of war aimed at producing morally mature states as a realistic goal rather than the romantic notion of a war to end all wars. One cannot be sure of the latter, that is, the last war, but one can make constant sense of the former, that is, aiming at fostering moral maturity.

This leads to the practical issue of how does one foster moral maturity in a morally immature world? Here is where Kant's historical views become relevant. In their pursuit of self-interest, all nations eventually seek commercial expansion. As Kant puts it, as the *spirit of commerce* takes hold, it cannot exist side by side with war. To spell this out graphically: the growth of commerce or capitalism leads to peace, peace leads to commercial success, commercial success leads to Republican government, and Republican government leads to freedom and dignity, that is, moral maturity.

Let us sum up Kant's position. Perpetual peace is only possible when all nations have arrived at moral maturity. Moral maturity is marked by the recognition of the categorical imperative expressed as the doctrine that human beings are to be treated as ends and not as means only. To treat someone as an end requires recognition of individual autonomy. Individual autonomy can only flourish in a state with a Republican government and a free economy. The immediate goal of any foreign policy is to promote the conditions which foster Republican government and free economies and to oppose non-Republican forms of government and centrally planned economies. In order to do this a state must have a strong and free economy and a strong military posture (the technological project is relevant here) which by its very existence, strength and self-confidence goads morally immature states to approximate the conditions which lead to the recognition of the categorical imperative.

> The spirit of trade cannot coexist with war, and sooner or later this spirit dominates every people … financial power may be the most reliable in forcing nations to pursue the noble cause of peace (though not from moral motives); and wherever in the world war threatens to break out, they will try to head it off through mediation. (Kant 1795, *Perpetual Peace*, paragraph 368)

A NEW DEFENSE OF LIBERTY: KANT'S CATEGORICAL IMPERATIVE

There have been four definitions of liberty in the history of Western Civilization. The classical world thought an individual free when he/she subordinated himself/herself to the social good as determined by some elite; the liberal definition of liberty, first advocated by Hobbes and Locke, is that human beings are free if they are not subject to arbitrary external constraint; the Rousseau doctrine is that an individual who willingly identifies himself/herself with the social whole is free. Kant provides a fourth.

Kant introduces a distinction between 'liberty' and 'freedom'. 'Liberty' is an external condition subject to limitation, but the defenders of the Liberty Narrative have heretofore been unable to specify the limitations. 'Freedom' is an internal condition reflected in all three dimensions of the categorical imperative – I cannot make an exception of myself and I must recognize the autonomy of others.

Liberty as a means to freedom: Kant's definition of freedom is that an individual is free if he/she lives a life of self-imposed rules, that is, an autonomous life. Previous defenses of the Liberty Narrative are inadequate because they treat liberty as a means to something else (prosperity, and so on), and they view liberty as something seen from the outside rather than as an internal moral achievement. To view freedom as something external is first of all to see the problem of peace as well as every other problem as one requiring externally induced solutions, that is, purely political solutions. It is to miss completely the moral dimension of these problems. To view liberty as something external and not internal is to be unable to make a distinction between the morally mature and the morally immature. Failure to distinguish the morally mature from the morally immature leads to an inability to see the gulf that presumably separates us from our adversaries, and lacking this perception it is but a short step to the conclusion that our adversaries are just like us. If they are just like us, then we are just like them. And if we are just like them, then we have no claim to moral superiority. Without a sense of moral superiority there is no reason to think that what we stand for is any better than anything else, and finally that it is certainly not worth defending.

It is important that we reassess our conception of liberty and its relation to freedom. It is important that we see the alternative account and most especially Kant's notion of freedom as autonomy. Kant's categorical imperative is not the dry, dusty and obscure abstraction of philosophical textbooks. On the contrary it may be the single most important defense of liberty.

Instead of agreeing with the ancients that we have a telos, instead of trying to prove that everyone is better off in a market economy, which may be true for the whole but not necessarily for every individual (otherwise we commit the logical fallacy of composition), and instead of avoiding the question of spiritual as opposed to material values, Kant tackles the problem differently. The most important thing about us is our freedom; all other values flow from it; and freedom is not zero-sum. Hence, there is no problem of how my true self-interest is compatible with the true self-interest of everyone else, even internationally. "I cannot reconcile myself to the following … . 'Mankind in general is not yet ripe for freedom of belief' … to proceed on the principle that those who are once subjected … are essentially unfit for freedom … is to usurp the prerogatives of Divinity itself, which created men for freedom" (Kant [1793] 1960, *Religion Within the Limits of Reason Alone*, p. 176, n7).

In his essay on *Perpetual Peace* Immanuel Kant provided (a) a moral vision, (b) a philosophy of history, and (c) a conceptual elucidation of the conditions necessary for understanding and justifying a federation of European nations. Kant is seen as both historically prophetic and programmatic. The major elements of Kant's position are autonomy, commerce, and representative government. Correctly understood, autonomy requires, and in turn is fostered by, a free market economy and a republican form of government. Autonomy also militates against the necessity for an international super-state and, along with a free market economy and representative government, fosters international peace and prosperity. Peace is not simply the product of economic, legal, or political means but requires moral progress as well.

Kant buttresses the Liberty Narrative by showing the connection between liberty and freedom, the latter understood as personal autonomy. In doing so, he provides a serious response to the Equality Narrative. Adherents of the Equality Narrative chide adherents of the Liberty Narrative on the grounds that liberty is a sham if people do not have the resources to pursue what they desire. This is both a straight forward materialistic argument by egalitarians and a demand for the redistribution of resources. Kant's response is twofold. In the first place, what is fundamental to human beings is freedom not material advantages. This places the Liberty Narrative on the high moral ground. In addition, the forced redistribution of resources treats some human beings as means to the material ends of other human beings. Looking further down the evolution of the narratives, when adherents of the Equality Narrative talk about the psychologically debilitating effects of inequality they will emphasize the extent to which some feel cheated because they are looked down upon by others. Here again, Kant's espousal of liberty as a means to freedom provides adherents of the Liberty Narrative with a response: self-respect is what individuals grant to themselves by becoming autonomous; to be focused on self-esteem is to see oneself through the eyes of others, and this is both morally immature (heteronomy) and a subtle form of envy.

HEGEL: THE 'CORRECTION' OF THE LOCKE NARRATIVE

Reading and interpreting Hegel (1770–1831) is a serious challenge given his style of writing, the breadth of his thought, the complex and convoluted nature of his system, and until recently the partisan readings of Hegel by scholars. Recent scholarship has rescued him from the authoritarians of both the left and the right who have for so long buried the insights of his book *Philosophy of Right* (Hegel 1820).

We begin by placing Hegel squarely within the Lockean Liberty Narrative.

Technological Project: The first important element of the Locke Liberty Narrative is an endorsement of the technological project (control nature for human benefit rather than conformity to nature; in Hegel this comes out as remaking the world in the human image); as Hegel put it:

> Through work ... the bondsman becomes conscious of what he truly is ... and thereby becomes *for-himself*, something existing on its own account ... . Through this rediscovery of himself by himself, the bondsman realizes that it is precisely in his work wherein he seemed to have only an alienated existence that he acquires a mind of his own. (Hegel 1807, *Phenomenology of Spirit*, 195–96)

Work not only allows us to liberate ourselves from nature's dominance but to develop our self-consciousness and sense of freedom. We not only impose meaning on nature but discover our autonomy in the act of self-disciplined creation. Hegel has taken Locke's insight about labor one step further and developed it into the new thesis that the Technological Project is the spiritual quest of modernity.

Market Economy: It should come as no surprise that Kant who proclaimed 'unsocial sociability' and Hegel who relished the 'cunning of reason' had both read and been influenced by Smith, especially the metaphor of the 'invisible hand'. Anyone who understands what Hegel meant by 'dialectic' should not be surprised to find that he endorsed the notion that a market was a perfect example of the logic of competition and cooperation. Hegel's system comprises numerous Lockean elements, such as private property, the rule of law, free choice of profession, extensive religious toleration, liberty of conscience, and freedom of opinion and of the press.

Limited Government: In Hegel's philosophy of history, there is an evolution from despotism to individual freedom:

World history is the record of the spirit's efforts to attain knowledge of what it is in itself. The Orientals do not know that the spirit or man as such are free in themselves. And because they do not know that, they are not themselves free. They only know that *One* is free ... . The consciousness of freedom first awoke among the Greeks, and they were accordingly free; but, like the Romans, they only knew that *Some*, and not all men as such, are free ... . The Germanic nations, with the rise of Christianity, were the first to realize that *All* men are by nature free, and that freedom of spirit is his very essence. (Hegel 1837, *Lectures on the Philosophy of World History*, paragraph 54)

The appropriate form of government for Hegel's own time was a British style constitutional monarchy. In his other writings, Hegel expresses disdain both for Jacobinism and the rabble.

The main source of confusion on the part of scholars is Hegel's conception of the 'state.'

The 'state' in Hegel is not the government. Hegel strongly disapproved of the ancient Greek polis. Providing public services and administering the law are functions of civil society and not the 'state' in Hegel's sense. A classical collectivist conception of society is out of sync with modernity. Like Smith, Hegel overcomes the individual versus community debate by arguing for how individual freedom is best realized in a certain kind of community (*Sittlichkeit*) involving what we would now call the intermediate associations of Tocqueville or civil society.

Rule of Law: Hegel articulated an early version of the *Rechtsstaat*.

Culture of Personal Autonomy: Hegel looked upon individualism in the form of modern subjective freedom as the final stage of history. Building on Smith and Kant, Hegel recognized what he termed the three stages of objective spirit as follows: in stage one (Smith's ethics) there is the recognition of individual rights, along with contract and property; in stage two (Kant) there is the development of morality or the sense of our duties to others; in stage three (Hegel) the tension between individual rights and social obligation is overcome in a higher synthesis.

What is that higher synthesis? That synthesis is embodied in the state. The state embodies the ideal that autonomous individuals are not part of a zero-sum world, that there is no conflict between ultimate self-interest properly understood as the autonomy of any one person with that of all other persons; that the pursuit of autonomy by each enhances the conditions of autonomy for all – something Kant alluded to in the categorical imperative, but more importantly an expression of Smith's unseen hand expressed in Germanic vocabulary. There is in Hegel no substantive collective goal; the collective goal is procedural = the norm of maximizing every individual's autonomy.

There are problems in modern market societies. The specific problems are poverty, the distribution of resources/opportunities and the otherwise social dysfunction of some members of market societies ("rabble"). Market societies are incompatible with traditional morality or some people's expectations (Piketty). To be sure the lack of autonomy is a problem within market societies, but the real question is whether this reflects market failure or the failure of some people to adapt to markets and to embrace autonomy. Hegel's discussion of the "rabble" sees the latter as failures rather than as victims. Interpreting the poor as victims is Rousseauean. Hegel's discussion of the "rabble" was quite possibly the inspiration for Oakeshott's delineation of the anti-individual as someone who chooses not to embrace autonomy.

Finally, we turn to Hegel's metaphysics in order to clarify why Hegel was not an authoritarian. Kant's Copernican Revolution in philosophy abandoned classical philosophy for the epistemological view that order and meaning is what the human mind imposes on nature. This still raises questions about the status of the mind. What Hegel added to Kant was the claim that the human mind has evolved historically. Kant too had taken history seriously and had maintained in Smithean fashion that nature, in the form of the economy, moved through stages. What Hegel added to Kant was the claim that nature and mind are two aspects of an all-encompassing Geist that evolves dialectically. Only the divine Mind (or Geist) is fully rational and self-conscious. Neither in history nor in a market society does everyone achieve consciousness of personal autonomy (individual freedom and responsibility). The failure of the rabble to achieve autonomy does not negate the notion that personal autonomy is the ultimate goal.

CONCLUSION: REFLECTIONS ON THE 'CORRECTION'

We have joined Tocqueville, Kant, and Hegel together as examples of fellow travelers within the Liberty Narrative yet 'correcting' the previously laid foundations of that narrative. Tocqueville's endorsement of the non-sublime "self-interest rightly understood" reminds us that individual liberty is best pursued through voluntary association with others without subsuming oneself in a mass society governed by a centralized administration. The concept of 'voluntary' participation will be echoed in Oakeshott's discussion of civil society. We should point out that Tocqueville's warning of self-interest wrongly understood has encouraged other writers like Robert Bellah and Robert Putnam to see a strong communitarian inclination in Tocqueville, one that could actually be used to support the Equality Narrative.

The same double-edged sword is present in the work of Kant and Hegel. We have argued that both Kant and Hegel are vital parts of the Liberty Narrative of personal autonomy and personal recognition. This hasn't prevented scholars and politicians since the nineteenth century from appropriating Kant's categorical imperative and Hegel's dialectic on behalf of the Equality Narrative. Two examples will suffice. First, twentieth century scholars interested in the issues of ethics in public policy contrast an egalitarian Kantian categorical imperative with self-interested Madisonian individualism. Second, Marx, as we shall see, appropriated the Hegelian dialectic on behalf of the Equality Narrative.

7.   Mill's Place in the Liberty Narrative

INTRODUCTION

John Stuart Mill and Karl Marx were the two great synthetic thinkers of the nineteenth century. It should come as no surprise that Mill articulated the clearest and most cogent version of the Liberty Narrative in the nineteenth century just as Marx will do so for the Equality Narrative. Not unsurprisingly, Mill's articulation of that narrative owes much to Tocqueville and Kant.

Mill (1803–76) was the son of James Mill and the godson of Jeremy Bentham, both radical reformers and utilitarians. In his *Autobiography* (1873), J.S. Mill documented an intellectual journey marked by a movement away from narrow utilitarianism and toward a deeper under-standing of liberty. He was the last major British philosopher to present an integrated view of the whole of philosophy and, like Kant and Hegel, to relate the theoretical and normative dimensions of his thought in a direct fashion. Mill understood his work in the technical areas of philosophy as a foundation for his social and political philosophy. His *Principles of Political Economy* (1848 and several subsequent editions; hereafter *PPE*) achieved the status of a canonical textbook. Nevertheless, Mill corrected Locke, Smith, Tocqueville and Kant.

MILL ENDORSES AND AMENDS THE LOCKEAN NARRATIVE

Mill endorsed and amended the Lockean narrative. First, he endorsed the technological project and economic growth. Mill's view on technology is expressed in his historical account of the stages of economic growth, a view which owes much to Scottish Enlightenment thinkers such as Hume, Smith, and Ferguson. Economic and social progress are marked by three stages: savagery, barbarism, and civilization. 'Civilization' means a modern industrial and commercial society like Great Britain with a liberal culture. The development of civilization is dependent upon the natural stages of progress, upon the diffusion of reading, and the increase of the facilities of human intercourse. The third stage of *Civilization*, in Mill's essay of that title (Mill 1836), is marked economically by industry, politically by limited government and the rule of law, and socially by liberty. Examples of these combined features can be seen in military operations, commerce and manufacturing, and the rise of joint-stock companies. The consequences of the rise of civilization are economic, political, social, and moral. Economically there has been a vast increase in wealth in which the masses (a visible economic phenomenon in the nineteenth century) and the middle class have been the greater beneficiaries as opposed to the obstructionist landed oligarchic aristocracy. Politically, power is shifting from a few to the masses. The new challenge, as Mill learned from Tocqueville, is to preserve liberty and progress in a mass based society.

He maintained that "We cannot … foresee to what extent the modes of production may be altered, or the productiveness of labor increased, by future extensions of our knowledge of the laws of nature, suggesting new processes of industry of which we have at present no conception" (Mill 1848, *PPE*, II, i, i). He agreed with Ricardo's critique of Smith that landlords were standing in the way of economic progress, but he was also influenced by Malthus' concern that the size of workers' families would outstrip economic gains. Mill was the first to include population control within the realm of political economy. As we shall see, and equally controversially, he advocated a tax on inheritance in order to undermine large feudal estates but not large productive private industrial enterprises.

Participation in a market economy informed by an individualist moral culture promotes a variety of forms of virtuous behavior. Nevertheless, Mill insisted that there had to be a moral purpose to the technological project. The desire to engross the whole surface of the earth in the mere production of the greatest possible quantity of food and the materials of manufacture, he considered to be founded on a mischievously narrow conception of the requirements of human nature. We note that among the many things that both Mill and his father had objected to most vehemently about the new industrial economy was the spoiling of the countryside by all of the new, and in many cases unnecessarily duplicative, railway lines. As inveterate hikers, they were especially sensitive to the destruction of natural beauty and the disappearance of solitude. Mill was a critic of both the focus on production and the static view of distribution. Wealth is not an end in itself; it is a means to human fulfillment and individual liberty. Income is not merely a means to consumer satisfaction and an incentive, but also a means to accomplishment. Growth for growth's sake was a perversion (Mill 1867, *Inaugural Address at Saint Andrews, Collected Works* XXI, p. 253).

Mill also addressed the issue of the stationary state, that is, an economy that no longer grows (a concern for classical economists but not neoclassical economists). Mill did not think that we had arrived at that state, so more growth was, in the foreseeable future, both necessary and probable. However, he did not believe that a stationary state was necessarily bad. He argued that wealth is not an end in itself but a means to human fulfillment and individual liberty. Even if there were a stationary state of zero growth, liberty would not necessarily be lost or suffer. Growth is important, but less important than liberty.

MILL AND THE MARKET ECONOMY: *PRINCIPLES OF POLITICAL ECONOMY*

Mill's most well developed response to the political economy issues of his day was in the *Principles of Political Economy* published in 1848. It is a work that redefines the relationship between economics and politics. The work has a methodological and an ideological dimension. Mill stated in the Preface that "there are perhaps no practical questions ... which admit of being decided on economical premises alone" (Mill 1848, *PPE*, II, p. xci). Policy decisions depend upon the explication of fundamental values followed by scientific consideration of means and consequences. Political economy comprises a set of economic policies based upon a unifying normative principle. For Mill, that principle is personal autonomy. Mill evaluates policies along two axes: (1) efficiency, and (2) the promotion of autonomy. The *Principles of Political Economy* was written to "rescue from the hands of such people the truths they misapply, and by combining these with other truths to which they are strangers, to deduce conclusions capable of being of some use to the progress of mankind" (Letter to William Conner, September 26, 1849, in *Collected Works* XIV, p. 37). The production, distribution, and consumption of wealth are necessary but not sufficient conditions for autonomy.

The great practical question of Mill's time was the social crisis created by the Industrial Revolution, namely class conflict. This crisis was exacerbated in Mill's mind by the perceived coming of an increasingly democratic society. Mill identified several possible solutions.

The Tory solution (that is, the policy of those who spoke for the landed aristocracy) was a defense of the status quo permeated by an attitude of paternalism toward the working class. Mill was vehemently critical of this response. In the famous chapter of the *Principles of Political Economy*, he begins by contrasting the feudal-paternalistic view of Disraeli and Carlyle with autonomy:

According to the former theory, the lot of the poor, in all things which affect them collectively, should be regulated for them, not by them. They should not be required or encouraged to think for themselves, or give to their own reflection or forecast an influential voice in the determination of their destiny. It is supposed to be the duty of the higher classes to think for them, and to take the responsibility of their lot, as the commanders and officers of an army take that of the soldiers composing it. (Mill 1848, *PPE*, III, p. 759)

Given the classical economists fears about the choking off of economic progress by landlords, and given Tocqueville's warning about the rising challenge of democracy, Mill believed that the only way to maintain the benefits of the Industrial Revolution along with preserving freedom was to reduce the power of the aristocracy. Hence, he advocated breaking up the old estates by ending entail and primogeniture, and by limiting how much could be inherited (an inheritance tax is not to be confused with an estate tax) by one individual. Mill went so far as to advocate government ownership of the landed resources as long as this governmental 'taking' was not an expropriation but a policy for which compensation was provided. He also added the qualification that moveable wealth, as opposed to landed wealth, should not be government owned nor should large and successful enterprises in moveable wealth be broken up. (See *PPE II*, p. 225: BK. II, Chapter II, section 4, note appended to the 1865 edition.) Moreover, he did not want to penalize through taxation the inclination to save that is the basis of capital formation on which economic progress depended. In short, what Mill tried to achieve was a balancing act in which wealth was maximized in such a way as to increase the possibilities of entrepreneurship and autonomy.

Most interesting is Mill's critique of classical political economy's response as represented by his father. Mill faulted that response because it blithely ignored that there was a potentially serious conflict between the entrepreneurial middle class and the workers, a conflict that would be exacerbated by the growth of democracy. Sooner or later there would be some public policy concerning the production and distribution of wealth, and given the views of Comte and others, Mill worried that it would be a coercive oligarchy. Moreover, classical political economists never questioned their own personal presumption of Puritanism and hence ignored the extent to which the single-minded pursuit of wealth in production led inexorably to a hypocritically disguised and corrosive materialism. Finally, the inadequacy of the methodology of classical political economy, notably its presumption of *homo economicus*, would eventually undermine the ideals of social cooperation and the notion of a common good. With the latter, class conflict was inevitable and destructive of the whole structure of liberal culture.

Toward this end, Mill introduced his strategic distinction between production and distribution. Political economy is a science to the extent that it can make true generalizations about the production of wealth. However, the current patterns of distribution reflected historical accident. Mill was not ignorant of the interrelationship of production and distribution. Mill never suggested or thought that distribution or redistribution did not itself have consequences for productivity. "Society can subject the distribution of wealth to whatever rules it thinks best: but what practical results shall flow from the operation of those rules, society cannot choose, but must be content to learn" (*PPE*, First edition (1848), II, p. 200). Mill recognized that changes in the way production was organized could alter patterns of distribution. Hence we could contemplate alternative schemes designed both to increase productivity and to increase the number of people who engaged in entrepreneurial activity and benefited from it.

The production of wealth is not the only or highest human objective. Mill stressed that while political economy usefully employs the notion of the pursuit of self-interest (*homo economicus*) as a construct this construct does not exhaustively characterize human nature. Mill's priorities are quite clear in that autonomy is the highest good. Economic efficiency is a means to autonomy. The Industrial Revolution and a free market economy are infinitely superior to feudalism precisely because they liberate the human potential for autonomy. On the other hand, if we lived in a world where we were forced to choose between autonomy and more material benefits, there is no question that Mill would favor autonomy. Mill reminds us that autonomous laborers were more productive so that autonomy was itself a means to efficiency. The growth of a commercial and industrial economy with a free market created the possibility for a world where all could be free and responsible. It was the purpose of political economy to help all of us realize the potential of the new order.

The third response to the problem of class conflict was that of Socialism/Communism. This response to the class problem was to close the gap by endorsing collective ownership and state control of the whole of the economy. Mill's response to it is telling:

> The principal of private property has never yet had a fair trial in any country; and less so, perhaps, in this country than in some others. The social arrangements of modern Europe commenced from a distribution of property which was the result, not of just partition, or acquisition by industry, but of conquest and violence … . The laws of property have never yet conformed to the principles on which the justification of private property rests [Locke] … if the tendency of legislation had been to favor the diffusion, instead of the concentration of wealth … the principle of individual property would have

been found to have no necessary connexion with the physical and social evils which almost all Socialist writers assume to be inseparable from it ... the decision [between Communism and private property] will probably depend mainly on one consideration, viz. Which of the two systems is consistent with the greatest amount of human liberty and spontaneity. (Mill 1848, *PPE*, II, pp. 207–208)

Mill endorsed an industrial market economy as expounded by Smith, Ricardo, and Say. In Book I, Chapter V, of the *Principles of Political Economy* Mill advances Four Fundamental Propositions respecting Capital. The first proposition is that "industry is limited by capital" and therefore it is a *mistake* to believe "that laws and governments, without creating capital, could create industry." Moreover:

[t]here is not an opinion more general among mankind than this, that the unproductive expenditure of the rich is necessary to the employment of the poor. Before Adam Smith, the doctrine had hardly been questioned ... [namely, that] there would be no market for the commodities which the capital so created would produce. I conceive this to be one of the many errors arising in political economy ... [on the contrary] the limit of wealth is never deficiency of consumers, but of producers and productive power. Every addition to capital gives to labor either additional employment, or additional remuneration; enriches either the country, or the laboring class. (Mill 1848, *Principles of Political Economy*, *Collected Works* II, p. 66)

"A second fundamental theorem respecting Capital relates to the source from which it is derived. It is the result of saving" and hence "to increase capital there is another way besides consuming less, namely, to produce more." Third, Capital is kept in existence "from age to age not by preservation, but by perpetual reproduction" (Mill 1848, *Principles of Political Economy*, *Collected Works* II, p. 68). The fourth proposition, with due attribution to Say and Ricardo is that what "supports and employs productive labor, is the capital expended in setting it to work, and not the demand of purchasers for the produce of the labor when completed." Demand for commodities is not demand for labor. Demand for labor (job creation) depends upon "the amount of the capital, or other funds directly devoted to the sustenance of labor." By ignoring the importance of wealth creation we injure the long term well-being of everyone but most especially the poor.

Nevertheless, the question of Mill's relation to socialism continues to puzzle scholars. There are good reasons for this. Mill described himself in the *Principles of Political Economy* as an "Ideal Socialist," but later wrote in the *Chapters on Socialism* (Mill 1879) a scathing critique of socialism.

The term 'socialism' came into use around 1830 and was applied to three movements deriving respectively from Saint-Simon (1760–1825), Fourier (1772–1837), and Robert Owen (1771–1858) in England. These writers, referred to as 'Utopian' Socialists, are the ones that Mill discussed most thoroughly and always had in mind. Saint-Simon himself (and later Auguste Comte) proposed having the entire social world organized and run by a technical elite. The society would be a thorough-going meritocracy. Fourier was a proponent of a workers' cooperative consistent with private ownership of property and prices set by a market. Other French figures who influenced Mill's thinking on socialism were Pierre-Joseph Proudhon (1809–65), advocate of producer's cooperatives without centralized control; and Louis Blanc (1811–82), another advocate of worker cooperatives, initially funded by the government, but thereafter independent of government control.

'Utopian' Socialism is the kind of socialism Marx and Engels rejected. In explaining why their manifesto was 'Communist' and not 'socialist' Engels said:

> By socialists, in 1847, were understood, on the one hand, the adherents of the various utopian systems: Owenites in England, followers of Fourier in France, both of them already reduced to the position of mere sects, and gradually dying out; on the other hand, the most multifarious social quacks, who, by all manners of tinkering, professed to redress, without any danger to capital and profit, all sorts of social grievances, in both cases men outside the working-class movement and looking rather to the 'educated' classes for support ... . Thus socialism was, in 1847, a middle-class movement, communism a working class movement. (Marx 1888, *Communist Manifesto* [English edition], preface)

Utopian socialists were critical of what 'capitalism' meant in the nineteenth century: (1) the assumption that human beings were primarily motivated by self-interest narrowly understood; (2) a permanent (and adversarial) division in society between two classes, owners and workers; and (3) the assumption that class membership was determined exclusively by birth. Capitalism in the twentieth and twenty-first centuries has come to mean something very different. In the contemporary context utopian socialists would not be considered socialists but capitalists, or more accurately, advocates of a free market economy. Marx and Engels clearly understood this.

Mill identified, in fact, with the utopian socialists. What this meant, first, is that he rejected psychological hedonism and egoism. Fourier was the great exponent of the idea that the natural passions properly directed (self-interest properly understood – Tocqueville) resulted in social harmony. Second, Mill advocated cooperatives. Mill's 'socialism' is the doctrine that workers should pool their savings and borrow on the open market in order to set up cooperatives, and everyone in a cooperative should be shareholders (for example, the contemporary Silicon Valley startup). Associations of individuals who own property, for example, publicly traded modern corporations, would be 'socialistic' in Mill's sense, but not in the contemporary context of state socialism. The world in which Mill lived was one in which property was largely owned by a few individuals, primarily by families. Until 1855, Parliament had proscribed all but a few limited liability joint-stock companies. We note as well that Mill anticipated Hayek in maintaining that no one could foresee the future permutations of a market economy.

MILL ON THE ROLE OF GOVERNMENT

It would be ludicrous to identify the author of *On Liberty* (Mill 1859) and *Representative Government* (Mill 1861), as well as the critic of Comtean totalitarianism as an advocate of anything but limited government. Mill took seriously Tocqueville's warning about the tyranny of the majority as well as the dangers of a democratic culture from his reading and review of Tocqueville. The social crisis created by the Industrial Revolution was class conflict. This crisis was exacerbated in Mill's mind by the perceived coming of an increasingly democratic society, the most serious consequence of which has been the decline of individuality. The future of civilization depended upon the masses exercising their power in such a responsible way that we shall continue to enjoy the benefits of civilization. Civilization would not endure unless the masses came to understand and appreciate the moral foundations of liberal culture. Unlike the Philosophic Radicals, and unlike orthodox Marxists, Mill was not an economic determinist. The moral world was not a mere product of material forces. The very functioning of the economy presupposed certain virtues. Herein is the explanation of Mill's economic position in the *Principles of Political Economy*; the germ of the recommendations of *Representative Government* (1861), and the project of *On Liberty* (1859).

Mill calls attention at the very beginning of *On Liberty* to the radical Rousseauean change in the meaning of the concept of 'democracy' that prompted in part his writing of that work.

'Democracy' means something different in each narrative. For Lockeans, following Madison in *Federalist 10*, democracy is a negative device. There will always be a plurality of competing interests in a market economy; in order to prevent one economic interest from dominating, a majority of the other interests can restrict or block the hegemony of that interest. What the majority wants is not necessarily good. As John Stuart Mill pointed out (following Tocqueville) the term 'democracy' meant in the eighteenth century a protection from government tyranny. In the nineteenth century, following Rousseau, 'democracy' acquired a positive function, namely, a consensus on the common good understood as the collectivist General Will. Lockeans, like the American Founders, worry about the tyranny of the majority and try to protect the rights of all individuals through constitutional guarantees; Rousseaueans, like the French Revolutionaries, believe that a democratically elected government is the voice of the people and that the people do not need protection from themselves. He concluded further that:

> We all know what specious fallacies may be urged in defense of every act of injustice yet proposed for the imaginary benefit of the mass. We know how many, not otherwise fools or bad men, have thought it justifiable to repudiate the national debt ... think it fair to throw the whole burden of taxation upon savings, under the name of realized property ... . One of the greatest dangers, therefore, of democracy, as of all other forms of government, lies in the sinister interests of the holders of power: it is the danger of class legislation. (Mill 1861, *Representative Government, Collected Works* XIX, pp. 442–46)

PERSONAL AUTONOMY

Rousseaueans are far less at home with the virtues of competition, emphasizing instead what they see as the vices of competition such as selfishness, greed, fraud, luxury, and anarchy. What pulls this Rousseau narrative in the direction of equality of outcome is the human sense of compassion, or deep-seated natural sympathy for others, and our duty toward the well-being of other humans. There is a compatible development in the world of politics and religion, an emphasis on the rule of the General Will rather than the rule of law and the substitution of a civil religion, or secular humanism, for the rule of individual conscience.

Mill believed himself to have joined a conversation that was defined directly by Kant. "Kant ... holds so essential a place in the development of philosophic thought, that until somebody had done what Kant did, metaphysics according to our present conception of it could not have been continued ... he has become one of the turning points in the history of philosophy" (Mill 1865, *An Examination of the Philosophy of Sir William Hamilton, Collected Works* IX, p. 493n).

No one was a more adamant advocate of Kantian personal autonomy than Mill, especially in the essay *On Liberty*. Mill did not share the Rousseauean inspired belief in the natural goodness of humanity nor the assumption that all social evil was the result of environmental/social circumstances. The belief that human beings are fundamentally good and corrupted only by their environment is shared not only by many socialists but by many anarchist libertarians. The former often believe that government must control all the major institutions in order to eradicate evil, and the latter believe that all evil is the result of attempts by the government to control all major institutions. Mill would disagree with both of those positions. Mill objected to Robert Owen's environmental determinist position and was sympathetic to Fourier's conception of cooperatives because the latter recognized individuality. There is an element of free will in human choice, and nature contains no teleology directing human beings to their good. Becoming a decent human being is a lifelong struggle against basic impulses. He went out of his way in the essay *Nature* (Mill 1874, *Collected Works* X, p. 395) to critique Rousseau who delighted "in decorating savage life, and setting it in advantageous contrast with the treachery and trickery of civilisation." Mill remained fervently pro-market; where he advocated reform it was not to correct market failure but to overcome the failure of individuals to be fit participants in a market economy:

> The commonest self-control for one's own benefit [self-interest rightly understood] ... this is most unnatural to the undisciplined human being; as may be seen by the long apprenticeship which children serve to it ... and the marked absence of the quality ... in nearly the whole of the poorer classes in this and many other countries. (Mill 1874, *Nature*, *Collected Works* X, p. 395)

Recall as well Mill's views on sexuality and his condemnation of men who abuse women; in a letter to Florence Nightingale in 1860 he reiterated his almost Manichean and Hegelian conception of the human predicament: "the world is a battlefield between a good and a bad power or powers, and ... mankind may be capable by sufficiently strenuous cooperation with the good power, of deciding, or at least accelerating, its final victory" (Mill, *Collected Works* XV, p. 709). Mill held a fundamentally secularized form of the Presbyterian view that human beings had self-destructive impulses as well as wholesome ones and that our duty was to amend or improve ourselves and the world we found through internally apprehended standards. Mill never romanticized the working class. Lewis Feuer has suggested that by the time Mill wrote the

Chapters on Socialism (1879), Mill had come to recognize that revolutionary socialism was permeated by an unhealthy ferocity and hatred.

Inequality and exploitation had hurt the working class, but many members of the working class had failed to implement self-discipline and had made the wrong choices on their own. Mill attacked the presumption that anyone should:

> rivet firmly in the minds of the laboring people the persuasion that it is the business of others to take care of their condition, without any self-control on their own part; [and] that whatever is possessed by other people, more than they possess, is a wrong to them, or at least a kind of stewardship, of which an account is to be rendered to them. (In a letter to McVey Napier, the editor of the *Edinburgh Review*, November 9, 1844. See *PPE, Collected Works* III, pp. 643–44)

Mill was appalled by wealthy women whose engagement with charitable activity was based on the assumption that the poor were dysfunctional only because they lacked material resources. There is no victimization thesis in Mill. In fact, he supported the New Poor Law of 1834 which banned 'outdoor relief' and insisted that paupers could receive relief only in workhouses with less than pleasant conditions (diet, confinement, separation of men from their families) designed to incentivize the poor to seek employment and restrict the size of their families. Mill insisted that "not only our conduct, but our character, is in part amenable to our will" (Mill 1865, *Hamilton, Collected Works* IX, p. 466) and that "we can, by a course of self-culture, finally modify, to a greater or less extent, our desires and aversions" (Mill 1865, *Hamilton, Collected Works* IX, p. 467).

RESTATING THE CASE FOR LIBERTY

Socialism is not just an economic or political position. It is a social doctrine as well. As a social doctrine, socialism offered an analysis of Europe in transition from a feudal economy to an industrial economy: the world divided between those who own capital (capitalists) and those who do not (working class); this division was originally based upon historical accident or worse; the members of both classes exhibit dysfunctional and pathological lifestyles. Fundamental to socialism is a critique of what it understands as capitalist inequality. Society as a whole is marked by exploitation, *inequality*, and the failure to maximize the potential (moral, aesthetic, and economic) of every individual. Mill inherited from his father and Bentham a shared concern with understanding the transition from feudalism to a modern industrial and commercial economy, along with the recognition of its accompanying social disruption. But Mill also saw new and welcomed opportunities, for example, the emancipation of women. Here we already detect a difference between Mill and socialism. Mill did not see himself in the posture of an adversary to all of modernity. As a public intellectual, Mill sees his role as Socratic: there is much about the modern world for which to be thankful and to be preserved; and his perspective is one of how to keep the good part and minimize or eradicate the bad part.

Mill faced two tasks. First, he had to address the *social question*, that is, the unequal distribution of wealth. He realized that a "correction" to Adam Smith was needed. He was cognizant of the vast and growing socialist literature (for example, Mill uses the terminology "the laborers and the capitalists" with such ease whereas these terms are absent from Locke and Smith. Similarly Mill's two predecessors never used the French term laissez-faire). Recall that Adam Smith defined the objective measure of the wealth of a nation as the amount of the necessities and conveniences of life divided by the number of people to which this product is to be consumed. Smith placed his emphasis on increasing production – the numerator – rather than controlling population, or the denominator. Malthus's "dismal" message was that the optimism is misplaced because the denominator – size of the population – will increase exponentially even though the numerator – size of the total production – will increase arithmetically.

Mill made both the increase in production and the control of population vital aspects of his approach to political economy. In this regard, he anticipated John Maynard Keynes although he arrived at a different conclusion on how this was to be done, namely, through the emancipation of women rather than government control. The "production of wealth" can be subject to scientific analysis whereas the "distribution of wealth" is in part "a matter of human institution." Mill concedes to the Equality Narrative that the current distribution is a reflection of historical accident. If one can make the distinction between the deserving and undeserving poor – which Mill and other classical liberals do make – is it not also reasonable to make the distinction between the deserving and undeserving rich? This is the challenge that Mill bequeathed to the twentieth and twenty-first century Liberty Narrative.

Mill was fully aware of the fact that deliberate changes in the distribution of wealth would impact overall productivity. Nowhere does he recommend a change that he believes will lead to an overall decrease in wealth. Improved distribution does not lead to equality of outcome. Market efficiency is inevitably accompanied by inequality of outcome.

Neither efficiency nor absolute equality can be the ultimate end. What Mill insisted upon was a moral argument in defense of private property.

Feudalism had distributed property on the basis of force and/or primogeniture. Locke argued that private property is legitimate because it is the result of personal effort (labor). The Socialists have argued that the actual distribution of property under capitalism is neither in accordance with economic science nor the Lockean individualistic work ethic. Mill considers the socialist critique of private property to be compelling since wealth distribution in the UK seems to be in accordance with tradition rather than contribution. This does not make Mill a socialist. What it does is to show that Mill is a friendly critic of capitalism. Mill, in effect, is saying what is wrong with the Lockean argument that the earth belongs to the living and to those who are industrious and rational. The Liberty Narrative has become complacent about defending the right to private property.

Mill's second task was to restate the case for individual liberty on different intellectual grounds. He abandoned natural right and the labor theory of value in order to provide a richer and deeper understanding of the Lockean narrative, one that had a much greater impact on the subsequent development of the Liberty Narrative. He refused to accept the notion of Locke, Hume, and Smith (as well as others like James Madison), all of whom had espoused the Liberty Narrative on efficiency grounds – it produces more wealth (a rising tide raises all boats).

Rousseauean defenders of absolute equality relative to a collective good must accept the position that even if there were a net loss of economic benefits, the non-economic social benefits (for example, the lack of envy) would far outweigh that loss. It has been suggested that if the wealthy voluntarily chose to redistribute their wealth to the less wealthy or to the poor there would be no loss of wealth and a lot less misery as well as more happiness. This suggestion fails to take into account that such a voluntary redistribution would affect future productivity.

The efficiency argument on its own has been under attack since the early nineteenth century. Constant, in his famous essay *The Liberty of the Ancients compared with that of the Moderns* (Constant [1819] 1988) voiced this concern even before Tocqueville. The increasing call in the nineteenth century for an absolute equality, now understood as the call for the recognition of a collective good – the equality and fraternity of the French Revolution – that subsumed the individual good, raised the same alarm that it had in the eighteenth century. Critics such as Tocqueville and Mill warned of a conflict between equality and liberty.

For both Tocqueville and Mill, equality and not liberty is the default position of modernity. Thus, liberty is in constant need of being defended and equality is in constant need of being moderated. Tocqueville warned that modern man had a great inclination to support the centralization of government which, given the history of the French Revolutions of 1789, 1830, and 1848, is the way to tyranny. This is what Hayek later called the road to serfdom.

The argument in favor of individual liberty and against absolute equality is presented by Mill as an argument in favor of freedom or autonomy (understood here as self-rule or self-governance). The assumption that we have free-will is a precondition of intelligible action. Mill insists that "not only our conduct, but our character, is in part amenable to our will" (Mill 1865, *Examination of the Philosophy of Sir William Hamilton*, *Collected Works* IX, p. 466) and that "we can, by a course of self-culture, finally modify, to a greater or less extent, our desires and aversions" (ibid., p. 467).

> The appropriate region of human liberty … comprises, first, the inward domain of consciousness … liberty of thought and feeling; absolute freedom of opinion and sentiment on all subjects … . The liberty of expressing and publishing opinions … . Secondly … liberty of … framing the plan of our life to suit our own character … so long as what we do does not harm [others] … . Thirdly … the liberty within the same limits, of combination among individuals; freedom to unite … . The only freedom which deserves the name, is that of pursuing our own good in our own way, so long as we do not attempt to deprive others of theirs, or impede their efforts to obtain it. (Mill 1859, *On Liberty*, Chapter 1)

> … the sole end for which mankind are warranted, individually or collectively, in interfering with the liberty of action of any of their number, is self-protection … to prevent harm to others … . There are good reasons for remonstrating with him, or reasoning with him, or persuading him, or entreating him, but not for compelling him, or visiting him with any evil … . Over himself, over his own body and mind, the individual is sovereign. (Ibid.)

In further elaborating the meaning of harm, Mill insisted, like Kant, that we "must never forget to include wrongful interference with each other's freedom" (Mill 1861, *Utilitarianism*, *Collected Works* X, p. 55). Moreover, "even in those portions of conduct which do effect the interest of others, the onus of making out a case always lies on the defenders of legal prohibition" (Mill 1848, *PPE*, BK V, Chapter 11, section 2).

Even if there were no net economic loss, there would be an end to freedom of speech and eventually freedom of thought and freedom of religion and the right to choose the government under which we live. We would see the triumph of mediocrity or a narrow public opinion imposing the same capricious and arbitrary standards on everything and everyone. These freedoms or liberties are considered good because they are instrumental to self-expression, personal autonomy, and the pursuit of happiness. For theorists like Mill, freedom trumps efficiency and that is why he is so often, incorrectly, identified with the egalitarian narrative. He argued that the defense of liberty requires more than the case for efficiency. For Tocqueville and Mill – just as it had been implicitly for Locke, Smith, and the Founders before, and forthcoming from Hayek and Friedman – freedom of choice trumps fraternal equality and economic efficiency. The US *Declaration of Independence* sees equality before the law as the necessary condition for liberty, and in this respect we have turned away from outcome egalitarianism pointing toward fraternity and returned to foundational egalitarianism pointing toward individual liberty. Autonomy is an intrinsic end, along with the pursuit of happiness, for foundational egalitarians. Wealth is important not as an end in itself nor as a means to consumerism but because it serves as the means for personal accomplishment (Hegel). This is the new argument of the Liberty Narrative. Wealth maximization and efficiency considerations are important only because in the end we need to know if such policies are maximizing opportunities for more and more people to become autonomous.

The belief in, and advocacy of, a collective good in which individual good is subsumed does not seek to preserve liberty because the purpose of liberty in the Rousseau narrative is to lay the foundation for equality-as-fraternity. Rousseaueans insist upon controlling any institution and practice that contributes to individual fulfillment within the collective good. Liberty, for them, is the necessary condition for equality, which is the avenue to fraternity.

Defenders of liberty, on the other hand, justify removing or relaxing external constraints because they presume that there is some kind of basic internal psychological need for something like personal autonomy. The defenders of liberty are reasserting in secular fashion the Christian doctrine of the dignity of the individual soul. This is what is behind Mill's defense of individuality. The case for individual liberty is that it is the condition for the individual pursuit of happiness. Like Kant and Hegel, Mill avoids such abstract notions of the original individual located in a state of nature.

Mill distinguished between the "theory of dependence and protection," and the theory of "self-dependence," when considering "the probable futurity of the laboring poor." Mill claimed that the laboring poor will come to love the taste of liberty that comes with the theory of self-dependence or self-reliance and will reject the government paternalism that comes with the theory of dependence.

Mill's *Political Economy* anticipated his *On Liberty* and *Subjection of Women*. Mill sees an analogy between the competition for goods and services with competition in the marketplace of ideas. His critique of the theory of the dependence of the poor on the rich is analogous to his critique of the dependence of women on men. The abuse of power by those over whom one has control through unmerited status is not only endemic to landed aristocracies but to the relationship between men and women. Status had to be earned through self-denial, self-control and hard work, and when properly earned transformed human beings into individuals whose self-definition necessarily precluded the exploitation of others. Women who are not autonomous cannot raise children who will be autonomous. Mill's distinction in *Political Economy* between authoritative and advisory interference by government in the economy is a key addition to the Liberty Narrative. Mill always insisted that the onus has to be put on those who propose the regulation. Liberty is the default position.

In *On Liberty*, Mill says he does not rely on "the idea of abstract right," and contract theory in his defense of liberty. Rather, he turns to what he calls the idea of "utility in the largest sense." He tries to stay away from all versions of natural rights. He has an understanding of social contracts that is critical of long-term contracts, including marriage. This conscious "correction" of Locke and Smith away from an appeal to nature, long-term contracts, and material well-being, marks what Mill sees as an improvement in the Liberty Narrative.

In *On the Subjection of Women*, Mill equates the status of women with the status of slaves, whereas the writers of the Equality Narrative in the French Revolution tradition equate the status of the poor with the status of slaves. There is however a critical difference between the two narratives. Mill makes the argument that competition and not custom should sway in the relationship between men and women. He also claims that he is not asking for "protective duties and bounties in favor of women; it is only asked that the present bounties and protective duties in favor of men should be recalled" (Capaldi and Lloyd 2011, p. 383). This would seem to place Mill in the non-affirmative action camp in terms of contemporary public policy. For the first time, the equality of women becomes an issue in political economy.

It is the family that prepares autonomous individuals to participate in civil society. Hence, the market economy cannot be expected to function independently of a reform in family life that promotes equality of

opportunity and autonomy, both of which will encourage more responsible procreation as well as provide civil society with the talents of women
who are currently excluded. Reform in family life must be accompanied
by political changes such as allowing women to own property in their
own right and to have the franchise. These are the kinds of things that the
'state' can do to promote autonomy. It is ludicrous to view this function
of the state as a form of collective authoritarianism. Autonomy entails
devotion to the welfare of others, but most especially to their achievement of autonomy. This is not only a romantic and Hegelian theme but a
very Victorian conception of high-mindedness.

The market economy of the Industrial Revolution in Britain is historically contextualized in a 'capitalist' system that created a class conflict
between employers and employees. 'Socialists' critiqued the dehumanizing aspects of capitalism and sought to overcome them but only at the
risk of undermining other liberating practices such as competition. Rather
than be an apologist and defender of the status quo, rather than merely
blaming others and assuming that the destruction of the old automatically
produces utopia, Mill opted for a synthesis which preserves the virtues of
a market economy without the class struggle and without surrendering
competition and liberty. His vision of liberal culture is the synthesis. The
title of Mill's most famous work is not On Equality; the title is *On
Liberty*.

8. The Scientific Socialism of Marx and Engels

Karl Marx was born in Trier, Prussia in 1818. He studied law and philosophy at the University of Berlin where he joined a group known as the Young Hegelians. His philosophy thesis earned him a Doctorate from the University of Jena in 1841. He then became a journalist for the radical journal *Rheinische Zeitung* in Cologne. When the paper was suspended by the government, he moved to Paris in 1843. While there he met and became a lifelong friend and collaborator of Friedrich Engels (1820–95), a wealthy German socialist. Engels had just published *The Condition of the Working Class in England* (Engels 1844). Marx moved to London in 1849. In 1864, Marx became involved in the International Workingmen's Association (also known as *First International*). He died in London in 1883.

Notable works by Marx include the 1844 *Economic and Philosophic Manuscripts* (not published until the twentieth century – dismissed by orthodox Marxists but taken seriously by humanist Marxists); *Theses on Feuerbach* (1845); the 1847 *German Ideology* written with Engels (not published until 1932); *The Poverty of Philosophy* (1847), a critique of the French anarchist socialist Pierre-Joseph Proudhon's book *The Philosophy of Poverty* (1847); *The Communist Manifesto* (1848) co-authored with Engels (an intra-Marxist scholarship over the status of Engels developed only in the mid twentieth-century); *The Eighteenth Brumaire of Louis Napoleon* (1852) focused on the French Revolution of 1848; articles for the American workers audience of the then progressive *New York Tribune* (1852–61); in 1859 Marx published *A Contribution to the Critique of Political Economy* (in which he embraced Ricardo's labor theory of value); *Theories of Surplus Value* (1860s but published posthumously, a history of economic thought going back to Adam Smith); the first volume of *Das Kapital* was published in 1867 (volume II in 1893 and III in 1894 both published posthumously by Engels). Marx commented on the Paris Commune in 1871 in his *Civil War in France* which marked the demise of France as a focus of attention in his thought and its replacement by Bismarck's Germany. Before he died he prepared the 1884 publication of *The Origin of the Family, Private Property and the State*. In addition to

The Condition of the Working Class in England (1844), Engels authored *Socialism: Utopian and Scientific* in 1880.

In his 1883 Graveside Speech, Engels asserted that Marx made three important scientific "discoveries": (1) "Just as Darwin discovered the law of development of organic nature, so Marx discovered the law of development of human history: the simple fact, hitherto concealed by an overgrowth of ideology, that mankind must first of all eat, drink, have shelter and clothing, before it can pursue politics, science, art, religion, etc." (2) "Marx also discovered the special law of motion governing the present-day capitalist mode of production and the bourgeois society [the bourgeoisie are the urban social class which owns the means of production and whose economic focus is private property and the preservation of capital] that this mode of production has created." This discovery was the doctrine of surplus value. "The discovery of surplus value suddenly threw light on the problem, in trying to solve which all previous investigations, of both bourgeois economists and socialist critics, had been groping in the dark" (Tucker 1978, pp. 681–82). Engels, harkening back to Marx's 'correction' of the earlier tradition, expressed clearly in *The Eleventh Thesis on Feuerbach* that "the philosophers have only interpreted the world, in various ways; the point, however, is to change it," concludes his speech: (3) "Science was for Marx a historically dynamic, revolutionary force ... . Marx was before all else a revolutionist. His real mission in life was to contribute, in one way or another, to the overthrow of capitalist society and of the state institutions which it had brought into being" (Tucker 1978, p. 682).

In *Socialism: Utopian and Scientific*, Engels says that with the first two discoveries – "the materialist conception of history and the revelation of the secret of capitalistic production through surplus value ... Socialism became a science. The next thing was to work out all its details and relations" (Capaldi and Lloyd 2011, p. 459). That's where revolutionary politics fits in. All of this is to be found in the ten-point program outlined in the *Communist Manifesto* (Marx 1848).

MARX'S PLACE IN THE EQUALITY NARRATIVE

Marx's intellectual gift was the ability to synthesize ideas from previous thinkers into a powerful version of the Equality Narrative. In addition to Rousseau, he incorporated the views of Locke (labor theory of value), Smith (division of labor, alienated worker), Hegel (history is a progressive process wherein struggle is essential, that is, dialectical), Feuerbach (materialism as opposed to idealism), Saint-Simon (class struggle),

Proudhon (property is robbery), and Fourier (the alienation of the technological project).

In a manner of speaking, Rousseau's version of the Equality Narrative was *Platonic* in the sense that it appealed to timeless ideal truths (for example, "General Will"). Marx's version, on the other hand, besides benefiting from and responding to the intermittent revisions and debates, is Aristotelian in the sense that the truth is understood to be dynamic, developmental, and teleological. In addition, Marx was also a modern thinker greatly influenced by the Scottish Enlightenment developmental view of history (that is, a natural history), and more importantly by Hegel who provided a model of human history as both developmental and teleological. Rather than a static and endlessly repeating cycle, all of history moves through time toward a specific telos or goal.

Two overt changes in the narrative are worth mentioning. First, Rousseau began with an idyllic depiction of the pre-modern condition and follows this with a critique of the market economy and the problems it had created. Nowhere does he provide any evidence of the existence of this idyllic pre-modern condition. Second, Rousseau had unequivocally and unconditionally critiqued the modern market society based on the technological project. By introducing a developmental account, Marx was able to show that no stage was idyllic and that each stage was an improvement on the previous stages. There is a great deal to like about the technological project and market economies even if they are flawed and doomed to be replaced. Every element in the narrative had to be rethought: (1) the technological project is a good thing; (2) the market economy has a specific flaw that needs to be identified and explained; (3) politics needs to be revolutionary not deliberative; (4) the rule of law is a form of bourgeois oppression; (5) unequivocally, there has to be one overall secular enterprise association in order to overcome alienation, and this means that all forms of religion come in for a serious critique. Also important is his substitution of freedom from religion for freedom of religion as a solution to the question: What to do with the question of the Jews in a Christian state? He specifically rejects Tocqueville's answer of religious toleration in favor of the abolition of religion. Finally, all future versions of the Equality Narrative must be in the form of overcoming some form of oppression (for example, Beard, Zinn, and so on).

It is useful to conceptualize Marx's position as a response to Hegel's articulation of the Liberty Narrative. Marx started writing in 1843 an unfinished critique of Hegel's *Philosophy of Right*. Whereas Hegel saw history as a movement away from ancient community to modern individualism, Marx sought to revive, recapture and update the ancient conception of community. Where Hegel saw Christianity (in its Protestant form) as contributing to the development of autonomous individuals, Marx saw Christianity as undermining ancient community. Where Hegel postulated the 'state' (not equivalent to the government) as promoting something like universal civil association, Marx will claim that the purpose of government is to promote and sustain a communal identity. Where Hegel worried about workers becoming part of the dysfunctional 'rabble' (Oakeshottean anti-individuals), Marx under the influence of Engels will see the workers as agents of positive social change. Where Hegel saw the role of commerce in civil society as a further expression of ethical life, Marx will see commerce as undermining morality by emphasizing private economic interests, especially in the realm of property, contract, marriage, and civil society.

In *Das Kapital*, Marx announced that he found the dialectic with Hegel standing on its head. "It must be turned right side up again, if you would discover the rational kernel within the mystical shell" (Tucker 1978, p. 302). In the 1840s, Marx was part of the Young Hegelian group that read Rousseau through French Jacobin eyes, emphasized that the Hegelian historical dialectic was still working through the various riddles and more changes awaited the human race. The "Old Hegelians" had focused on Hegel's claim that this process of change would come to an end in the form of a coherent synthesis. The Old Hegelians thought that Hegel had already provided a comprehension of everything. The "Young Hegelians," however, thought Hegel's strength was to provide a critique of everything. But what is important to carry away from this framework is that revolution rather than criticism is the driving force of history. To cite *The eleventh Thesis on Feuerbach* again: "The philosophers have only *interpreted* the world, in various ways; the point, however, is to *change* it" (Tucker 1978, p. 145). Marx attributed the failure of the French Revolution to lead to real reform to the fact that the Revolution was inspired and guided by philosophical abstractions (for example, "rights") rather than a true understanding of how the world works. In addition, he viewed the 1789 *Declaration of the Rights of Man and the Citizen* as a rationalization of bourgeois property rights.

Two consequences follow from this. For the young Hegelians and Marx, the focus needs to be on the collapse of the existing order into something new and better. The old Hegelians were satisfied that the riddles of history had been solved in Prussian Germany under the guidance of the Lutheran church. What Marx contributed to the dialectical part of Hegel was a material base. The reality of economics rather than the concept of ideas should be the point of departure. In the *Economic and Philosophic Manuscripts*, Marx talks a lot about the alienation of life in terms that might seem Hegelian. He never mentions

Darwin. But there is no doubt that by the time of his death, Darwin had replaced Hegel as the true articulator of the dialectic. Secondly, life is not determined by consciousness but consciousness is determined by life. This, we will argue, is central to the Equality Narrative. Private property is seen by Marx as the epitome of alienated man and hence the Western parliamentary system underscores the unacceptable distinction between the state and society.

The *Economic and Philosophic Manuscripts* emphasized alienation or estranged labor as if the real problem with capitalism is the production side. In other words, the division of labor was the problem. What Marx sets out is the basic theme of the Equality Narrative: labor and not private property is at the center of the study of political economy. Man, not profit, is at the center of the study. Accordingly, classical political economy with Robinson Crusoe fighting for existence is a mere fiction. The center of the world is the mortal combat between two classes. We would add here that the emphasis on the battle between two classes rather than the individual versus authority is vital for Marx's expression of the Equality Narrative.

TECHNOLOGICAL PROJECT

Lacking historical perspective, Rousseau had opined, in part, for a return to the pre-technological project, a pre-industrial, agricultural economy. On the contrary, the technological project is part of the key to the historical process.

For Marx, there are five identifiable stages of history, and in each stage the key concepts are the nature of the economy and the corresponding form of social organization:

1. Pre-historical: agrarian + communal ownership. For the Young Hegelians as well as Feuerbach, the ancient community was undermined by religion and the pursuit of private economic interests.
2. Ancient World: agrarian (country) + commercial (city) + private property (including slavery or ownership of other human beings).
3. Feudal World: agrarian + communal ownership (joint-ownership by the lords and serfs) but no slavery (serfs have 'rights').
4. Bourgeois Capitalism: industrial (technological project) + private property (the bourgeoisie own the forces of production but not human beings); history does not end here. Capitalism is also characterized by development, growth in the form of industrialization, urbanization, technological progress, increased productivity

and growth. The capitalist class is one of the most revolutionary in history, because it was both responsible for the overthrow of feudalism and for constantly improving the means of production. Capitalists have an incentive to reinvest profits in new technologies. At the same time, new technologies are in part responsible for the increase in production that leads to gluts and ultimately the downturn of over-production.

5. Communist Utopia: industrial (TP) + communal ownership (no economic classes, no wages, and no 'state' but the "free association of producers under their [own] conscious and purposive control"). "[T]he historical trend of our age is the fatal crisis which capitalist production has undergone in the European and American countries where it has reached its highest peak, a crisis that will end in its destruction, in the return of modern society to a higher form of the most archaic type – collective production and appropriation ... the vitality of primitive communities was incomparably greater than that of Semitic, Greek, Roman, etc. societies, and, a fortiori, that of modern capitalist societies" (First draft of a letter to Vera Zasulich [1881]. In Marx–Engels *Collected Works*, vol. 24, p. 346).

MARKET ECONOMY

'Capitalism' is generally used as a term to indicate private ownership in a competitive market. In Marxist theory, and in much of the literature of Continental Europe, 'capitalism' also connotes (a) the need for capitalists, the owners of property, to maximize profit, usually by cutting production costs, increasing sales, and monopolizing markets, (b) wage labor, and reinvesting the surplus of the labor product and (c) a corresponding social/political class structure based on the distinction between owners and workers.

'Socialism' is not simply an alternative economic position. Socialism is a set of economic, social, political, and policy doctrines. As a social doctrine, socialism offers an historical analysis of Europe in transition from a feudal economy to an industrial economy. It sees a world divided between those who own capital (capitalists) and those who do not (working class). Because this division is originally based upon historical accident or worse, members of both classes exhibit dysfunctional and pathological lifestyles. As a social doctrine, socialism is this critique of what it understands as capitalist inequality: society as a whole is marked by psychological egoism, exploitation, *inequality*, and the failure to maximize the potential (moral, aesthetic, and economic) of every individual and society as a whole. Socialism presumes that individuals are fundamentally good and corrupted only by their environment. As an economic doctrine, socialism attributes the evils of modern life to the unequal distribution of the means of production in the form of private property. There are several different socialist responses to this state of affairs, all involving either doing away with or greatly limiting, private property rights.

As described above, socialism is more of a philosophical and social doctrine. That is how Marx and Engels understood it in the *Communist Manifesto*, and that is why they chose to identify their position as 'communist.' What's the difference? More accurately, Marx and Engels shared with socialists the critique of capitalism, but what they thought they were adding was a 'scientific' account of how the capitalist economic system functioned and why it would, in a manner of speaking, self-destruct. That is why they later identified their position as 'scientific socialism.'

What makes Marx's account of economics scientific? A science, based on the model of physical science, explains, predicts, and controls. Socialists prior to Marx and Engels 'complained' rather than explained; and when they did explain, their explanations lacked predictive power and did not generate a policy to control the outcome. 'Scientific' socialism claims to provide an explanation, a prediction, and control.

What are the specific policy recommendations? According to the *Communist Manifesto* there are ten:

1. Abolition of property in land and application of all rents of land to public purposes.
2. A heavy progressive or graduated income tax.
3. Abolition of all right of inheritance.
4. Confiscation of the property of all emigrants and rebels.
5. Centralization of credit in the hands of the state, by means of a national bank with state capital and an exclusive monopoly.
6. Centralization of the means of communication and transport in the hands of the state.
7. Extension of factories and instruments of production owned by the state; the bringing into cultivation of waste-lands, and the improvement of the soil generally in accordance with a common plan.
8. Equal liability of all to labor. Establishment of industrial armies, especially for agriculture.
9. Combination of agriculture with manufacturing industries; gradual

    abolition of the distinction between town and country, by a more equable distribution of the population over the country.

10.   Free education for all children in public schools. Abolition of children's factory labor in its present form. Combination of education with industrial production, and so on.

The key components of Marx's economic theory are: his understanding of Locke's labor theory of value (goods are exchanged at rates decided by the amount of labor that went into the production); Ricardo's iron law of wages (labor will only ever be paid subsistence wages; Marx praised Ricardo as the last 'scientific' political economist); profit (labor produces goods worth more than wages, and this difference goes to the capitalist); the misery of labor, contra Rousseau, Smith, and Malthus, is not the result of either the moral failings of the working class or the wickedness of capitalists – it is the result of economic laws which turn even capitalists into victims.

    Contrary to the Lockean narrative, the market economy does not work toward equilibrium or to consistent progress. Instead, capitalism is inherently unstable and digs its own grave. (Henceforth, for all adherents of the Rousseau/Marx Equality Narrative, every downturn in the economy is 'the' potential crisis that will undo capitalism.) Thus depression rather than improvement is the normal condition of the working class. The law of inevitable collapse replaces the law of supply and demand as the central concept of how to understand economics. For Marx, 'labor' and 'capital' are not abstract variables to be inserted into a productive system that can be understood according to economic laws. Rather an economic system is dynamic and has an inner logic as it moves through phases. Whereas the very concept of classical political economy (Lockean Narrative) presumes that there is an end to history with the arrival of capitalism, Marx's enterprise is to show, both morally and scientifically, that this system will collapse.

    Marx accepts the distinction between use value and exchange value that we saw in both Smith and Mill, but he places a higher worth on use value than exchange value. In fact, we get the impression that exchange value neither measures true value nor adds value. Use value has true value because the commodities are produced to satisfy human needs, and value is created by labor power. In labor, the use value to the purchaser always exceeds the exchange value or what the laborer is paid.

    Every commodity has a true value that is measured by the socially necessary labor time it takes to bring the commodity to market. Marx seems to have 'corrected' Locke and Smith by showing that only a pure labor theory of value uncontaminated by the false claims of landlords and capitalists to a share in the product of labor is a true measure of worth or value. Isn't this an argument that property is theft by another means? But don't landlords and capitalists contribute to the creation of the product? Would it be fair to say that a pure labor theory of value makes sense only in the most primitive society or one where the production problem has been solved?

We don't think it is stretching Marx's approach to suggest that the ideal communist society would be in accordance with formula C-M-C where M is money used as a medium of exchange to facilitate the circulation of commodities that meet human needs. This C-M-C ideal is the alternative to his harsh version of an exchange economy based on manipulation and greed, or M-C-M'.

Marx's version of an actual market economy is the M-C-M' formula where M' is greater than M and thus money has been turned into capital by the buying and selling of commodities, and the creation of capital is equivalent to the creation of profit. So it doesn't matter, in the end, what the commodity is since turning money into capital is the alpha and omega of the exchange system. We suggest, in other words, that there is a strong moral side to this formulation. This becomes even clearer when we realize that the production of commodities is actually determined by those who own the means of commodity production (demand does not reflect what consumers really want or need). Property is not an expression of personal autonomy or to be measured in income earned. Rather property is the stock of industrial wealth owned by the captains of modern industry.

C-M-C is praised by Marx for meeting human needs and M-C-M' is criticized for creating profit through the marketing of commodities. This is the equivalent of saying that exchange value is "fetish" value, or illusionary value, or, to adopt the language of the earlier *Economic and Philosophic Manuscripts*, exchange value is alienated or estranged value. Put differently, we suggest that the fetishism of commodities articulated through the M-C-M' formula is Marx's more scientific way of articulating his earlier philosophical concept of the alienation or estrangement of labor. For the next step in the argument is to show precisely how this takes place.

It turns out that one of the commodities in the M-C-M' formula is labor where labor power is bought and sold like any other commodity. And thus as a commodity, there must be socially necessary labor time needed to bring that commodity to market. In other words, what time in the laboring day would it take for the laborer to spend to feed, house, and clothe his family? Let's say four hours. But the capitalist determines the length of the working day. Let's say ten hours. It turns out that the capitalist gets these six hours for free. This surplus value is profit and is based on force and fraud. Again the Equality Narrative is fortified by the notion that property is theft.

The irony here is that the worker is and is not paid what he is worth and that is the ultimate "contradiction" of capitalism. He should be getting ten hours' pay but he is getting, according to the labor theory of value, and the socially necessary labor time concept, the four hours' pay he needs to preserve his family! This amounts to the exploitation of the laborer. Later, as we shall see, Piketty will also argue that labor, as opposed to capital, is treated unequally and hence unfairly. In both cases, what we see, allegedly, is an objective and scientific account of the unfairness along with the claim that the unfairness is constitutive of the economic system under capitalism.

Marx's discovery of the doctrine of absolute surplus value has had a profound impact on the work place aspects of public policy and the strategy of trade unions. No wonder so many disputes between management and labor turn on the length of the working day.

Marx also discovered the doctrine of relative surplus value. If the length of the working day is shortened – say from ten hours to eight hours – as a result of union activity and/or government policy, the capitalist's absolute surplus value has declined from six hours to four hours. The capitalist now introduces machinery that does two things: (1) it reduces the socially necessary labor time for the worker to cover the cost of the necessities of life from say four hours to three hours and (2) he can fire several workers who have been made redundant by the machinery.

Marx does not see the capacity to truck, barter, and exchange as part of the natural way humans improve their condition. Instead, he considers exchange as the mechanism by which one set of humans – the owners of the means of production – exploit other humans – the many who have only their labor to sell on the market. And far from seeing the natural course of the economy being toward (1) growth and equilibrium and (2) the improvement in the condition of the working class – as do Locke, Smith, and Mill – Marx predicts the decline in the condition of the working class and the ultimate collapse of capitalism. Nor does Marx consider the contributions of the capitalist (either as owner, management, or entrepreneur).

In *Das Kapital*, Marx incorporates his earlier comments about alienation without an appeal to Hegel. So, in Volume 1, Part III we learn that "the elementary factors of the labor-process are 1, the personal activity of man, i.e., work itself, 2, the subject of that work, and 3, its instruments" (quote retrieved on January 4, 2016 from www.marxists.org/.../marx/

…/burial.htm, section 1). In Part IV, Chapter 12, we learn further that this process leads to "the cheapening of labor itself." There is also his sarcastic reference in Part IV, Chapter 14 to Adam Smith's solution of "homeopathic doses" of state education to what both agree are the dehumanizing effects of the division of labor. Substantial portions of Parts IV and V are devoted to a critique of Political Economy especially its apparent lack of concern for the "crippled" worker "mutilated" by the division of labor and mechanization in the modern factory system.

Because of these internal contradictions or inevitable tensions, a market economy, says Marx, inevitably leads to socialism. The technological project and the appropriation of surplus value by capitalists lead to an ever larger scale and monopoly. The result is a continuous concentration of wealth in fewer and fewer hands and a clear division of society into capitalists and proletarians. When all production is finally completely socialized (one giant monopoly) there will be a revolution.

As in Rousseau, there is a strong ethical dimension to Marx's argument. A market economy is incompatible with the alleged morality of personal autonomy in the Lockean narrative. The owners of the means of production appropriate a larger share of production than is warranted by their contribution. Moreover, labor is treated as a commodity (commodification) just like non-human commodities. This is incompatible with human dignity.

GOVERNMENT

The whole historical process is rational, that is, it can be understood and conceptualized. Human beings, however, are not rational, that is, they cannot stand self-critically outside of themselves. Every human being reflects where he/she is both historically and economically. In one sense this is obviously true, and in another sense it is profoundly insightful – we all always operate within an inherited context. It is also true that there is no Archimedean contextless external standpoint. It also seems to be the case that the context evolves. That is why one can say that "reason" has a history. What remains controversial is the relationship of individuals to the inherited and evolving context. For Marx, the relationship is deterministic. To have a larger perspective is merely to be further along in the evolutionary process. There is no way that someone who is further along can persuade the 'retardee' to view things differently. This is why Parliamentary argumentation is a waste of time. This raises the important question originally faced by Hegel of whether History does come to an end (teleology) and how would we know that we have reached that point?

Meaningful change only comes about through action, especially violent action. The essence of historical materialism is that the mode of production of the material means of existence determines both individual human consciousness and social relationships. Philosophy therefore must give up its pretensions; it is a symptom of social malaise; it is the opiate of intellectuals. In the *Critique of the Gotha Programme* (1875), Marx opposed the attempt to compromise with state socialism in the interests of a united socialist party. He also repeated all of Rousseau's arguments against representative democracy, namely, its representation of special interests rather than the collective common good. In his 1871 *Civil War in France*, he lauded the Commune for not making a distinction between legislative, executive, and judicial functions. The Lockean conception of the rule of law was a fiction in which judges appointed for life (*Federalist Papers*) to interpret the *Constitution* actually preserved the interests of the capitalist class.

Marx and Engels maintained that between capitalism and the establishment of a socialist/communist system, there would be a dictatorship of the proletariat, namely, a period during which the working class would exercise political power and forcibly socialize the means of production. Marx conceded the possibility of a peaceful transition in some countries like Great Britain and the US because of the presence of democratic institutional structures, but in countries with centralized governments, notably France and Germany, there could only be revolution.

With Marx, the established Equality Narrative takes on a new and revolutionary tone. In fact it is difficult to distinguish between the Equality Narrative and the revolutionary narrative in Marx. There is a strong dismissive tone in the writings of Marx and Engels to previous articulators of the Equality Narrative. The French Socialists were utopian, or reactionary, or opportunists. There is here a dismissal of the religious dimension of Owen and Saint-Simon. It is not possible to advance the Equality Narrative by reform. We need revolution. Politics and ideas are the mere playthings of those with power, and this is defined as those who own economic property. Accordingly, all politics and ideas are the result of the dictatorial imposition by the few over the many. Thus one is tempted to think that winning the battle for democracy is no more, and no less, than the dictatorship of the many over the few; that the rule of law is simply the advantage of the stronger.

This position raises some serious questions about the sense of social justice and fundamental fairness that undergirds the Equality Narrative. Are fairness, equality, and social justice in any sense objective? Do we know for sure that they reflect the final or end stage of moral thinking? Are they something more than rhetorical guilt buttons to be pushed by activists?

Crucial to the Equality Narrative is the belief that there must be one all-encompassing collective whole in order to *eliminate* conflict. That is why even workers' cooperatives in either Fourier's or Mill's sense were, to Marx and Engels, an unacceptable economic compromise because those cooperatives would compete with each other in a market. Crucial to the Liberty Narrative is the belief that conflict (faction in Madison's sense) cannot be eliminated, and therefore, the object of government and the rule of law is to *manage* or minimize conflict. There could be for Marx and Engels no such thing as Tocquevillean self-interest rightly understood or Madisonian ambition counteracting ambition. Marx and Engels have modified both the scope and the content of the Equality Narrative.

Engels introduced a vital concept near the end of *Socialism*, that the state will wither away. Technically what this means is that the state/government is merely an institution that allows one class to oppress another. When there are no longer economic classes, oppression, and thus the state, has "withered away." Does this mean that the Equality Narrative has come to an end because equality has been fulfilled? The answer is not exactly, because there will be a government that administers or manages things, and clearly in this new relationship some people (administrators) will have a different status from others ('administratees'). The government of the people has been replaced by the administration of things. Presumably, no one will feel that the difference in status amounts to a new kind of class differentiation.

In the *Communist Manifesto*, Marx maintained that the central feature of communism is the abolition of private property. Put differently, it is to abolish the center piece of the Liberty Narrative. As we have seen, ever since the French Revolution, various authors have advocated at least regulating private property and doing something about the unequal distribution of property. Thus in the 10 point program "to win the battle of democracy" the plan is to make "despotic inroads on the rights of property." What Marx also said is that "these measures will be different in different countries" (Tucker 1978, p. 490). And this phrase has given cover to two movements: (a) the development of an egalitarian socialism that attempts to bring about the end result by peaceful and parliamentary means including but not limited to the regulation of private property, and (b) the need for an extension of Marxism beyond the initial perspective of an advanced European economy. So Marx the revolutionary not only wants to smash private property but also wants to smash political liberalism. Thus he reserves some of his most hostile remarks for "Petty-Bourgeois Socialism." But these forms while pointing out the "crying inequalities in the distribution of wealth" (Tucker 1978, p. 493) are ultimately out of touch with the revolutionary march of history. In the words of Engels, these forms of socialism are utopian rather than scientific.

INDIVIDUAL AND COMMUNITY

Marx acknowledges that Locke and Hegel understood that humankind fulfills itself through labor. But the dignity of work is lost once it is sold or bargained away. To give up ownership of one's labor, one's capacity to transform the world, is to be alienated from one's own nature. It is a spiritual loss. This loss is commodity fetishism, the subordination of human beings to commodities. Marx further differentiated between the economic base and the cultural superstructure. Once the two are out of synch there is social conflict. This is what later came to be called the atomization of the individual, cutting individuals off from their larger social context. From the Marxist perspective, the Lockean narrative and its praise of rights is the preeminent expression of alienation. It also leads to various forms of social pathology marked by the pursuit of satisfaction of artificial and self-destructive needs (what later came to be called 'consumerism' spurred on by spurious advertising). In a healthy society, Marx espouses what the Apostle Luke had espoused, "From each according to his ability, to each according to his need." Even if a communist economy underperformed a capitalist economy, it would still be superior in that it did not produce socially destructive products and services. The Equality Narrative does not guarantee a universal increase in living standards.

Hegel had been the first to identify civil society, that intermediate realm of the economy that hovers between the family and the state. Marx viewed all of the institutions of civil society (Tocqueville's intermediate institutions) as defective. For example, in his senior thesis, Marx had originally argued that religion had as its primary social aim the promotion of solidarity. Spiritual alienation was really a form of social alienation. Later, Marx saw the social function of religion as preserving the economic and political status quo of inequality. It is the *opium* of the people. The abolition of religion as the illusory happiness of the people is the demand for their real happiness.

If Marx is correct, the advancement of the Equality Narrative requires that the world be viewed as a class struggle to end class divisions in contrast to a Liberty Narrative that sees life as an individual struggle to retain autonomy. In the *Economic and Philosophic Manuscripts*, also known as the *Paris Manuscripts*, *On the Jewish Question*, and *The*

German Ideology all of which preceded the *Communist Manifesto* of 1848, we find the critique of (1) private property, (2) the division of labor, and (3) toleration of religion along with the rare articulation of what the fulfillment of the Equality Narrative might look like. In the *Manuscripts*, Marx speaks about the "alienation" or "estrangement" of labor from the end product and the process of production under a system of private property. It is as if he were making central what Smith made peripheral in his warning about the downside to the division of labor in Book V of *The Wealth of Nations* (Smith 1776). He also offers a glimpse of life without the division of labor in *The German Ideology* (1847):

> In communist society, where nobody has one exclusive sphere of activity but each can become accomplished in any branch he wishes, society regulates the general production and thus makes it possible for me to do one thing today and another tomorrow, to hunt in the morning, fish in the afternoon, rear cattle in the evening, criticize after dinner, just as I have a mind, without ever becoming hunter, fisherman, herdsman or critic. (Tucker 1978, p. 160)

Can we say that to the extent that there is a liberty component in the Equality Narrative that it is on the production side of economics? Thus the concern with the division of labor is a production question where the worker is reduced to a cog in the machine. Thus freedom means being liberated from the division of labor in order to be free to do things as one has a mind to do so. The difference between Locke and Marx on freedom is that under Marx one cannot be free and still have to live a life of necessity. So in the ideal world, and Engels makes this very clear, we enter a new world where politics is replaced by the administration of things. It is no longer increasing the size of the pie but making sure that it is distributed in accordance with a notion of equality because there is enough to go around if only we plan properly and distribute fairly.

Critics are apt to point out that the condition of workers is vastly improved since Marx's time. Not only do workers enjoy a high standard of living, but they also enjoy many of the benefits Marx talks about, including leisure time, profit sharing, and so on. What the critics miss is that as long as these benefits take place in a competitive market economy there will continue to be, according to Marx, social dysfunction nationally (everything from drug addiction to strikes to racism, and so on) and internationally (for example, illegal immigration, refugees, and so on). The only way these problems will be solved is through central planning in a world government led by those who understand the big picture.

Critics also point to the fact that most if not all of Marx's predications turned out to be wrong. Specifically, alleged communist revolutions did not take place in advanced capitalist countries but in countries trying to move from feudalism (for example, Russia in 1917, China, 1949, Cuba 1959, and so on). To be fair to Marx, by the 1870s he came to believe that the future could be best seen in Russian village communes! Moreover, instead of being the most humane societies, alleged communist countries like the Soviet Union, Mao's China, Castro's Cuba have been among the most inhumane. As astute as these criticisms are, they fail to reckon with the power of the Equality Narrative both to appeal and to evolve. Lenin was to maintain that colonialism allowed advanced bourgeois societies to placate workers at the expense of the oppression of developing economies (for example, sweatshops, and so on). Stalin would identify "capitalist encirclement," the attempt by Bourgeois powers such as the US and UK to undermine communism as requiring an internal police state.

It has become customary to distinguish three successor versions of Marx's Equality Narrative. First, there is the social democratic version which espouses evolutionary democratic socialism (for example, Bernstein, Kautsky, De Leon, Progressives, Piketty, and so on). Second, there is the hardline orthodox materialist and deterministic version (Engels *Anti-Dühring*, Lenin, and Stalin). Third, there is the idealist version which emphasizes the theme of alienation from the early manuscripts and the sociology of knowledge (for example, Lukacs, most European and primarily French 'Left' intellectuals).

Lenin spoke about the same problem between the opportunists and revisionists like Bernstein and the real revolutionaries in Russia who were convinced by the later Marx's work on the 1871 third French Revolution and by Engels that the bourgeois state had to be smashed in order to complete the revolution against private property. In fact, Marx in *Economic and Philosophic Manuscripts* (1844) argues that "equality is nothing but a translation of the German 'Ich=Ich' into the French, that is, political form. Equality as the groundwork of communism is its political justification, and it is the same as when the German justifies it by conceiving man as universal self-consciousness" (Marx 1844, *Economic and Philosophic Manuscripts*, 99). The question of action is this: can this be achieved through the bourgeois state or must that state be smashed and replaced by a unified and revolutionary party apparatus?

Mao argued exactly the same point in his "Combat Liberalism" (1937) and "Long Live Leninism" in 1960. The role of a united and revolutionary Communist party was necessary to combat the stubborn resistance of the bourgeois around the world. So instead of focusing on revolutionary activity versus parliamentary activity within the stage of advanced capitalism in Europe, Lenin and Mao expanded the two class model to a two world model where the oppressed of the world need to take the fight to the monopoly capitalists and imperialists of the world. The model to avoid is the opportunist Tito's former Yugoslavia where the revolutionary spirit of communism has been replaced by the unprincipled compromises with the bourgeois world. One can only wonder at the opportunist and revisionist experiments of cooperation with the bourgeois that China has undertaken since the death of Mao in 1966.

We do not intend to suggest that revolutionary ideologues building on the work of Karl Marx and Friedrich Engels – who dropped the word economics in the title of their works – are inconsequential to the development of economics as a field of action. We have in mind the works of Lenin, Stalin, Mao, Castro, which has a rich history all the way down to Hugo Chavez's endorsement of "Open Veins" in the twenty-first century. This turn to political ideology puts the Equality Narrative in the default position. But it also does two other things: it suggests that equality can be reduced to a collectivist issue, and it hides the problem that community good needs to be reconciled with individual liberty.

9. Charles Beard, the Progressives, and Roosevelt's New Deal

THE PROGRESSIVES: THE CHALLENGE TO THE LIBERTY NARRATIVE

The development of economics as a thoroughly scientific study and the implementation of economic goals as a feature of political ideology is a turn away from the retrieval of the conversation in political economy. In the remaining chapters, we focus on the extent to which the Liberty Narrative and the Equality Narrative are still operative in the twentieth century and the extent to which these narratives will take part in the twenty-first century.

The early Progressive era in the United States, for our purposes, runs from 1860 to 1928. Although there are many dimensions to the phenomenon called Progressivism, there are three common threads that stand out. First, there is an ambiguous disposition toward the American past as revealed in the writings of Herbert Croly (1869–1930), Charles Beard (1874–1938), and Frederick Jackson Turner (1861–1932). There is an ambiguity toward the *Declaration of Independence* (Croly) in the sense that it holds out an egalitarian promise although that promise has been derailed or unfulfilled. There is also an ambiguity toward the *Constitution* (Beard) in the sense that it is an undemocratic and irrelevant document. In the right hands, churning out the loosest of interpretations of the *Constitution* and overcoming the impediments of the separation of powers and old-fashioned federalism, that document can be turned into an instrument for Progressive reform. For example, the interstate commerce clause can be used to build an independent regulatory network and the necessary and proper clause can be utilized to provide cabinet level status to the agricultural, labor, and commercial sectors of the economy under the guiding hand of the President.

Second, there is the notion that American exceptionalism, in the form of the unlimited frontier and lucky isolationism, is over and that it is time to face the issues of a modern industrial society with teeming urban centers. Central to this account is that, in effect, the Liberty Narrative may have been appropriate for an earlier time and place, but that narrative is now empirically false and normatively bankrupt. For individualism and laissez-faire have become the refuge of the robber barons, railroad tycoons, newspaper owners, all operating together in smoke filled rooms or sneaking around in hotel lobbies cutting deals with legislators contrary to the public good. We need a new narrative, one that sees government as a solution rather than a problem, and one with an agenda that addresses what since the French Revolution has been called "the social problem." And at the core of the social problem is the relationship between capital and labor on the one hand and the role of the federal government in advancing a concept of social justice on the other hand. Labor Day became a national holiday under the Progressives' influence in 1887. President Cleveland specified the first Monday in September to avoid identifying with socialist May Day.

The third common dimension to the Progressives is their belief that cooperation among the various elements in society should replace competition among these elements. There is something both inefficient and unseemly about competitive markets. The Progressives were not particularly opposed, for example, to monopolies because there was a certain advantage in terms of economies of scale as well as a greater ease in forming a cooperative approach toward the common good between a monopoly in economics and a monopoly in government. And this is particularly true if politics becomes administration and the locus of government shifts from self-serving special interests in the legislature to public serving certified experts in the administrative state. The Progressives' 'correction' of the Equality Narrative is to introduce the regulatory state to the American scene.

BEARD: ROUSSEAU AND MARX COME TO AMERICA

Charles Beard's most influential book was *An Economic Interpretation of the U.S. Constitution* (Beard 1913). The Croly/Beard view became the prototype for the ongoing Rousseauean reinterpretation of American history, especially the founding era.

Beard understands his economic interpretation – "the theory of economic determinism" – as a challenge to three other theories of historical interpretation: (1) Bancroft's "higher power" at work in human affairs theory; (2) the Teutonic understanding that the Anglo Saxon race is superior; (3) an absence of any hypothesis historical school. Actually, we might well say that (1) is the object of his attention. There is a sort of Bancroft jurisprudence theory that he is challenging. Bancroft's theory suggests that the *Constitution* is the product of we "the whole people" introducing abstract justice rather than a class of the people securing their own property. What Beard is really interested in showing is that there is a fundamental difference in economic holdings between those who supported and those who opposed the *Constitution*. He ends with the statement that the "compelling motive" was "the economic advantage which the beneficiaries expected would accrue to themselves first, from their action. Further than this, economic interpretation cannot go" (Beard 1913, pp. 17–18).

He claims that his economic interpretation can be found in Madison's political science of *Federalist 10* which is "a masterly statement of the theory of economic determinism in politics" (Beard 1913, p. 15). He quotes *Federalist 10* as his source. However, Beard's view of economic determinism is closer to Marx than it is to Madison's emphasis on the presence of, even durability of, economic issues.

"The whole theory of the economic interpretation of history rests upon the concept that social progress in general is the result of contending interests in society – some favorable, others opposed, to change" (Beard 1913, p. 19). Thus he wants to know what classes and social groups existed and the key is to examine property: (1) Real Property: small debtor farmer (Luther Martin), manorial lords, southern slaveholders; (2) Personality Property – money and public securities, Society of Cincinnati, personality in manufacturing and shipping (Fitzsimons, Clymer, McHenry, Daniel Carroll and the Boston folks); (3) small mortgaged farms; (4) owners of Western lands (Hugh Williamson, George Washington, R. Morris, and so on); (5) manufacturing establishments. There were four disenfranchised: slaves, the indentured, property-less working class, and women.

Beard is correct. The underlying political science and political economy of *The Federalist* is to be found in *Federalist 10* and *51* dealing with property interests and the separation of powers. Beard, however, incorrectly states that "A majority of the states placed direct property qualifications on the voters, and the other states eliminated practically all who were not taxpayers" (Beard 1913, p. 71). Important for Beard is the fact that "not one member represented in his immediate personal economic interests the small farming or mechanical classes" (Beard 1913, p. 149). "Above all, it is to the owners of personality anxious to find a foil against the attacks of leveling democracy, that the authors of *The Federalist* address their most cogent arguments in favor of ratification" (Beard 1913, p. 154). There are "two fundamental parts: I. A government endowed with certain positive powers, but so constructed as to break the force of majority rule and prevent invasions of property rights by minorities. II. Restrictions on the state legislatures which had been so vigorous in their attacks on capital" (Beard 1913, p. 154).

As far as the structure of the government is concerned, "the keystone of the whole structure is, in fact, the system provided for judicial control – the most unique contribution to the science of government which has been made by American political genius" (Beard 1913, p. 162). "Equally important to personality as the positive powers conferred upon Congress … were the restrictions imposed on the states" (Beard 1913, p. 178).

Beard focuses on the prohibition of paper money and the obligation of the contracts clause in personality versus agrarianism (Beard 1913, p. 178). "The authors of *The Federalist* carry over into the field of international politics the concept of economic antagonisms which lie at the basis of their system of domestic politics" (Beard 1913, p. 183). In his concluding paragraph, Beard maintains that:

> Enough has been said to show that the concept of the *Constitution* as a piece of abstract legislation reflecting no group interests and recognizing no economic antagonisms is entirely false. It was an economic document drawn with supreme skill by men whose property interests were immediately at stake; and as such it appealed directly and unerringly to identical interests across the country. (Beard 1913, p. 188)

The ratification process was a *coup d'état*. This was in the same league as what Napoleon did in 1803 (Beard 1913, p. 218). The process of ratification adopted by the framers was a "revolutionary departure from their instructions" (Beard 1913, p. 222). Beard examines "what methods were employed in calling these conventions and setting the seal of approval of the Philadelphia assembly" (Beard 1913, p. 225). Beard points out the precipitous nature and "speedy dispatch" of certain state conventions and how in Pennsylvania "the Federalists continued their irregular practices" (Beard 1913, pp. 232, 234). He also suggests that "a reputable historical writer" claims that a sufficient number of members of the Massachusetts Convention "were bought with money from New York to secure ratification in Massachusetts" (Beard 1913, p. 228).

Beard contends that the idea that the *Constitution* was adopted by "a whole people" is inaccurate (Beard 1913, p. 239). The ratification was not a popular act. Property qualifications barred a considerable portion of white males. And a small portion of the eligible actually voted, especially in the rural areas. The true estimate is that only 25 percent of the eligible voters participated. "Talent, wealth, and professional abilities were, generally speaking on the side of the Constitutionalists" (Beard 1913, p. 251).

We need, says Beard, to "individualize" those people who supported and those who opposed ratification. "Holders of personality saw in the new government a strength and defense to their advantage" (Beard 1913, p. 290). The adoption of the new system was due to the influence of the security interest within personality. "The opposition to the *Constitution* came from the agricultural regions, and from the areas in which debtors had been formulating paper money and other depreciatory schemes" (Beard 1913, p. 291). The key to understanding 1787–1789 is that there "was a deep-seated conflict between a popular party based on paper money and agrarian interests, and a conservative party centered in the towns and resting on the financial, mercantile, and personal property interests generally" (Beard 1913, p. 292). In the pamphlet literature, "we find the most frank recognition of the fact that one class of property interests was in conflict with another." Beard's conclusion: a small group of active men with personality interests – "money, public securities, manufactures, and trade and shipping" – called for the Convention and the rest of the people had no say in who went there (Beard 1913, p. 324).

Ironically, Charles Beard both reviled and revived interest in *The Federalist*. Douglass Adair has shown that *Federalist 10* was rarely cited in the nineteenth century. Thus Beard made it more important than it had been. *Federalist 51* provides the institutional or constitutional framework for the operation of *Federalist 10*. There is nothing in *The Federalist* to encourage the direct will of the people ruling; it must be the deliberate sense of the community. That is what Madison means by the rule of law rather than the rule of men. The latter was seen as the very essence of tyranny. But for the Progressives the institutional framework was a mere façade for the rule of the upper over the lower class.

CROLY/BEARD AND THE BATTLE FOR DEMOCRACY

Beard's objective was to win the battle for democracy. Interestingly, one might have expected that Jefferson would have loomed large in the heroic figures of the Progressives. Wasn't he the democrat par excellence of the Founding? He authored the *Declaration of Independence* and wasn't present at the creation of the *Constitution*. While Jefferson might have been a democrat, according to popular histories, he had an under developed understanding of democracy, namely, he put his emphasis on individual freedom and not social justice or community (Croly). Didn't he oppose the upper class system being proposed by Hamilton? Yes, but the Progressives think they can cure Hamiltonianism of upper classism and keep his nationalism. The solution is a national democracy. Croly reminded Americans that the *Declaration of Independence* is a myth because the dream of individualism will never occur. Beard decried the *Constitution* because it entrenched oligarchy.

Beard suggests that historians have misplaced the difference between Hamilton and Jefferson as the great divide in American politics, that it was not the battle of agrarianism against capitalism. Rather he is interested in how a bunch of investors and property owners won in 1787 and the *Constitution* and ratification is a reflection of the stacking of the deck.

Federalist 10 does say that the most common and durable source of faction is the property question. And that is what makes a conversation between the Founding and the Progressives possible. For Locke and Smith, private property is a legitimate reward for personal effort. It also leads to the improvement of the human condition. For Rousseau and Marx, private property is theft and is the symbol of human alienation. Linked to the property question is the question of what is the proper role of government. For Marx, all politics and government is about power, and power ultimately is economic power which in turn is about the few who own and the many who don't own property.

There is consequently a link to Lincoln and the Civil War and the amended *Constitution*. The Progressives play up the notion that the origin of real progress in America is only constitutionalized by the 13th Amendment which prohibits one human being from owning another human being. At issue is whether or not that is a reversal of the ill-founded nation or a fulfillment of a well-founded nation. Lincoln replaces both Jefferson and Hamilton as the Founder of modern America where human rights are more important than property rights. Thus the *Declaration* becomes more important than the *Constitution*; if anything the *Constitution* is a reaction to the *Declaration*. That is the Progressive narrative.

But once you have passed the 13th and then the 14th and the 15th Amendments what is there for you to do and what is the lesson for the next generation? Hamilton is a half hero of the Progressives because they see him as a nationalist willing to use the power of the federal government. The economic theory of Beard is a mild form of class war, and the social question is at the heart of the Progressive approach to politics. And certainly with the Progressives, equality replaces liberty as the central concern of politics. The role of the federal government is to regulate interstate commerce, hence the Interstate Commerce Commission and the emergence of the three new cabinet departments.

So the Progressives are against the improved science of politics and the extended commercial republic as articulated by the Founding generation. They think that America is ill-founded. They would rather have a parliamentary form or system governed by a centralized administration and a society that holds to the values of social justice or communal freedom than an individual liberty that seems to reinforce the selfish side of human nature. Competition implies market failure whereas government intervention suggests government solution. And there is no sense saying that local government is better because, according to the Progressives, the social problems do not recognize state boundaries. Thus, in addition to the separation of powers and checks and balances, the Progressives have no attraction to federalism.

Coordination rather than competition leads to good outcomes and leadership is linked to the notion of knowledge. There is a Progressive inclination to believe that there is a body of knowledge that can be certified by an advanced degree as in schools of public policy (Enlightenment Project as opposed to the Technological Project) somehow independent from special or personal interests. These public servants will seek the common good, and since commerce and the common good do not go together it is the job of government to reign in the self-interested few who would exploit us unsuspecting and innocent many.

The conventional interpretation of American history was Lockean. The great divide in American politics was the difference between Hamilton and Jefferson. The battle for America is capitalism against agrarianism, hence the inevitability (Tocqueville) of the Civil War and the triumph of capitalism (Technological Project in its military dimension). In Beard's eyes, this interpretation is a mistake. Instead he imported a European model, specifically Rousseauean, aided by some soft Marxism, to interpret America. Progressive historians and subsequent scholars have emphasized the conflict between the "democratic" Bill of Rights and *Declaration of Independence* on the one hand, and the "aristocratic" *Constitution* on the other hand.

HOOVER, ROOSEVELT, AND THE GREAT DEPRESSION

The New Deal has had a profound impact on how Americans engage in the conversation about public policy. In order to understand that conversation, it is necessary to return to the "Great Depression." Triggered by the New York Stock Market crash of October 29, 1929 (known as Black Tuesday), a worldwide economic downturn ensued and lasted until the advent of World War II. Worldwide GDP fell by 15 percent; international trade declined by more than 50 percent; personal incomes, tax revenues, profits, and prices all declined; unemployment in the US rose to 25 percent.

Needless to say, there have been, and will always be, many competing explanations of the causes of the Great Depression. We shall not discuss them except to note briefly in broad terms the extent to which they reflect, in part, Lockean and Rousseauean narratives. Among the Rousseauean narratives we find Marxism (boom and bust as permanent features of capitalism and the 'inevitable' collapse of capitalism); neo-Rousseauean (the unequal distribution of wealth led to an economy where production exceeded demand – the position of the early Herbert Hoover); and Keynes (lower aggregate expenditures leads to a demand-supply gap that needs to be closed by government managed expenditures – the Roosevelt position). On the Lockean side we find Austrian Business Cycle theory, espoused by Rothbard and Hayek (the latter predicted in February of 1929 that the actions of the Federal Reserve would lead to a crisis starting in the stock and credit markets) in which you let recessions work themselves out in the market or they turn into a 'Great' Depression when exacerbated by government intervention; and monetarists (Friedman) in which the alleged failure of the Federal Reserve to inject liquidity led to undermining the banks and credit (not enough help to capitalist institutions).

Herbert Hoover, originally a Progressive Republican, was elected President in 1928, but he was soundly defeated by Franklin Delano Roosevelt in 1932. Roosevelt was re-elected three times and served until his death in 1944. It was Roosevelt who initiated the New Deal. In the ensuing years, a quasi-debate emerged between Hoover who more and more reflected the Lockean narrative and Roosevelt who espoused the Rousseauean narrative in the American context.

Herbert Hoover delivered two important, and seemingly contradictory, campaign speeches in the Fall of 1928. Both occurred during the Roaring Twenties and a full year before the Great Depression was even a twinkle in the eyes of just about anyone. Thus, in these two speeches, we have a summary of his pre-Great Depression position on the relationship between individual liberty and positive government.

The first speech is the Madison Square Garden Speech delivered on October 22 where he warned about the dangers of big government. He is criticized by the Democratic Left, during the Great Depression and beyond, for his spirited defense of "rugged individualism." It is, to continue this leftward retrospective interpretation, as if Hoover's rugged individualism, and the supposed affiliation with narrow self-interest, was the cause of the financial and moral crisis. This rugged individualism, supposedly shorn of any connection to a view of the responsible role of government, is sufficient justification for Roosevelt's (hereafter FDR) solution of beneficial governmental regulation, by selfless planners, over an anarchistic market.

The second speech is Hoover's November 2, St Louis Speech, just days before the 1928 Presidential election which Hoover won over-whelmingly. Here he articulated the case in favor of the positive role of government within the individualism of the American System. He is criticized by the Libertarian Right, which emerged after the New Deal and became more articulate after the Great Society, for his deliberate endorsement of "constructive government." It is, to pursue the rightward critique, as if Hoover's "constructive government" opened the door to the arrival of the New Deal and the problems associated with federal government programs in the last half of the twentieth century and beyond.

We reject both of these seemingly coherent, but one-sided, interpret-ations of Hoover in the late 1920s. These interpretations actually require choosing one speech over the other as the articulation of the "true" Hoover. He is either a rugged individualist, who degrades the role of federal government in American life, or he is a governmental supporter, who undermines the role of the individual in American life. Hoover intertwined rugged individualism, equality of opportunity, and the march of progress in opposition to the paternalistic and failed system of Europe. In his Presidential Nomination Address of August 11, 1928, Hoover anticipated this connection: "This *ideal* of individualism based on equality of opportunity to every citizen is the negation of socialism ... . Equality of opportunity is a fundamental principle of our nation. With it we must test all our policies. The success or failure of this principle is the test of our government" (Lloyd 2006, *Two Faces of Liberalism*, hereafter TFOL, p. 34). And to underscore this interconnection, Hoover states in the Madison Square Garden Speech that the European system "would extinguish equality of opportunity." Fortunately, "for a hundred and fifty years liberalism has found its true spirit in the American system, not in the European system" (TFOL, p. 38).

Hoover is not oblivious to the negative connotations that accompany the use of the phrase "*rugged individualism*." It is not code words, says Hoover, for "devil-take-the-hindmost" or a "system of laissez-faire" even though, we hasten to add, that is how "rugged individualism" is com-monly viewed. Nor is he oblivious to the need for a role for government that is consistent with the Liberty Narrative. According to Hoover, "there are three potential fields in which the *principles* (ideas) and *impulses* (ideals) of our American system require that government take construc-tive action" (TFOL, p. 41, italics added). Note that Hoover uses the word 'require' rather than 'useful' or 'compatible.' So what does Hoover see as required "leadership" from the federal government? We can list these under three headings: (1) "public works such as inland waterways, flood control, reclamation, highways, and public buildings"; (2) "education, public health, scientific research, public parks, conservation of natural resources, agriculture, industry, and foreign commerce"; (3) "assistance of the government to the growing efforts of the people to co-operation among themselves to useful social and economic ends" (TFOL, p. 41).

FDR in 1932 articulated the alternative vision of "the forgotten man" whose condition it was the role of government to alleviate (TFOL, p. 67). We need to have "faith once more in the forgotten man at the bottom of the economic pyramid" (ibid.). "It is high time to get back to funda-mentals. It is high time to admit with courage that we are in the midst of an emergency at least equal to that of war. Let us mobilize to meet it" (TFOL, p. 69). Is this the replacement of what Oakeshott will call civil association with enterprise association? Certainly by the time of the New Deal the word 'democracy' had become less associated with individual liberty, decentralized government, and more with majority rule and with the Progressivist understanding of collective cooperation, centralized government, and the public good.

So we have a Rousseauean redefinition of democracy away from the political understanding of majority rule, whether that be direct or indirect rule, and a move toward everyman, everybody, the people, the public good, the general welfare. "Clearly, all this calls for a re-appraisal of values." FDR claims that "the day of the promoter" is over and "the day of enlightened administration has arrived" (TFOL, p. 121). Our task is to rise, in our actions, to the utopian level of "[the first] Roosevelt and Wilson" (TFOL, p. 123).

Roosevelt explains in sarcastic oratory: "mere builder ..." the old way of getting yourself out of an economic hardship was to build more things; it's over (the frontier is over) you cannot produce your way out of this problem – part of the economic lesson he is giving is our problem is not a production problem, we produce more than we need, the problem is a distribution problem. We have enough to go around. The depression is caused because there is not enough money in people's hands, and the solution is putting money in people's hands. The reason for the recession is the unequal distribution of income and wealth.

In his Oglethorpe University Speech, May 22, 1932, FDR addresses graduating students who are clearly not better off than they were four years ago when they entered college. They entered, FDR reminds them, with the expectation that there would be a job waiting for them when they graduated. They are in this situation due to no fault of their own. They are victims. The reason for this terrible situation, says FDR, is the lack of planning. This situation, however, makes a new approach possible. "I believe that we are at the threshold of a fundamental change in our popular economic thought, that in the future we are going to think less of the producer and more about the consumer. We must do what we may have to do to inject life into our ailing economic order; we cannot make it endure for long unless we can bring about a wiser, more equitable distribution of the national income" (TFOL, p. 74). So FDR clearly links economic recovery with economic reform and this has been a liberal-progressive mantra for over a hundred years. Perhaps the American narrative has changed: the forgotten man has replaced the rugged individual. Thus the language of individual rights has been replaced by the language of group rights and the value of individual autonomy replaced by the commitment to social justice.

In his Presidential Nomination Address, July 2, 1932, FDR reiterates that the failure of "Republican leadership" to deal with our troubles "may degenerate into unreasoning radicalism" (TFOL, p. 96). The reactionary "Toryism" that favors the few, and hopes that their prosperity "will leak through" to labor and so on, is over and encourages "wild radicalism" (TFOL, p. 96). We need to realize, that contrary to the republican leaders' utterances, economic laws are not "sacred, inviolable, unchangeable," but "made by human beings" (TFOL, p. 102). It is time for the federal government to "assume bold leadership in distress relief" (ibid.). This Address clearly calls for a new deal and a new order, and it is democratic in the sense that it is to assist the American people. The language of "war" and "crusade" rings through the speech on behalf of "a new order." It is time to fight for everyone, and that is what republican leadership overlooks. Also here we find a bold challenge to abandon classical microeconomic theory and engage in something else.

In retrospect, it appears that Roosevelt did not have a specific set of plans, and it is unlikely that he is at that time embracing Keynes per se because Keynes did not come up with the final version of what he had in mind until the publication of the *General Theory* in 1936. It makes much more sense to see this as a reflection of the ongoing Rousseau narrative as previously articulated by the Progressives.

We need to be clear on how FDR and Hoover differ on these two points: (1) Both are saying that reform of something in the system is needed for economic recovery. Are they aiming at the same reforms for recovery? Hoover is calling for reforms in the areas of banking, transportation and power. Is this different from FDR six months later? (2) Certain reforms reinforce the values of the American system – the Hoover position – and certain reforms help in the reappraisal of the values of the American system – FDR.

ROOSEVELT, HOOVER, AND THE NEW DEAL

In his acceptance speech of the 1932 Democratic nomination for president, Franklin Roosevelt promised "a new deal." "Throughout the nation men and women, forgotten in the political philosophy of the Government, look to us here for guidance and for more equitable opportunity to share in the distribution of national wealth ... I pledge myself to a new deal for the American people. This is more than a political campaign. It is a call to arms." What ensued was a host of programs designed to deal with what historians called the "3 R's": Relief for the unemployed, Recovery of the economy to 'normal', and Reform of the financial system to prevent future depressions. We shall follow the practice of historians by distinguishing between the "First New Deal" (1933–34) and the "Second New Deal" (1935–38).

Again, we shall for the most part ignore the interminable debate about whether the New Deal was a success or failure. There is no independent laboratory to test which theories are correct. One can say that things were better (or worse) at a given date or a different date but only after we define 'better' or 'worse.' For example, the economy improved during the first term, but there was a downturn in 1937. Roosevelt took credit for the improved pre-1937 economic performance, but that backfired in the recession of 1937. There is no independent way to measure what would have happened without New Deal programs, and there is no independent way to measure what would have happened if there had been an even more vigorous New Deal. Even the historical fallout is subject to endless debate. When do we stop measuring the 'long-term' effects of the New Deal? For example, between 1926 and 1940 only the top 3 percent paid income tax. Today it is much higher. Is that an effect of the New Deal?

What does seem incontrovertible is that there has been a dramatic increase in the reach of the federal government and what has been called the rise of the 'imperial' presidency, that is, the executive branch has become the center of authority within the federal government. Never before Roosevelt was a president measured by their first 100 days in office, and this 100 day period became a touchstone, a measuring rod for how successful you are going to be as president. Our concern is to focus on the role played by the two narratives in the words of Roosevelt and Hoover in these developments.

Roosevelt's rhetorically intoxicating First Inaugural Address famously begins "that the only thing we have to fear is fear itself." This statement summarizes the subtle shift in language from individual rights and liberties that frequent Hoover's writing to a language of communal responsibilities and freedoms that are familiar to Roosevelt's audience. 'We' are all in this together. Roosevelt's Freedom from Fear and Freedom from Want in his 1942 State of the Union Message is the culmination of a ten year plan ultimately to shift the meaning of the Bill of Rights away from supporting limitations on the reach of the federal government to supporting – perhaps guaranteeing – an expansion of the reach of the federal government. All this Inaugural hinting is a decade before Roosevelt's famous Four Freedoms for the world Address.

THE FIRST INAUGURAL

To begin the First Inaugural with the notion that the central "leadership" objective is to establish freedom from fear is, in fact, to elevate the social over the political role of the federal government. Accordingly, the government henceforth is to be concerned with actively securing the general social welfare, and perhaps even eliminating the causes of faction, rather than being the neutral umpire of the collisions and collusions that occur among individuals and groups operating within what Madison in *Federalist 10* called "civilized societies."

Roosevelt maintains that we need "national planning" based on the new realization of "our interdependence on each other." Apparently, the old order of individual independence is over. A key to the Progressive Agenda, then, is the substitution of mutual interdependence for individual independence. The lesson of the dark days we have endured, says FDR, is that we must put the mad chase for profits behind us. "Our true destiny is not to be ministered unto but to minister to ourselves and to our fellow men" (TFOL, p. 161). And, thus, we have the substitution of rational "national planning" for what is perceived to be the irrational market forces that were the very cause of the Great Depression. "Our *Constitution* is so simple and practical that it is possible always to meet extraordinary needs by changes in emphasis and arrangement without loss of essential form." Put differently, the time for constitutional interpretation has arrived. Roosevelt asks for war powers. "I shall ask the Congress for the one remaining instrument to meet the crisis: broad executive power to wage a war against the emergency, as great as the power that would be given to me if we were in fact invaded by a foreign foe" (ibid.).

The most prominent word in this speech is "discipline" – he uses it five times – and he means the discipline of the people. That is, apparently what the people have asked for! "They have asked for discipline and direction under leadership" (TFOL, p. 164). This emphasis on discipline of the people must have resonated with Hoover. His remarks that the New Deal is attempting to regiment the people of America makes sense in the light of FDR's remarks. And Hoover's parallel of the New Deal to European Fascism also makes more sense. The idea that FDR's First Inaugural is a "frank" call for a theory of executive leadership – against the traditional separation of powers in the general government and division of powers between the levels of government – over a disciplined people – rather than a self-governing people – ought to strike Lockeans as dangerous to the existing American System. Should we be surprised that the two back to back "fear" comments are the ones that come to our mind rather than mentioning "disciplined" five times?

Hoover wants to conserve the *Constitution* of both Washington and Lincoln from the *Constitution* according to the Roosevelt Progressives. On *Constitution* Day 1935, Hoover talks about the Bill of Rights as a "phase of the *Constitution*." We think this is an important lesson for twenty-first century Lockeans to remember, namely Hoover's assumption that the *Constitution* and the Bill of Rights are compatible. And that for Hoover, the original *Constitution*, and Bill of Rights, and the Civil War Amendments, together, are the core documentary *Constitution* under assault by the Progressives. What seems clear, following Hoover's appeal to Lincoln, is that any discussion of the *Constitution* must be informed by an appeal to the fundamental values of the American Order, and that "system is based upon certain unalienable freedoms and protections" that are beyond the reach of government.

These freedoms in the Bill of Rights that are beyond the reach of government are so obviously and unambiguously stated that "it does not require a lawyer to interpret those provisions. They are as clear as the Ten Commandments" (TFOL, p. 58). From Hoover's point of view, the language of the *Constitution* and the contemporaneous documentary evidence are such that a reasonable citizen would agree with Hoover that a lawyer is not necessary to interpret the language of the *Declaration*, the *Constitution* or the first ten Amendments because the language is abundantly clear.

Furthermore, these rights, "were established by centuries of struggle" and when "our forefathers … wrote the *Declaration of Independence* they boldly *extended* these rights" (italics added). And later they were "incorporated in black and white within the *Constitution* – and so became the Bill of Rights" (TFOL, p. 59). The interrelationship between these founding documents, the *Declaration*, the *Constitution*, and the Bill of Rights, and the Civil War Amendments is the American system of liberty. The Progressives to the contrary notwithstanding, these four documents of the American heritage are not in mortal conflict with each other. That is Hoover's Lockean position, one that is an intellectually and politically defensible response to the Progressives. This is how Hoover put it in the 1935 *Constitution* Day speech:

> Liberty never dies from direct attack. No one will dare rise tomorrow and say he is opposed to the Bill of Rights. Liberty dies from the encroachment and disregard of its safeguards. Its destruction can be no less potent from ignorance or desire to find shortcuts to jump over some immediate pressure ... . In our country, abdication of its responsibilities and powers by Congress to the Executive, the repudiation by the government of its obligations, the centralization of authority into the Federal Government at the expense of local government, the building up of huge bureaucracies, the coercion or intimidation of citizens, are the same sort of first sapping of safeguards of human rights that have taken place in other lands. Here is the cause of anxiety and concern to the thinking citizens of the United States ... . George Washington in his Farewell Address had warned that one method of assault may be to effect, in the form of the *Constitution* alterations which may impair the energy of the system and thus undermine that which cannot be directly overthrown.

A LOCKEAN RESPONSE TO THE NEW DEAL

A solid Lockean narrative then would argue that the New Deal has: (1) taken America off its normal course of Constitutional conduct, by the "sapping of safeguards" to the *Constitution*; (2) these "sappings" of interpretation have stretched the *Constitution* to fit these new deals; (3) since [World War I] the Great War, the people of Europe have been "surrendering their freedom for false promises of economic security ... . Every day they repudiate every principle of the Bill of Rights"; and (4) the analogy to nineteenth century slavery: "Here is a form of servitude, of slavery – a slipping back toward the Middle Ages" where "the citizen has no assured rights." In Europe, we are witnessing the playing out of "the most fundamental clash known to mankind ... men who are slaves of despotism, as against free men who are the masters of the State." We can foresee here Hayek's *Road to Serfdom* (1944).

Hoover, in effect, accuses the national planners in the FDR administration of sacrificing personal liberty to accomplish the end of national planning. Hoover's coverage suggests that when faced with a choice between economic progress and primary liberties, a Lockean should choose liberty. Why? Lockeans like Milton Friedman would probably say we don't have to make the choice between economic efficiency and personal liberty because economic efficiency can only be achieved by a system of personal liberty. Thus the national planners, by way of unintended consequences, have actually chosen economic inefficiency and a reduction in personal liberties!

So, at one level, like Hayek, Hoover is totally giving away to the philosophers of national planning the economic efficiency, economic progress and general welfare argument. And thus any talk of the common good and general welfare is an invitation to impose an outside standard on the otherwise factually neutral value system. In the end, however, we think that Hoover ends up pretty much like Friedman: market driven economic efficiency, as opposed to economic efficiency as defined by the planners, is compatible with economic freedom. The Bill of Rights is not "a fetter upon progress." And the reason why he thinks the Machine Age (technological project), properly understood as an attachment to economic progress, and the "living principles of liberty" go together is because "the initiative of men, their enterprise, the inspiration of thought, flower in full only in the security of these rights." Hoover reminds us that future economic security of the "underprivileged and unemployed" depends on promoting "the creativity and stimulants of free men" rather than turning free men into regimented men in the name of a false understanding of economic efficiency. Hoover's Constitutional Day Address, then, is an invitation to his audience to use their imagination and locate the New Deal within the new philosophies of Europe that are antagonistic to the Bill of Rights and thus the *Constitution* (quotes from the *Constitution* Day speech, *New York Times* 1935).

MARCH 1933: A NEW BIRTH OF EQUALITY

In FDR's, Annual Message, January 3, 1936 (State of the Union), we see that New Deal I has "established a new relationship between Government and people" effective March 1933 (TFOL, p. 258). That is the month and year of change for FDR, "Government became the representative and the trustee of the public interest." The rule of the people replaced the rule of the few autocrats. But the "unscrupulous money-changers" then defeated, now "seek the restoration of their selfish power" (ibid.). So what "shall we" (repeated 12 times) say to this attack "on our affirmative action" (TFOL, p. 260). We shall recall March 1933 and we shall also say that we do "not want to return to that individualism of which they prate … [because] advantages under that system went to the ruthless and strong" (ibid.). We have changed that with the introduction of "a people's Government" (ibid.). "Their weapon is the weapon of fear. I have said, 'The only thing we have to fear is fear itself.' That is true today as it was in 1933" (TFOL, pp. 260–61). Look at the extent to which FDR marks

1933 as the start of a revolution, and the revolution is against individualism because that is a cover for autocracy. This is critical for our thesis that Hoover is trying to defend individualism properly understood from a revolutionary understanding of the role of government.

Hoover, at the Republican National Convention, June 10, 1936: We are gathered "to determine the fate of those ideals." Hoover makes the parallel between the "march of European collectivism" and "regimenting the people into a planned economy" under the direction of the "personal power" of the President. There has been an attack on freedom by the New Deal during the last four years in America in terms of the violation of the separation of powers, growth of spoils politics, and the consolidation of government (TFOL, pp. 272–73). Thank Goodness, so far, for the *Constitution* and the Court and the press. And here is the issue: "There are some principles that cannot be compromised. Either we shall have a society based upon ordered liberty and the initiative of the individual, or we shall have a planned society that means dictation, no matter what you call it or who does it. There is no half-way ground. They cannot be mixed. Government must either release the powers off the individual for honest achievement or the very forces it creates will drive it inexorably to lay its paralyzing hand more and more heavily upon individual effort" (TFOL, p. 278). What is remarkable in this speech is that there is no attempt to blend traditional liberalism with the progressivism that we saw in 1928. And there is no fluffy reference to values and so on. Here in 1936, there is a choice and freedom is at stake and it is a principle. "Fundamental American liberties are at stake" (TFOL, p. 279). So, this piece actually nails down our thesis that the New Deal woke up Hoover to the notion that the alternative to the European system was not the blend but the rejection of the Rousseau narrative.

THE SECOND INAUGURAL

In his Second Inaugural Address, January 20, 1937, FDR harkens back to 1933:

> we dedicated ourselves to the fulfillment of a vision – to speed the time when there would be for all the people that security and peace essential to the pursuit of happiness. We of the Republic pledged ourselves to drive from the temple of our ancient faith those who had profaned it, to end by action, tireless and unafraid, the stagnation and despair of that day. We did those first things first. (TFOL, p. 307)

Here in the opening paragraph, we have the whole point of the New Deal: it is not primarily about recovery but about reform and the reform is articulated as the abolition and prohibition of some evil force. But this kind of project is never over. There is always another dragon to destroy. FDR repeats his notion that 1933 introduced "a new order of things" based in "social justice" (TFOL, p. 309). It is more than simply economic reform; it is about getting rid of the "bad morals" of "heedless self-interest" on behalf of "a morally better world" (TFOL, p. 309). "The greatest change we have witnessed has been the change in the moral climate of America" (ibid.).

So what is the second New Deal all about? Getting to "our happy valley." What is the challenge? "Millions" of people, perhaps up to "one-third of a nation ill housed, ill clad, and ill nourished" (TFOL, p. 310). So "Today we re-consecrate our country to long-cherished ideals in a suddenly changed civilization" (TFOL, p. 311). The Forgotten Man is also Everyman; or, as Hoover calls the objective of the New Deal, the Average Man. However we want to categorize the New Deal Man, he is not the Rugged Individual. The man of the New Deal is not the Individual Man except as an object of criticism. FDR: When "seeking for economic and political progress as a nation, we all go up; or else we all go down, as one people" (TFOL, p. 311). So much for the positive benefits of personal individualism!

10. Keynes and Hayek: the Road to Serfdom

UTILITARIANISM: A TURN TO ECONOMIC SCIENCE

Broadly speaking, utilitarianism is the view that social policy can be reduced to a kind of calculation of the consequences of alternative courses of action. Just exactly what is being calculated and how one measures those anticipated consequences is itself a matter of dispute among holders of utilitarianism. The well documented problems with utility can be summarized as follows: we cannot appeal to consequences without knowing how to rank the impact of different approaches with regard to different moral interests (liberty, equality, prosperity, security, and so on); we cannot appeal to preference satisfaction unless one already grants how one will correct preferences and compare rational versus impassioned preferences, as well as calculate the discount rate for preferences over time; appeals to disinterested observers, hypothetical choosers, or hypothetical contractors will not avail because if such decision-makers are truly disinterested, they will choose nothing. If we choose in a particular way, we must already be fitted out with a particular moral sense or a thin theory of the good. Any intuition can be met with contrary intuitions; any particular balancing of claims can be countered with a different approach to achieving a balance; in order to appeal for guidance to any account of moral rationality one must already have secured content for that moral rationality. In short, it begs every question.

Jeremy Bentham was among the first to proclaim utilitarianism, and he influenced the development of economics in the latter half of the nineteenth century and the twentieth century. Specifically, he influenced the development of economics as an allegedly pure science. A turn to economic science seems to presume that the case for economic liberty, and its relationship to political and social liberty, no longer has to be made. And it also does two other things: it suggests that the issue of liberty can be reduced to an efficiency issue and it hides the problem that individual liberty needs to be reconciled with community good. It suggests that equality can be reduced to a collectivist issue and it hides the problem that community good needs to be reconciled with individual liberty. We shall not discuss Bentham, but we do want to note that Bentham was in some ways the "grandfather" of macroeconomics. Dicey was the first to point out that Bentham's system evolved into a form of collectivism, thereby crossing the boundary between libertarian and democratic socialist versions of positivism. Bentham's principle of utility could give justification to collectivism: the majority was the poor, and the society should be organized for their benefit. In his book, *Lectures on the Relation Between Law and Public Opinion in England during the Nineteenth Century* ([1885] 2008), in Lecture IX, "The Debt of Collectivism to Benthamism" Dicey spells out how "the socialists of today have inherited a legislative dogma, a legislative instrument, and a legislative tendency from Benthamism."

The most important figures in the development of economic science prior to Keynes were Jevons, Sidgwick, and Marshall. William Stanley Jevons (1835–82) was a Christian utilitarian who rightly observed that J.S. Mill was not, strictly speaking, a utilitarian, and worse yet, had abandoned Bentham's utilitarianism. Jevons, a mathematician and economist, devoted a large part of his career to arguing against Mill. He aimed to replace the influence of Mill's *Principles of Political Economy* (Mill 1848) with his own book, *A General Mathematical Theory of Political Economy* (Jevons 1862). It was this book that marked the advent of a purely mathematical economics.

Henry Sidgwick (1838–1900), economist and philosopher of ethics, wrote on political economy from a utilitarian perspective. Alfred Marshall, founder of the Cambridge School of Economics, would describe Sidgwick as his "spiritual mother and father." It was Sidgwick who reluctantly admitted that there was no rational foundation to basic moral beliefs.

Alfred Marshall (1842–1924) did succeed in replacing Mill with his own book, *Principles of Economics* (Marshall 1890). Under the influence of Jevons and Sidgwick, he too was concerned with improving the condition of the working class. The Revolutions of 1848 had focused the attention of Mill and all subsequent British economists on the plight of the working class. Just as Smith had been forced to come to terms with Rousseau, so Marshall as well as his pupil and successor Keynes, would be forced to do likewise.

Following Say, J.S. Mill had assumed along with all classical political economists that the great issue was how to increase "the wealth of nations," that is, how to increase living standards. The answer was to increase the productivity of labor by increasing the accumulation and the investment of capital. Value depended upon capital. The higher the underlying productiveness of the economy, the higher will be the level of employment for any given real wage. In short, supply creates demand. As a consequence, "What supports and employs productive labor, is the capital expended in setting it to work, and not the demand of purchasers for the produce of the labor when completed. Demand for commodities is not demand for labor" (Mill's Fourth Proposition on Capital). Jevons challenged Mill and argued that value depended upon demand. Marshall combined these two positions and concluded that *in the short run*, supply cannot be changed and market value depends mainly on demand. This, as we shall see, leads directly to Keynes.

KEYNES: THE CASE FOR A THIRD WAY

John Maynard Keynes (1883–1946) begins *The End of Laissez Faire* (Keynes 1926) with a frontal assault on the "abstract" principles articulated by Locke, Smith, and Tocqueville as pretty much nonsense. He borrows Bentham's "forgotten but useful nomenclature," articulated in Bentham's 1843 *Manual of Political Economy*, without falling into what he portrays as Bentham's assumption that government interference was "generally needless" and "generally pernicious." The task of economics should be "to distinguish afresh the *Agenda* of Government from the Non-Agenda." The task of politics is "to devise forms of Government within a Democracy which shall be capable of accomplishing the Agenda" (Keynes 1931, *Essays in Persuasion*, pp. 312–13).

In 1926, Keynes does not endorse "state socialism" as the alternative to laissez-faire. State socialism is "little better than a dusty survival of a muddled version of just the same philosophy as underlies nineteenth-century individualism." So, according to Keynes, we need a fundamental correction in both narratives since they are both preoccupied with freedom. The task of government should be to address the issue of the "great inequalities of wealth" which is a great cause in the "unemployment of labour" (Keynes 1931, *Essays in Persuasion*, pp. 317–18). What he has in mind, he says, supports a role for intermediate communities and the state that neither currently do. Given his inclination toward a new and additional role for the state on behalf of equality, we would have to place him as a new kind of supporter of the Equality Narrative.

Keynes acknowledged not only the major philosophical shortcoming of utilitarianism but that there could never be a satisfactory utilitarian response to the Rousseauean critique: "private and social interest do not coincide" (Keynes 1932, *Collected Works*, IX, p. 305). Even more important, in *The General Theory of Employment, Interest and Money* (1936, Chapter 24, part 1), Keynes changed the focus of economics largely because of a perceived "arbitrary and inequitable distribution of wealth and income." The focus is now on short-run employment creation rather than long-run wealth creation as the central aim of economic policy. The causes of economic growth are at best an afterthought.

Keynes argued that it was "aggregate demand" which determined economic activity. Inadequate aggregate demand leads to high unemployment. In order to moderate the "boom and bust" cycles of economic activity, and to achieve full employment, government regulation of the demand side of the economy was needed. For the market to reach its full potential (telos equilibrium), we need full employment. Because of price stickiness (workers often refuse to lower their wage demands), government needed to adjust aggregate demand and aggregate supply. One way in which government could stimulate demand in times of high unemployment, was by spending on public works. Public works were not a form of redistribution; they were intrinsically valuable, indirect means to the creation of wealth, and a temporary measure for exceptional circumstances like the Great Depression. He did not advocate government spending financed by borrowing but insisted upon balanced budgets.

Keynes also had his version of "perpetual peace." If market economies can be managed successfully on the domestic level then the same could be true internationally (for example, a coordinated international monetary system). He advocated and worked tirelessly in the post-war period (World War II) for a global market economy rather than the prevailing mercantilism. Later writers such as Galbraith believed that the termination of Keynesian policies during the global debt crisis of the early 1980s increased inequality worldwide.

Was Keynes a Lockean or a Rousseauean? In his own mind, he was undoubtedly at least a 'corrected' Lockean. He was firmly committed to the technological project; he thought he was repairing the market economy based on his understanding of the relationship between demand and supply; he believed in limited government (opposing state sponsored social democracy in favor of management by an intellectually and morally qualified elite) and he advocated world peace; the role of the state is not the ownership of the means of production but management of investment (not production but distribution with the expectation that this would lead to full production); he supported the rule of law; and most certainly presumed the sanctity of individual autonomy. To the extent that he acknowledged the social problem his response was no different in kind from that of Smith or perhaps Mill – amelioration and evolution not revolution.

No doubt, Keynes, in his own mind, thought of himself as a breakthrough thinker for a new century. But having corrected, even demolished the status of the Lockean narrative, has he not left himself open to the temptation of the Rousseau narrative? Like Rousseau, his unit of analysis is the society as a whole rather than the individual. There is no defense, never mind an ambiguous defense, of private property, free conscience, and limited government. The structure of government is a means to secure the public good determined by experts rather than a means through which the deliberate sense of the community emerges. His deep concern with inequality rather than liberty surely leaves him open to the Rousseau narrative. No wonder then that Keynes has been more appealing to subsequent lovers of the Equality Narrative than those who hold liberty in the highest regard.

HAYEK: THE REVIVAL OF LIBERTY

Friedrich August von Hayek (1899–1992) was an Austrian born economist greatly influenced by his philosopher cousin Ludwig Wittgenstein and by fellow Austrian economist Ludwig Von Mises. He accepted a position at the London School of Economics in 1931. In 1944 he published *The Road to Serfdom*, an answer and warning to his friend Keynes.

In Chapter 1 of *The Road to Serfdom*, "The Abandoned Road," Hayek presumes there was a road to freedom that was abandoned. The first chapter focuses on when, where, and why that road was abandoned. He says that German intellectuals of the 1870s abandoned the freedom road in favor of the socialist road of control and then ultimately embraced the totalitarian road. They argued that we could not have spontaneous order; we needed a specific central planner. However, says Hayek, knowledge is too diffused and dynamic to be available to the planner, and, in fact, one can learn by making mistakes. The German intellectuals also deemed Western ideals to be "shallow." It seems that the only real choices available when he wrote the book were among various kinds of socialism.

Hayek wants to reintroduce another alternative. By 1932, he says, both the UK and the US were no longer liberal. Protectionist policies were widespread. But there is a chance for the revival of freedom in these two countries. And the revival rests on the revival of "freedom in economic affairs without which personal and political freedom has never existed in the past" (p. 13; all references are to the original 1944 edition published by Routledge). Like Friedman, Hayek thinks that liberty is freedom from coercion. He adds that freedom is important for the "discovery process." This has become known as "evolutionary economics," one that produces good outcomes by way of competition. Planning, by contrast results in unanticipated (and bad) outcomes.

Hayek was still operating in the intellectual world where socialism meant ownership of the means of production and government central planning. He is addressing British socialists as the war is ending. Hayek was fighting hard core European socialism and in that regard had a profound impact on Margaret Thatcher. It is only later in the 1970s that socialism came to be known as equal income redistribution. In other words, equality became a revised goal of post-World War II socialists; they softened their authoritarianism by appearing to advance the cause of freedom in adopting equal distribution of wealth as their project.

It is important to note Hayek's intellectual debt to Tocqueville and not only in the title of the book. The content argues that the socialists can only achieve their new servitude doctrine through "arbitrary administrative coercion." This new despotism is administered by what FDR would praise as the enlightened administrator. But Tocqueville warned, and Hayek repeats the warning, that the choice is between equality with liberty or equality with slavery or servitude (Hayek 1944, p. 28). In most democracies, folks still think that socialism and freedom can be combined (Hayek 1944, pp. 33–34). Socialists want to replace individualism with collectivism. Planning can be understood as a displacement of competition on the grounds that free enterprise is chaotic. By 1944, Hayek abandons using laissez-faire to describe his alternative because laissez-faire had become such an indefensible phrase (Hayek 1944, p. 37). Moreover, the idea that there is a third way is a fallacy (Hayek 1944, p. 43).

His definition of planning is a "deliberate organization of the labors of society for a definite social goal" (Hayek 1944, p. 59). But the social goal is code for the common good which, in turn, is code for a planned society determined by the planner's views. He, very similar to Hoover, argues that the key to losing democracy is that the Legislature invariably delegates decision-making to bodies that are independent of the Legislature (Hayek 1944, p. 72). This is actually delegating sovereignty. It is only within a capitalist system that democracy is possible (Hayek 1944, p. 73). The real loss is not democracy but liberty (Hayek 1944, p. 74).

The rule of law for Hayek is a great liberal principle – an ethical code – encompassing pre-established rules within which individuals are free to make decisions. The economic argument is that the government should lay down general rules and not micro manage economic decisions. These rules are more like sign posts than orders. The political argument is that we should have an impartial state rather than a moral state or the substantive state. Hayek repeats that liberalism is not identical to laissez-faire. Friedman, in the Introduction to Hayek's *Road to Serfdom*, praises Hayek for capturing the timeless choice: collectivism and central direction (serfdom) versus individualism and voluntary cooperation (freedom).

HAYEK ON WHY ROUSSEAUEAN (SOCIALIST) ECONOMICS RESTS ON A MISTAKE

Many economists, Rousseauean and otherwise, do not understand the market economy. Their first mistake is that they apply the wrong model for understanding a market economy. There are three models: mechanical, organic, and social. Mechanical order applies to physical objects. As such, the whole is reducible to its constituent parts (inputs = outputs), the part retains its identity (a spark plug can go in Ford, GM, and so on), and it can be represented spatially. Market economies are clearly not mechanical orders because they constantly produce unanticipated consequences. Living things in general are not mechanical which is why in the practice of medicine doctors must be aware of side-effects. So, perhaps markets can be understood as an organic form of order.

In organic order, the whole is greater than its constituent parts (for example, the human hand cannot be understood except as part of how it functions within the human body); the whole has to be understood as having a purpose or goal (teleological), so for example, animals and plants are understood to aim at survival; and although you cannot simply reduce them to spatial relations you can represent them temporally, that is, they grow and develop and often decay. The Scottish Enlightenment thinkers including Smith to some extent had an organic theory of the market in their natural history approach. But none of them asserted a telos. It was Marx who attributed a telos to the market economy. As we have seen, one of Hayek's theses is that a market economy does not have a telos (and hence cannot be planned or managed). Even if one is not a Marxist, the treatment of the market economy as some kind of whole, as in macroeconomics, leads to the idea of managing the economy to achieve its "end."

The market economy is a social phenomenon and exhibits spontaneous order. Spontaneous does not mean instantaneous. It means the order was not the product of human design. For example, natural languages such as English were not created – that is there was no originating committee with subcommittees on grammar, syntax, spelling, and so on that designed the language. People did not originally know they were speaking English or using participles, and so on. In retrospect, and as the result of discovering tensions, people started to make explicit what had originally been implicit. And, in the case of living languages, they continue to evolve in unpredictable ways requiring more retrospective elucidation and explication. There is no inherent teleology in natural language and by extension in any form of social order including the market economy.

The goal of socialist economic planning is the construction of "a rational economic order" (Hayek 1945, "The Use of Knowledge in Society," p. 77). According to Hayek, socialist economic planning assumes (1) the possibility of perfect knowledge on the part of economic planners, (2) the ability to define, without reference to the understandings of individual economic actors and their contexts, an objective hierarchy of preferences, and (3) the ability to determine the relative values of all means and ends available to the planner. For socialist economic planning to work, the following would have to be true: (a) everything I 'really' want as an individual is compatible with everything else I 'really' want (presumably experts on human nature would know this and could overrule my misperceptions or self-deceptions); (b) everything each individual 'really' wants is compatible with everything that everybody else 'really' wants ("general will"); (c) everything that 'we' really want forms a neat hierarchical system which enables us to prioritize these wants (teleology) and thereby enables us to resolve potential conflicts objectively; and (d) 'we' or the experts at least can objectively determine which means or programs or policies can implement this hierarchy. Even if we cannot agree on individual 'real' wants, perhaps the economy as a whole has some sort of telos or aims at an equilibrium point like full employment (Keynesian macroeconomics).

None of these things according to Hayek is true. There is no such information. Even if there were a super-computer in which we input our lists of wants, those lists would be in a constant and dynamic state of change as we discovered what other people wanted and modified our wants accordingly. The belief that a group of experts knows what we 'really' want or should want and that these wants form a neat teleological system leads to totalitarianism.

A more modest proposal is that democratic elections determine the overall goal. In practice, this simply means that a majority or a coalition of interest groups imposes its will on others. In practice, as public choice economics argues (Buchanan), the overall goal or goals are determined by the private interests of politicians, and hence the rise of crony capitalism. Periodic democratic elections keep shifting the goals and the prioritization, and this infuriates the technicians or bureaucrats who, if they believe in macroeconomics, will impose their latest collective model.

The intellectual source of this monumental blunder is a false metaphysical and epistemological view that we have previously identified as the Enlightenment Project and what Hayek recognized as nineteenth century positivism. This is the belief that there is a social science analogous to physical science and therefore there can be a social technology. This false metaphysics and epistemology is what his cousin Wittgenstein railed against in philosophy.

Curiously, there is a Romantic (nineteenth century) version of this. According to some romantics, there is no structure to things; you can mold things the way you want them to be; reality does not have a form which can be studied, written down, learnt, communicated or treated in a scientific manner; there are no laws of economics beyond human control. We can 'will' socialism into existence (for example, we can 'will' progressive taxation and 'will' that this won't create resentment or become a disincentive).

HAYEK AND THE WITTGENSTEIN CORRECTION

Let us return to Wittgenstein. Ludwig Wittgenstein (1889–1951) rejected epistemological realism, the view that knowledge is the mirroring of an external structure understood as a structure independent of human beings; as a consequence, he rejected scientism, the view that science was the whole truth about everything. He also rejected the notion that philosophy was itself a cognitive discipline, and insisted that philosophy was not the locus of theories. The task of philosophy was the explication of norms inherent in our language (practice). There are no hidden rules, no hidden logic, and no discoveries about the real meaning of the expressions we use. Philosophical problems arose only when we confused the grammar of one kind of expression (or practice) with the grammar of another.

Language is a tool, but scientism distorts the conception of language as a tool by making referential use basic. The distortion takes the form of likening language to a telescope in which we can only talk about the way in which the world appears using different sets of lenses. Scientism refuses to ask questions about the telescope itself, or the user of the telescope, or the interpretation of what is seen, or all of the *uses* to which it is put. If it did ask such questions then we would see that the uses and the meaning of the results of the uses are molded by our culture. Wittgenstein further denied that the semantic and pragmatic dimensions of language can themselves be explained by some further science (for example, psychology, brain physiology, and so on).

Wittgenstein denied the realist position that reality determines the structure of language; rather language determines our view of reality. More accurately, the relation of human beings to external things (and to other human beings) is mediated by language in particular and culture in general. 'Thought' itself is immersed in social life and social action. As a consequence, practical reason takes primacy over theoretical reason. Language cannot be understood as a pictorial process. For something even to be a picture there must be an implicit interpretation of it as a picture, that is, there must be picturing. Picturing is not a structure but the activity of a cultural agent. All of this is, with some qualification, a restatement of Hume and Kant, who happen to be Hayek's favorite predecessors.

The ability to use language presupposes the ability to follow rules, but language cannot be equated with rule following. Wittgenstein asked what it meant to understand a rule. Wittgenstein denied that there was a special and unique epistemological act by which rules were grasped. Instead, in order even to follow a proof in mathematics we must be able to recognize when a rule is applied. This recognition is not the same as an explicit formulation of the rule for at each transition we are free to reject a particular application, and none of this can be formulated in advance. The final acceptance of a proof is a new decision, not entailed by previous decisions. Wittgenstein's investigation of rule application led him to reject the notion of a mechanical application of a rule. No system of rules can contain a meta-principle for the development and application of the rules. How then does communication avoid constantly breaking down? Communication works because it is embedded in what we as social agents are doing. The glue is the grounding in social practice. All meaning and all necessity is grounded in *social practice*. That is why Wittgenstein placed great stress in the *Investigations*, on the contention that sensation words do not arise from a *private language*. The notion of a private language is *incoherent*.

Human actions are not purely natural events but symbolic events relying upon tacit agreements. Recall here Hume's example of two men rowing a boat who come in time to coordinate their strokes. The meaning of such events is dependent of how the agents involved in those events perceive or understand the events. There is an institutionalized cultural background. The agents' understanding of the events is not itself explicable at some other level by reference to objects independent of the agents' attitude toward those objects.

Wittgenstein compares language to a game and reminds us that *the participants in a game change the game or cause the game to evolve by adding on new interpretations of the rules.* While a game is open-ended and cannot be definitively analyzed, it can be studied historically, and it can continue to evolve, sometimes through the conscious efforts of its participants who seek to apply the historically inherited rules to new circumstances. For Wittgenstein, there is a pre-theoretical framework of social norms that are not a matter of individual choice but which have evolved historically. These rules bind us in a given context of the activities of life. That is why Wittgenstein is not a romantic!

Hayek, following Wittgenstein, claimed that "it is probably no exaggeration to say that every important advance in economic theory during the last hundred years was a further step in the consistent application of subjectivism" (Hayek 2010, *Studies on the Abuse and Decline of Reason*, p. 94). The Hayekian argument against the possibility of socialist economic planning is a critique of the realist epistemology implicit within the socialist enterprise.

What is significant is that both thinkers (Hayek and Wittgenstein) are engaged in a sort of philosophical therapy that is central to their respective projects, by which they mean to bring us back to the non-metaphysical use of language, and to show us how the movement from everyday use to metaphysics leads to confusion and to what they argue are false conclusions. Such confusions, Hayek argues, are behind those schools of thought that hold all rules or laws must have been invented or explicitly agreed upon by somebody and are thus subject to judgment according to how well they conform to the intentions of their inventors. Among these misleading associations are the ideas of social justice and a just price. The only condition that must be adhered to is the recognition that no single substantive purpose can be understood to be the goal of society as a whole. We must tolerate the existence of multiple organizations whose members may pursue goods contrary to the goods pursued by other organizations. However, internal to this conception is the idea that toleration does not extend to the pursuit of goods that are themselves inimical to the existence of other goods. An organization devoted to the destruction of the larger civil association cannot be tolerated.

HAYEK AND THE TASK OF ECONOMICS

For Hayek, the task of economics is to explain how individuals can use the "dispersed bits of incomplete and frequently contradictory knowledge," without any single individual commanding all of that knowledge (Hayek 1945, p. 77). This is the dilemma of economic planning, the question of *who* is to do the planning in the economy. According to Hayek, there are three possible institutional frameworks within which to approach this dilemma. Planning may be:

1. Central Planning or planning "by one authority for the whole of the economic system."
2. Monopoly Planning, or "the delegation of planning to organized industries."
3. Planning by Competition, or "decentralized planning by many separate persons."

Socialists accept the notion of a metaphysically unique economic equilibrium, an intersection of supply and demand that exists independently of the market itself. Hayek argues that this notion of equilibrium is a metaphysical confusion, and that we should henceforth use the concept of 'equilibrium' only to signify the state of affairs in which all of the plans of individual economic actors are in coordination with one another. Crucial to this argument is the notion that the market order as a whole is a spontaneous rather than a planned order. Consistent with his Wittgensteinian philosophy, Hayek argues that we cannot apply standards to the spontaneous market order that only have meaning within the context of a planned order.

In the 1937 essay "Economics and Knowledge," Hayek criticizes popular notions of equilibrium. The understanding of economics against which Hayek argues is characterized by Lord Robbins's famous definition of economics as "the science which studies human behavior as a relationship between ends and scarce means which have alternative uses, that is, economics understood as the study of the allocation of scarce resources among competing ends" (Robbins 1935, p. 16). This implies the existence of a substantive equilibrium condition the contents of which are deducible from the intersection of the supply of available resources and demand, that is, from the nature of the world itself without relation to the actual market. The assumed existence of equilibrium implies that economic outcomes can or should be judged according to how closely they approach that metaphysically unique equilibrium condition.

Hayek, on the other hand, believed that equilibrium as a concept does not refer to a unique state of affairs deducible solely from the nature of the world. Equilibrium can only refer to "a *state* of equilibrium at a point of time" (Hayek 1937, p. 41). This point has no larger metaphysical significance, "but it means only that the different plans which the individuals composing it [society] have made for action in time are mutually compatible" (ibid.). This state is not one that, once reached, will remain the same forever as the idea of a metaphysically unique equilibrium implies. Rather, "equilibrium will continue, once it exists, so long as the external data correspond to the common expectations of all the members of the society" (ibid.). For Hayek then, the use of the concept of equilibrium in economics should be limited to discussing the condition that obtains when the plans of various individuals are coordinated.

In addition to challenging realist metaphysics and epistemology, Hayek questions the objective theory of value of the classical tradition. Instead of a price theory that locates the meaning of prices in the objects themselves, Hayek enunciates a subjectivist theory of prices. Hayek raises the issue in the course of explicating the conditions necessary to make sense of the apparent ability of the market to coordinate the plans of individual actors. This is the other side of his criticisms of socialist attempts to construct a rational economic order. On the one hand, socialist economic theorists appeal to unrealistic standards in support of their proposals. On the other hand, Hayek himself simply seeks to *describe* the order that he already sees in existence, to understand it, and to assess its fitness by appealing to standards discoverable within the order itself. From this methodological perspective, Hayek is carrying out the Wittgensteinian (and Humean and Smithean) philosophical project in the realm of economic theory.

Prices act as signals, consolidating and transmitting information about the relative scarcity of diverse goods. They do not, contrary to the view of the classical economists, refer to any property inherent in the goods themselves. To make this point, Hayek draws some suggestive analogies according to which we may understand the nature and role of prices: By transmitting information that otherwise would be unavailable to economic actors because of its locality, complexity, or tacit character, prices allow individuals to dovetail their plans with the plans of others without having any direct knowledge of the whole arrangement of plans. The true function of the price system is to consolidate and communicate a vast amount of both explicit and tacit knowledge, but it does so in such a way as to make the resulting order 'seem' to have been arranged by a single mind (ibid., p. 87). It is not, moreover, the quantity of knowledge that in the first instance makes the price system so necessary to the maintenance of the extended order of human cooperation. This necessity is the result of both (a) "the unavoidable imperfection of man's knowledge" and (b) the existence of "a body of very important but unorganized knowledge which cannot possibly be called scientific in the sense of knowledge of general rules" that Hayek calls "knowledge of particular circumstances of time and place" (ibid., pp. 91, 80). Based on his rejection of the realist epistemology of the socialist enterprise, Hayek believes that economics "has demonstrated conclusively" that a single mind could solve the economic problem of coordination only through prices "which cannot be derived from any property possessed by that particular thing, but which reflect, or in which is condensed, its significance in view of the whole means-end structure" (ibid., p. 85).

HAYEK AND THE IMPOSSIBILITY OF SOCIALISM

Having examined the arguments of the theories against which Hayek aims his criticisms, we are now in a position to understand what Hayek means when he writes of the logical and factual impossibility of socialism. Hayek's revolution in economics culminates in a new conception of the nature and significance of the system of market prices. It had long been argued before Hayek that prices act as rates of equivalence, allowing market participants (both buyers and sellers) to judge the relative value of goods. However, among the classical economists beginning with Adam Smith there had been a general confusion about the significance or meaning of prices. Smith, like later classical economists, believed in two distinct values: value in use and value in exchange (rooted in the labor theory of value). In practice, prices expressed value in exchange, which had some connection with the supply and demand mechanism of the market. Value in use was believed to derive from the nature of goods themselves. The labor theory of value held by the classical economists is an objective theory of value. The labor theory of value, while neither necessary nor sufficient to ground a theory of socialist economic planning, has nonetheless been a historically important part of such a theory.

Hayek argues that the substantive arrangement of the components of spontaneous orders cannot rightfully be called just or unjust. This is because they are not intended to fulfill any particular purpose, but only to provide the conditions within which individuals may pursue their own purposes. Therefore, when Hayek criticizes the phrase "social justice" and claims that the market order cannot be judged according to external standards of justice, he does not rule out the possibility or the desirability of judging the actions of individuals within the order. Nor is he opposed to imposing what are regarded as rules of just conduct on participants in the market order, so long as those rules are not designed to bring about a particular arrangement of the components of the order. Because spontaneous orders do not aim at any concrete good, such an order cannot be "corrected" except by ensuring that the principles on which it rests are consistently applied. They may be called just only insofar as the rules governing the actions of individual members are universally and consistently applied. Oakeshott will make a similar point about the justice or injustice of law.

The success of the technological project had also encouraged the Enlightenment Project view that there could be a social technology. The latter was premised on the view that every effect had a cause, and therefore all human action is caused including what we 'mistakenly' think are free choices of the will. This was a problem with which Mill wrestled throughout his lifetime but he came down on the side of believing in free will. Individuals were ultimately responsible for the choices they made.

Nevertheless, there was a gradual transition from the early nineteenth century view that poverty was a moral problem involving individual responsibility (Mill and Charles Booth) to the twentieth century view, via the Fabians, that the poverty problem is really a social problem about the equality of the working class. Whereas early nineteenth century Protestants had emphasized the difference between the "deserving poor" and the "undeserving poor," in a post-Fabian world of neoclassical economics, the poor were victims requiring social policies of reform. This greatly weakens faith in and commitment to the Lockean narrative.

Keynes and his immediate predecessors were unwilling to give full allegiance to individual autonomy. And in a world in which professionals prided themselves on being 'scientific' and wanting economics to be a science, it was easier to acquiesce in a covert acceptance of determinism and not worry about the philosophical conundrums. Hayek, on the other hand, did not shy away from the equally difficult task of defending the freedom of the will in his philosophical works. Nevertheless, in his economic works, Hayek was content to focus on the incoherence and danger of social planning.

Hayek had a profound influence both politically and theoretically. His thought influenced Margaret Thatcher who was elected as Prime Minister of the UK in 1979 and promptly ended the dominance in policy by Keynesianism. Theoretically, political economists of all persuasions took seriously the Hayekian argument against central planning especially in the wake of dramatic reversals in the former Soviet Union and China. The Rousseau narrative would not be abandoned but it would undergo a reformulation in response.

11. Locke and Keynes Arrive in the Twentieth Century US: Galbraith, Harrington, Friedman, and Rawls

GALBRAITH: SOCIALISM FIT FOR AN AFFLUENT SOCIETY

The post-World War II economic boom in the US and the accompanying economic (general prosperity), social (vast expansion of higher education and the increasing role of women in the workforce), and political changes (formal end to legal segregation) not only made the Great Depression a distant memory, but it also made it increasingly difficult to sustain the Rousseau narrative in America. That narrative was refashioned by John Kenneth Galbraith (1908–2006), Harvard Professor and leading Rousseauean public intellectual in the US serving under four democratic administrations (Roosevelt, Truman, Kennedy, and Johnson).

In *American Capitalism: The Concept of Countervailing Power* (1952), Galbraith maintains that prior to the Great Depression the old narrative had some validity in that "big business" ran America. However, since then the American economy has been managed by a triumvirate of business, labor, and government experts. In addition, economic reality had changed and required a new conception of economics. In *The Affluent Society* (1958), Galbraith argued that we have moved from an age of material poverty to an age of material "affluence."

In the 1998 Introduction to *The Affluent Society*, Galbraith takes a swipe at what he refers to as two errors in contemporary economic theory: (1) the status of poverty, and (2) the independent demand curve. The first error is that, ironically, by retaining the long term interdependency between the assumption of scarcity and the development of economic theory, we have overlooked that we are actually living, certainly in post-World War II United States, in an affluent society rather than a poor and deprived economy. As a consequence of this blind spot, we actually neglect the poor and those who live on the margins of society and, instead, we get involved in consuming unnecessary items and building armaments of war to defend the affluence. Chapter 1 of *The Affluent*

Society discusses how economic theory has clung to this myth of scarcity rather than recognize the reality of affluence and the new opportunities and responsibilities that brings. This is what will link Galbraith and Harrington. Galbraith claims that an affluent society develops a comfortable (dis)regard for the poor, and we develop a comfortable doctrine to rationalize what Harrington will call the Other America.

The concept of "conventional wisdom" (*Affluent Society*, 1998, hereafter *AS*, Chapter 2) is defined by Galbraith as a notion that has acquired widespread "acceptability." Accordingly, the current conventional wisdom among economists that scarcity is the cornerstone of economic theory is wrong. Put in terms that Galbraith would endorse, it is "obsolete" and unrelated to what is going on in the world. The conventional wisdom is what has become "acceptable" and a familiar perception of the world. One is reminded here, although Galbraith does not mention it, of the work of Kuhn dealing with the dominant paradigm and how one shifts it by thinking outside the box against the tired science of peer group reviews of acceptable inquiry. According to Galbraith, the way conventional wisdom is transcended is not by other ideas "but the march of history" (*AS*, p. 11). Smith, Ricardo and Malthus were responsible for economics being called the "dismal science;" they reflected the world in which they lived. But there was a paradigm shift in the mid-nineteenth century. Right wing Ricardians remained with the market and pessimism while left wing Ricardians (Marx) became interested in the distribution of wealth and revolution (*AS*, Chapter 3). We would argue that this is not just a new paradigm but the evolution of the Rousseau "paradigm" in constant tension with the Locke "paradigm".

Let us return to his 1998 Introduction. Galbraith asks how one replaces an old conventional wisdom with a new conventional wisdom. Interestingly, he also claims that Keynesianism has derailed liberal-left political economy from its original concern with the distribution of income to the new concern with production of goods in order to reduce unemployment. Galbraith suggests that the liberal left needs to move away from Keynesian production-employment theory to a concern with quality of life issues. But that presumes, we might add, that high unemployment and persistent income inequality is not a long term issue! Galbraith belittles the importance of production by emphasizing the useless presence of fin tails on cars and what later became the "throw away" economy. According to Galbraith, a lot of what is produced is unnecessary and entices liberals into a new government sponsored production paradigm.

This leads him to comment on a major theme of the original *Affluent Society*: "the social balance" between the public sector and the private sector. Put bluntly, Galbraith would view post-World War II Keynesians as now part of the essential problem. He would also view the attempt by Hayek and Friedman as restoring the myth of markets and individualism. Friedman and Hayek are out of touch with the march of events!

Let us focus here on the fact that he is butting heads with liberals who focus on individual equality as the core of their agenda. Perhaps he draws too stark a difference from the left on this point, but what he is after is to increase the progressive income tax to enhance social services rather than to see the money go either into the military or in pursuit of securing individual equality. The moral dimension of Galbraith's work is to avoid a dependency on increasing useless production to secure the objective of full employment.

What we can draw from this 1998 Introduction is that Galbraith identifies at least four different kinds of socialist or left-leaning approaches: (1) ownership-of-the-means-of-production socialists, the nineteenth century form, because private property is theft (look at Britain up until Thatcher where steel, coal, and communications, were state owned. Why? If decisions are in private hands then decisions will favor the few and not the many); (2) progressive-income-tax-for-individual-equality socialists (Progressives, like F.D. Roosevelt, aren't interested in owning the means of production; they don't see mortal battle between labor and capital, just the need for more balance by introducing a progressive income tax); (3) Keynesian-stimulate-production-to-solve-unemployment socialists (Keynesian socialism, with an emphasis on production; dig ditches and build infrastructure, stimulate production in order to solve unemployment; all have some sort of "democratic" character to it. Keynes would respond by saying don't talk to me about quality of life issues when unemployment is at 10 percent); and (4) social-balance socialists with which Galbraith identifies the quality of life and, thus, the quality of the environment, as the critical agenda for socialists to pursue in an affluent society. He takes credit in the 1998 Introduction also for being influential in the creation of what we would call "environmental socialism."

The Equality Narrative now shifts from production and distribution to consumption. The Galbraith model is actively taking place now as we write. Obama's first stimulus package was not targeted at social balance, it was more Keynesian; but now he is shifting toward Galbraith. Social-balance people would be very upset about propping up Microsoft or the Chevy Malibu. They say we need hybrids and bike lanes and mountain trails and park benches planned every 20 yards or so surrounded by natural habitat. This sort of environmental policy from a Keynesian view point is a luxury. Keynesians don't do anything to stop "useless" production. Social balance persons, on the other hand, want to separate production questions from unemployment.

What is least likely to be successful today is the first or nineteenth century form of socialism. That is not to say that Americans are all center right, but American people have a tendency to give you only two years. Roosevelt was fortunate that he had longer than two years. Galbraith is a post Keynesian, not focused on creating jobs per se but on creating quality jobs. Similarly, the 'newer' left is interested in cultural issues, not just production. The role of government is far greater in the Equality Narrative than in the Liberty Narrative, and it grows even greater when equality expands to include the quality of life. If I am talking about social balance then I go green. Galbraith's criticism is of a throw-away society.

In Chapter 7, on inequality, Galbraith states that economic inequality has become a declining issue in modern social history. And the big reasons are that government regulation has replaced social revolution and that the call to do something about inequality has less pull in an affluent society. It is the increase in output in recent decades, not the redistribution of income, which has brought the great material increase in the well-being of the average person. And, "however suspiciously, the liberal has come to accept the fact" (*AS*, p. 79).

Anyone reading the *Affluent Society* today should not only ponder the above claim about the lack of material poverty but also read his early chapters on the emergence of economic theory as trapped in the myth of scarcity. Moreover, that is the myth to which too many contemporary economists are attached. One important consequence of the attachment to the conventional wisdom is that too many of us believe that the production of goods and services is the measure of progress and civilized living. The nature of poverty has also changed, although Rousseau and Marx presaged this as well. An increase in wealth is not a proof of economic and societal health. There is a comfortable disregard for those who are marginalized. Poverty is no longer central. The existence of poverty becomes even more shameful because old excuses don't work anymore.

There are still numerous social problems including environmental degradation. Galbraith explains why in *The New Industrial State* (Galbraith 1967). "Conventional wisdom" explains economic activity as a competitive market ruled by consumer sovereignty. On the contrary, businesses control consumers through advertising. Specifically in the industrial sector, large and powerful corporations control commercial culture, social values, and ultimately politics. It finances a huge military-industrial complex (Eisenhower). These corporations are primarily interested in increasing their personal wealth through increased commodity production. Markets are incapable of providing for public goods. So-called conservative thought (Lockean narrative) is no more than the search for a superior moral justification for selfishness.

The independent demand curve problem is probably his main contribution to economic theory both in the *Affluent Society* and in the *New Industrial State*. His main point is that first you produce the goods then you make the market. Supply only creates its own demand by advertising and salesmanship. Thus we need to abandon the myth of consumer sovereignty. This is a critique of microeconomic theory. He criticizes the assumption that one can draw a demand curve separate from a supply curve. Galbraith is saying this is a basic fallacy because things are produced and then you have advertising, which creates demand, so the basic demand curve and supply curve are not separate. At the core of Galbraith's Equality Narrative is that (some) people are unable to take care of themselves, including making basic choices concerning their income, living, and so on. Part of the reason is that the corporate world bamboozles them with ads, "buy, buy, buy!" It is not that people are just simply incapable but that they have been tricked. Part of the narrative is that the reason you can't take care of yourself is that the corporate world isn't letting you. The crucial issue between Hayek and Galbraith will boil down to this: the former thinks that people learn from their mistakes and the latter thinks that people don't understand their self-interest because they are being hood winked. This is Locke versus Rousseau revisited.

In his 1998 Introduction Galbraith admits that he did not foresee as much income inequality as persisted over the 50 years since the publication of his original volume. But we get the clear message that this underestimation of inequality is not a major concession to his original call for a shift in paradigm thinking. Keynesianism reintroduced the Smithean concern of production and moved the left from a nineteenth century concern with distribution. But the Keynes–Government alliance in the twentieth century has replaced, and successfully so, the Smith–Market alliance of the eighteenth century. Thus income inequality – an essentially nineteenth century socialist conventional wisdom distribution question – has been replaced by the twentieth century conventional wisdom of Keynesian production theory. It is time, Galbraith seems to be arguing, for political economists to return to the nineteenth century distribution issue and away from their flirtation with production questions (see Chapter 13 on Piketty, this volume). We need to turn away from recovery through production to reform through redistribution. But we need, Galbraith continues, a further redistribution paradigm for the twentieth and twenty-first centuries. And that is reform in the unequal distribution in physical resources and mental energy devoted to the public and private sectors. In short, what we need is redistributive environmental socialism.

With Galbraith, the Rousseau narrative has moved the focus from production, and even from distribution, to consumption. The problem is no longer the technological project, nor even the market economy when it is truly a market, nor limited government but what the government focuses upon. Of course, Galbraith wants uncoerced choices, but it is not clear whether he is advocating authentic choices (a la Kant and Mill) or fulfilling choices. If it's the latter, who gets to decide that? Galbraith wants social-balance political economy.

HARRINGTON: LIBERTY, EQUALITY, AND THE OTHER AMERICA

Michael Harrington (1928–89), originally a product of the Catholic Social Justice tradition, was best known as the leading intellectual voice of the 1960s Social Democratic movement in the US. Even after he lost his religious faith, he continued to believe that the whole of the human race was an enterprise association with a collective goal which obligated each and every one of us to be responsible for the whole of humanity.

Harrington made his way into the new left and built on Galbraith by assuming the age of affluence is here so what poverty remains stands out as a sore thumb that should be eradicated. Harrington consciously acknowledges the work of Galbraith and then urges us to move beyond Galbraith's articulation of "case poverty" and "insular poverty" in the *Affluent Society*. We have instead "*a culture of poverty*" rather than an affluent society that satisfies pseudo needs rather than real needs (Harrington 1962, *The Other America*, p. 158). This culture of poverty is the *Other America*. Poverty becomes more than an economic question; it's now a cultural question: The "other" America represents the culture of poverty against the culture of affluence.

Harrington was a socialist, driven by Catholic social justice, who embraced the role of non-governmental agencies rather than just an old fashioned socialist who thought the central government should own the means of production and run the entire show. True, he endorsed government planning, but what should not be overlooked is Harrington's belief that if the affluent American people only saw the "invisible poor," then their conscience would respond to the moral outrage and scandal of the situation. He defines poverty as "those who are denied the minimum levels of health, housing, food and education that our present stage of scientific knowledge specifies as necessary for life as it is now lived in the United States" (Harrington 1962, p. 175).

Harrington engaged in a protracted debate with fellow Irish-American Catholic Daniel Patrick Moynihan, who espoused the Lockean narrative and who Harrington dubbed a "neoconservative." What Moynihan doesn't see, according to Harrington, is that the issue is a systemic one located in the very culture of poverty. The issue for Harrington is not as it was for Moynihan a matter of parenting, or of legal and political equality. The poor are victims of a lack of resources; the resources are available in our affluent society; and the failure to extend those resources is neither exploitation nor even selfishness but a moral blindness. Americans should feel guilty, not about what they have done, but what they have failed to do and toward which they turn a blind eye.

Part of the problem of ending poverty, which even Galbraith does not capture because of his focus on affluence, is that there is "a culture of poverty" (Harrington 1962, pp. 16, 61). This culture is imposed by white racism (p. 71). "The Negro is classically the 'other' American" (Harrington 1962, p. 72). For the Negro to be equal requires a transform-ation of the basic institutional structure of America. This won't happen until the Negro is no longer poor. Harrington focuses on "The Rejects" of society. There is an "economic underworld" of "victims" in each city where both management and labor racketeers operate. They were born poor; America expects blacks to be poor (Harrington 1962, p. 24).

He says clearly that with respect to the poor, in general, we pay a high price for wives working, the impoverishment of home life, and less time for the children (p. 179). We need a cultural change (p. 79). Unfortunately, the "Great Society" program just hasn't worked he says in an appendix to a later edition of his book. He claims that a quarter of all Americans are living in poverty, and they are living hopeless and humiliating lives. Seemingly pointing back to FDR's claim that one-third were living in poverty, he says 50 million Americans are living in misery. This should be a moral outrage. The American people should be ashamed (pp. 176–91). We will not eliminate poverty, he says, until we accept the 100 percent solution. The notion of joining affluent America is not a reality for poor people; rather it is a "taunt" against the rejects (Harrington 1962, p. 28). America has rejected an entire class of people.

"In morality and in justice every citizen should be committed to abolishing the other America for it is intolerable that the richest country in the world should allow such needless suffering. But more than that, if we solve the problem of the other America we will have learned how to solve the problems of all America" (Harrington 1962, p. xxix). Unfortunately, there is a "smug moralism" in affluent America as if the poor actually have a choice! They can't move. More importantly, we have the technology to provide every citizen with a decent life.

Harrington takes on Adam Smith directly with regard to how to measure the economic condition: it is an indignity to tell the American poor that they are better off than the Indian poor or the tribesmen of Africa! (Harrington 1962, pp. 17, 158). New definitions of human standards of living emerge over time and we should keep up with that change: today in America, a considerable number of people suffer below what is possible (Harrington 1962, p. 178). In a manner reminiscent of Rousseau, Harrington warns that even if the standard of living of the poorest members of society is raised above subsistence their relative poverty leads to social unrest.

So what is his standard of measurement: how much better things could be only if we stirred? (Harrington 1962, p. 18). The Welfare State is simply not enough. We need a better vision. We need a passion to end poverty. The Welfare State wasn't built for the desperate and hopeless and violent. So there is no sense in making the poor the wards of the state. Yet he suggests we need to extend the Welfare State from covering one-third of the people to all the people (Harrington 1962, p. 167). We should have social security for all. We need a comprehensive medical program. We need to end the illusion that charitable contributions will end poverty. We need a social movement led by liberals and labor rather than party politics as usual. At the same time we need to create a new human environment. We need to house the Other America within affluent America (Harrington 1962, p. 167).

Housing is the crucial element in solving racial poverty (Harrington 1962, p. 79). How is the housing policy to be achieved? Planning rather than the invisible hand will solve the housing problem. We also need billions of dollars in social investment so that every citizen has what he is entitled to: a decent job or an adequate income. We also need a guaranteed income with a work incentive. "Every citizen has a right to a decent job or to an adequate income" (Harrington 1962, p. xxvii). That is how we end the outrage of the Other America. He says (Harrington 1962, p. xvi) that we need bold innovations that go beyond the New Deal. The objective is to eliminate poverty. And we need to realize that we are faced with a segment of the population that is "locked into a hopeless social existence acquired by accident of birth." Unfortunately, says Harrington, the anti-poverty program was undermined by the cost of the Vietnam War (Harrington 1962, p. xx). "The greatest opportunity for social change since the New Deal was sacrificed to the tragedy in Vietnam" (Harrington 1962, p. 205). There were also the deaths (assassinations) of Martin Luther King and Robert F. Kennedy. Harrington wished to go beyond the New Deal also in the area of planning: "There should be an Office of the Future attached to the Presidency" (Harrington 1962, p. xxiv).

A major part of the Appendices of Harrington's book is devoted to measuring poverty since the release of the book. Apparently Presidents John F. Kennedy and Lyndon B. Johnson were moved by Harrington's argument to end poverty in America. But, by 1969, Harrington declared the "unconditional war" against poverty by the Great Society to be a failure. In every crucial area, says Harrington, the United States provides its worst off citizens only a percentage of what they desperately need: food, housing, education, and social services. Some programs did work: unemployment declined, Food Stamps made a difference, so did Job Training, and social security increased. However, the same groups that were poor in 1960 are poor in 1970. The living conditions in the inner cities are simply intolerable. Concerning the 1980s, he says the evidence indicates that to win the war on poverty requires more radical departures in economic and social policy than President Johnson ever imagined. The problem is rooted in institutions and not programs. We can't accept 5 percent unemployment (as does Friedman) as full employment. The future political movements have to be more imaginative and more militant than those in the 1980s.

Harrington did not address the question of how we are to explain the existence of those Americans born under less than ideal conditions whose super achievements have made them into cultural heroes, nor does he explain the existence of those Americans born and raised in what many would consider ideal circumstances but who become members of the culture of poverty. Nor did he address the arguments (Charles Murray) that some government programs actually exacerbated the culture of poverty. Harrington never wavered in his faith in what we have called the Enlightenment Project, the belief that there could be a social technology. He remained committed to the therapeutic view that every social problem could be solved, and where previous programs had failed it was because we had not gone deep enough in understanding the problem.

Locke's *Second Treatise* and Smith's *Wealth of Nations* heavily stress the idea of improvement rather than perfection. By what means is this improvement to take place? And how will you defend yourself against the charge of a lack of compassion for the impossible dream of perfection? Why shouldn't there be a guarantee that everyone should benefit and that there be no losers? In response, Locke and his successors see that the arts and sciences (the practical arts and sciences) will be used to improve society. Locke would argue that this improvement would necessitate schooling in Business, Law, and Public Policy. They would also suggest that we do not fully understand and cannot repair some forms of social dysfunction.

In Keynes' version of the Rousseau narrative the focus was changed from the distribution of wealth to the production of wealth. In the versions of Galbraith and Harrington the focus was changed from the production of the wealth of the nation to the securing of the welfare of the nation through a proper consumption of wealth. In that respect, the Great Society was qualitatively different from the New Deal. Nevertheless, what all three thinkers have in mind is defining or redefining the nation in terms of some sort of great communal enterprise to be administered by experts like themselves.

LOCKE REDUX: FRIEDMAN AND THE FREEDOM TO CHOOSE

Milton Friedman (1912–2006) was an influential member of the economics program at the University of Chicago, a senior fellow at the Hoover Institution, and leading Lockean public intellectual of the Republican Party in general and President Ronald Reagan in particular. He was present at Hayek's founding meeting of the Mont Pelerin society in 1947. One could argue that from 1950 to 1980 the Liberty Narrative went underground and on the defensive, but Friedman remained its chief and best known spokesperson in the US.

Although a severe critic of Keynes, Friedman embraced a macroeconomic theory he called *monetarism*, in which there is alleged to be a natural rate of unemployment of 5 percent (contra both Galbraith and Harrington), that government could at best only increase employment above this rate, and that government could do this by increasing aggregate demand but only when inflation was accelerating. In principle opposed to the Federal Reserve, he sought to limit its damage by suggesting that there be only a small and steady increase of the money supply consonant with economic growth. In retrospect, the Great Depression was the result of a contraction in the money supply, a contraction for which Hoover's administration had been responsible. This is also why Friedman opposes the gold standard because it ignores the necessity for monetary growth.

Specifically, Friedman critiqued the Keynesian economist William Phillips and his formulation of the so-called Phillips curve. The latter asserted the existence of an inverse relationship between unemployment and inflation, such that unemployment could be reduced at a calculable cost to inflation. Friedman famously denied the existence of this relation-ship and predicted that unemployment and inflation (*stagflation*) could exist at the same time, and his prediction turned out to be true in the 1970s, paving the way for Reagan's defeat of Carter in 1980.

Friedman's most influential book, and his clear statement of the Lockean narrative, is *Capitalism and Freedom* (Friedman 1962). Fried-man saw a constructive role for limited government to play. But what he warned about was the alternative between a free society and a collectivist society. Accordingly, whether by coincidence or co-relation, Friedman claims that you cannot have a free society without a free economy. He never says that with a free economy must come a free society. It is a necessary but not a sufficient condition. Friedman states that political freedom is impossible without economic (and social) freedom. The two choices are the market or control. It is not clear that with economic freedom political freedom inevitably follows. His support of economic reforms in Chile is a positive example. He thought that Hong Kong was the ideal model. But that was before the take over and, even when he said so, it was a British colony. And how do we explain twenty-first century China in terms of economic freedom/control–political freedom/control matrix? His dichotomy is between individual liberty and collectivist control. Thus, he objected to John F. Kennedy's Inaugural Speech in 1961, which stressed "ask what you can do for your country." We need to emphasize that by political freedom, Friedman does not mean majority rule. Freedom, generally, he sees as a means to satisfy individual ends and reaching the highest indifference curve.

Friedman advances two main measures of the size of government and the corresponding level of freedom of the individual. The two work in opposite directions. One measure of freedom for Friedman is government spending as a percentage of national income. His goal is 10 percent; this last took place in 1928. By the end of World War II it was at 36 percent, but fell to 20 percent by 1947. By 1980 it was 40 percent which he calls the result of the galloping socialism of Medicare and the Welfare State. So it would seem that the bigger threat to freedom for Friedman was the Great Society rather than the New Deal. From the New Deal on, and we see this vividly in the post 1960s, the biggest excuse for the expansion of government programs has been to solve unemployment. This policy has been followed on the assumption that where the money comes from does not matter.

We need to compare the Keynesian brand of Socialism where govern-ment gets involved in solving unemployment with the other forms of socialism introduced by Galbraith, and Harrington. No kind of socialism can be justified on liberal principles, says Friedman. But do we know the

point at which a government exchanges freedom for one or another form
of socialism and collectivism? During the "Reagan Revolution" of the
1980s, and until 2005, the rate of government spending as a percentage
of national income fell to 35 percent. By 2008, it was back up to 40
percent and since 2010 plus 50 percent. Does this mean that we were
freer during the Reagan plus years and less free in the twenty-first
century? Friedman would say "yes."

The amount and kind of government regulation over our daily life is
the second measure of individual freedom. He has a list of 14 government regulations that he claims are inconsistent with a free society. Here
are the 14 items: (1) parity price supports; (2) tariffs; (3) output control;
(4) rent control; (5) minimum wage laws; (6) industrial regulation
(Inter-state Commerce Commission); (7) speech regulation (Federal
Communications Commission); (8) social security (Social Security
Administration); (9) licenses; (10) public housing (Federal Housing
Authority); (11) military conscription (since repealed); (12) national
parks; (13) the US Post Office; and (14) toll roads.

Not on the list is education, but Friedman devotes a lot of time arguing
against a government monopoly in education. He argues that vouchers in
both public and private schools are preferable to government control. The
real problem in education is that we combine the administration of
schools with their financing. Currently, there is an under-investment in
human capital relative to physical capital. We must avoid the government
interfering in the form of offering subsidies and engaging in redistribution. Similarly, licenses are a serious restraint on economic freedom.
Unlike registration and certification, licenses are the most difficult to
justify on freedom grounds.

He objects to government not only being involved in solving
unemployment, but also being involved in promoting the equality of
income distribution. He asks, what is the justification for the role of
government in this redistribution project? What is wrong with the
principle of from each according to his capability to each according to
his productivity? He thus rejects the Marx model from each according to
his capability to each according to his needs. Thus, he is not in favor of
a progressive income tax; rather he favors a flat tax in conjunction with a
negative income tax. He says: "one cannot be both an egalitarian ... and
a liberal" (Friedman 1962, p. 195). Furthermore, Friedman is uninter-
ested in the distribution question: the distinction between wealth acquired
by inheritance and wealth acquired by ability is untenable (Friedman
1962, p. 164).

On social issues, Friedman was a libertarian. Friedman was in favor of
legalizing marijuana. What bothers him is the issue of both government

and private monopoly, and there is a similar line in Smith. Friedman might suggest a health saving account rather than an Obama style health system. Friedman would not be in favor of pouring more money into education but rather parents getting vouchers. He would be happy with Fed Ex and UPS competing with the United States Postal Service. Some were surprised by Friedman's recommendation on the one hand that business leaders did not need to have a strong social conscience and that the family rather than the individual was the basic unit of analysis. Private philanthropy was where individuals could express their personal morality and where entrepreneurial business-models could flourish.

In the Conclusion, Friedman argues that intellectuals in the 1920s and 1930s became converted to an ideal collectivist society. They compared the actual with the ideal. But he invites us to compare the actual with the actual. How did Marxism play out in Russia? How have our own programs played out? Why do programs fail? They fail because the values of outsiders replace the values of insiders. The do-gooders spend our money for our good! And then they spin the yarn that "robber Barons" are the root of our problem. We need to change our idea of "social responsibility" back to the idea of "individual responsibility."

One might sum up Hayek and Friedman in the following way: Hayek was fighting hard core European socialism and in that regard had a profound impact on Margaret Thatcher. Friedman was fighting the regulatory state of the American Progressives and in that regard had a profound impact on Ronald Reagan.

THE IRONY OF INHERITANCE

Friedman's version of the Lockean Narrative (nowadays often referred to as classical liberalism) was great at breaking new ground, at challenging the then Keynesian status quo, but it wasn't as good at defending the ground it had broken. If labor is the cause of value – Locke and Smith for example argue this against the feudal and mercantilist theory of value – what happens when the Labor Theory of Value is appropriated by the Marxists? And what if the friends of the market turn to defending maximizing the highest individual preference curve regardless of the quality or morality of the curve of preference?

If one argues – as Locke and Smith most certainly did – against the rule of inheritance to distribute property – the feudal model – what happens when Friedman is no longer breaking ground against feudal property but defending 200 years plus of new ground defending work as the claim of private property? Do you become a defender of inheritance –

like Friedman – or do you, like John Stuart Mill, wrestle with the notion that the economic theory of distribution is of no help; is it simply who is in charge of social mores?

And why should the mores change – as surely they have changed for example under Friedman – to defend inheritance because the unit of analysis is not really the individual anymore but the family? That is why Friedman can argue against inheritance taxes. Is there not an irony here? Lockean individualism and the rugged individual sort of belong together. If we move from the individual to the family, are we talking about "rugged familyism"? But is this a good enough defense against inheritance taxes if other members of your family did not work a day in their lives? Where does the right of inheritance come from if not from labor and self-reliance and self-responsibility? If not then we are right back to the Middle Ages and the capitalist attack on the distribution of property under feudalism.

RAWLS: A NEW EGALITARIAN ORTHODOXY

John Rawls (1921–2002) was a Harvard political philosopher and Fulbright Fellow at Oxford. He was praised by President Bill Clinton for helping a whole generation of learned Americans revive their faith in democracy.

More importantly, Rawls contributed something very important to the Rousseau Narrative in the twentieth century in his highly influential book *A Theory of Justice* (Rawls 1971). As we saw in the previous chapter, utilitarianism proved to be a dead-end for rationalizing Keynesian macroeconomics. In this chapter we have seen so far how Galbraith and Harrington have moved the focus to the social issues; but their prescriptions for reform, as opposed to their diagnosis, seem to imply that Rousseaueans want some kind of orthodoxy rather than toleration in economics, politics, and religion. Is the real purpose of the left in the twenty-first century not to expand liberty but to impose a new orthodoxy in the name of everyone or the whole world? "Will" seems to replace choice and feelings replace judgment.

Normative thinking came back to life in philosophy or was officially and canonically resurrected in the work of John Rawls. Rawls is aware of the two narratives: "There is a divide between the tradition derived from Locke ... and the tradition derived from Rousseau" (Rawls 2001, *Justice as Fairness*, p. 2). He attributed to Rousseau the honor of being the first to acknowledge the importance of inequalities: "The first great figure on this subject seems to have been Rousseau in his *Discourse on Inequality*" (ibid., p. 130, n50).

According to Rawls, no Lockean, in fact no one, deserves what they have regardless of how they acquired it. The reason for this is that we are all products of the genetic lottery and the historically accidental family circumstances into which we were born. That being the case, we need a philosophical justification for any form of distribution; otherwise the powerful will simply impose one on the weak. Moreover, we are now in a position to explain the smug moral blindness that Harrington claimed was the rationalization for why the successful think they do not have to care about the unsuccessful. Lockeans are smug because they mistakenly believe they deserve their privileges because they earned them. The notion that certain privileged folks have constructed a false narrative in order to put one huge something over on the innocent and *victimized* many is central to the Equality Narrative. This is the Rousseauean origin of all victimization narratives. Citing Rousseau's *Emile*, Rawls asserts that the feeling of resentment in children is fundamentally correct because they sense when "they are unfairly treated … one could say to conservative writers that it is mere grudgingness when those better circumstanced reject the claims of the less advantaged to greater equality" (Rawls 1971, *Theory of Justice*, p. 540). Affluent and successful individuals who agree with Rawls' genetic and social determinism reflect what has been called "white guilt."

So what is the correct theory of distribution? What is the new social contract? Starting with the Rousseauean assumption that no social order is legitimate unless founded on an original unanimous consent to procedure, Rawls postulates a hypothetical "original position" in which individuals are said to choose principles of justice "behind a veil of ignorance." As in Rousseau, we enter society naked and give up all claims to previous property and advantages. Choices must be made with no knowledge of one's place in society, class position or social status; nor does anyone know his/her natural assets and abilities, intelligence, strength, or sex. What sort of knowledge can be the basis of the choices? The answer Rawls gives is general facts about human society and the laws of human psychology. Presumably, the social sciences provide us with those facts that will serve as the foundations of social and political theory. The veil of ignorance is meant to nullify the effects of specific contingencies which put men at odds and tempt them to exploit social and natural circumstances to their own advantage. This cannot mean their "real" advantage but only their "apparent" advantage. Hence, it is clear that Rawls presupposes that each individual would under natural or ideal

circumstances have a well-being that is defined relative to some harmonious holistic view of society (General Will). Rawls maintains that
everyone's well-being is dependent upon a scheme of cooperation
without which no one could have a satisfactory life. In making this
assumption, Rawls is relieved of the necessity for proving that self-
interest requires cooperation or coordination (something utilitarians cannot prove).

We might raise the question of why human beings would be tempted to
exploit specific contingencies. This cannot be a law of human psychology
because individuals behind the veil of ignorance will be allowed to know
all of the laws of human psychology. Hence, the temptation to exploit
circumstances must be one of those deterministic environmental circumstances which deflect individual human beings from their true ends. It is
also consistent with that part of the Rousseau narrative that presupposes
the existence of exploiters. We cannot see any basis for nullification
unless human beings have a natural teleology which defines their "real"
self-interest.

In the original position, choosers will operate with the *maximin rule*:
they will rank alternatives by their worst possible outcomes and adopt the
alternative the worst outcome of which is superior to the worst outcomes
of the others. There is a presumption here that human beings are
fundamentally risk-averse so that the fundamental consensus decision
protects us against the worst possible outcome. There is already here an
assumption that human beings are fundamentally risk-averse and a veiled
aversion to the notion of entrepreneurial economic growth. Keep this
assumption in mind when we discuss Oakeshott in the next chapter.

Two principles of justice then emerge:

1.   Each person is to have an equal right to the most extensive total
      system of equal basic liberties compatible with a similar system of
      liberty for all. These liberties are positive and require reference to
      some social whole (General Will) in order to resolve potential
      conflicts. Kant had argued for the primacy of liberty, and in this
      Rawls claims to be following Kant. As even friendly critics have
      pointed out, Rawls fails to establish the primacy of liberty. More-
      over, Kant had argued against the belief in both determinism and
      the view that justice was in any way concerned with teleology and
      self-fulfillment. Kant advocated fundamental human autonomy; he
      argued that redistribution treats persons as a means to the good of
      others. This is precisely where Rawls departs from Kant. Without
      some further Rousseauean notion of transcending individualism
      through membership in the ethical life of the community, Rawls'

position appears as no more than a popular though logically private political agenda. As Stuart Hampshire noted in his review, Rawls' analysis "is certainly the model of social justice that has governed the advocacy of R.H. Tawney and Richard Titmus and that holds the Labour Party together" (Hampshire 1972, *New York Review of Books*).

2.   Social and economic inequalities are to be to the greatest benefit of the least advantaged (*Difference Principle*). The difference principle is a response to socialist concerns about equality. It is a way of arguing that given the original position we understand how self-interest is tied to the interest of others.

The discussion of *maximin* does not differentiate between relative and absolute disadvantages (for example, basic versus minimal needs). This leads to the suspicion that for Rawls the main concern is with how each views oneself relative to others. This suspicion is borne out by Rawls' contention that the most important primary good is self-esteem coupled with the view that self-esteem depends upon how we see ourselves through the eyes of others. This is the exact opposite of what Kant and Mill had both said about personal autonomy.

A case can be made that in *Political Liberalism* (Rawls 1993) and *Justice as Fairness* (Rawls 2001), Rawls seriously qualified or even changed his position. Nevertheless, it is the *Theory of Justice* that has had the lasting impact.

12. Hayek and Oakeshott: Making a New Case for Liberty

INTRODUCTION: REVISITING THE PHILOSOPHICAL PILLAR OF LIBERTY

Readers might be surprised by the continued connection we draw among philosophy, politics, and economics. There are several reasons for revisiting Hayek even as we focus on Oakeshott in this chapter. Differences aside, both were deeply concerned with philosophical foundations and for a while were colleagues at the London School of Economics. It is the shared Wittgensteinian philosophical perspective that explains (1) their marginalization by the philosophic community, (2) their vehement rejection of the Rousseau Equality Narrative and (3) their trenchant critique of economic planning or government regulation. In addition, (4) they focused on an aspect of the two narratives that had been largely neglected until the late nineteenth century, namely, the 'rule of law'. They argued, in effect, that the Liberty Narrative needed a new philosophical foundation.

PHILOSOPHY IN THE TWENTIETH CENTURY

The academically dominant philosophical movements in the twentieth century were based on scientism, that is, the view that science is the whole truth about everything, and the job of philosophy is to spell out the implications of that view. One of the implications of that view is that there is or should be social science – the explanation, prediction, and control of social phenomena. This is the agenda of the Enlightenment Project, specifically to formulate and implement a social technology. The articulation, defense, advocacy or implementation of this social technology is what later adherents of the Equality Narrative have urged: for example, the Marx–Engels version of scientific socialism, the Progressives' notion of the administration of things, Keynesian macroeconomics, and so on. By its very nature, scientism looks for the alleged generic truths about humanity (Rawls), that the promise of human fulfilment consists in acting consistently with these truths, that is, in subordinating our will, and therefore these generic truths allegedly entail a harmonious collective conception of social organization. For all of these reasons, the ascendency of scientism poses a serious challenge to the Liberty Narrative.

The philosophic origins of scientism go back to classical Greek philosophy, specifically its espousal of the view that knowledge is the reflection of a structure independent of human beings. This conception of knowledge is called epistemological realism. Classical philosophy, the philosophy of the Greeks, Romans, and most of medieval thought asserted that knowledge is the grasping of an external structure in objects themselves. This view of knowledge is historically associated with adherence to the idea that society is a collective enterprise administered by elite wise men (philosopher kings or clergy) who alone are capable of grasping this structure. We say 'historically' because there is no necessary logical reason why, prior to actual empirical confirmation, we should assume harmony either within the individual or within a social whole. The harmony assumption reflected the classical belief (hope and faith) that explanation had to be teleological.

Modern philosophers as early as Descartes began chipping away at this view of knowledge, and this culminated in the works of Hume (alleged to be a skeptic) and Kant who proclaimed the Copernican Revolution in Philosophy. The latter two opposed epistemological realism and asserted that knowledge was a structure imposed upon experience by human beings. This view of knowledge is historically associated with the advocacy of the Liberty Narrative.

In opposition to this Humean/Kantian theory of knowledge, nineteenth century philosophical positivism reasserted epistemological realism and proclaimed physical science as the vehicle for accessing the objective structure of the world independent of human structuring. Moreover, it was postulated that science could totally explain human beings. The resurgence of epistemological realism in its positivist form gave new life to the eighteenth century program of the Enlightenment Project, designed to discover the objective structure of the social world along with enabling the derivative development of a social technology. In the nineteenth century, Auguste Comte, the major French social positivist (ultimately provoking Mill's ire) and Marx's scientific socialism are the premier examples. Curiously, even though this post-Newtonian scientism assumed that explanation had to be ultimately mechanistic instead of teleological, it also allowed that underlying mechanistic explanation was compatible with teleology.

In the twentieth century, the epistemological realism and a derivative social technology were espoused by the so-called Vienna Circle (Schlick, Carnap, Reichenbach, Neurath, Popper, and so on) whose members eventually migrated to the US as a consequence of the rise of Nazism and World War II. These positivists and their progeny not only dominated the discipline of philosophy but they had an enormous impact on the methodology of the social sciences. In the positivism of the Vienna Circle one sees optimism about how science is the successful elimination of superstition and nonsense and how philosophy is the intellectual overseer of the transition period to a totally scientific world view.

The *Manifesto* of the Vienna Circle endorsed the idea of regulating economic and social life according to rational principles. Carnap asserted:

> that the great problems of the organization of the economy and the organ-
> ization of the world at the present time, in the era of industrialization, cannot
> possibly be solved by the 'interplay of forces', but require rational planning.
> For the organization of [the] economy this means socialism in some form; for
> the organization of the world it means a gradual development towards a world
> government. (Carnap 1963, "My philosophical development," in P.A. Schilpp
> (ed.), *The Philosophy of Rudolf Carnap*, p. 83)

Neurath argued that after seeing the fruits of central economic planning during wartime (World War I), market economies would be replaced by a communal economy. "In a socialized economy the living standards and wages of everybody will be fixed by ... decrees ... they will not be decided by contract" (Neurath [1919] 1973, *Through War Economy to Economy in Kind*). Given human fallibility, Popper concluded that social technology should be used but central planning ought not to be. As we progress in scientific knowledge there should be a corresponding growth in the area that central planners can legitimately control. Although totalitarian control is unacceptable, we can have ever increasing growth by social planning. The totalitarian implications of Popper's conception of social engineering, despite its intention, has been duly noted and criticized by F.A. Hayek (*Law, Legislation, and Liberty*, 1973), despite the fact that Popper dedicated his book *Conjectures and Refutations* (Popper 1963) to Hayek.

THE PHILOSOPHY OF THE LIBERTY NARRATIVE IN HAYEK AND OAKESHOTT

Hayek and Oakeshott returned to the views of Hume and Kant's Copernican Revolution in Philosophy. In the *Critique of Pure Reason*

(1781), Kant rejected the classical epistemological notion that cognitive knowledge must conform to objects and replaced it with the exact opposite contention, namely, that objects must conform to our cognition. Standards are not external but internal. In the classical world, the epistemological challenge was to identify the alleged external standard, and the practical challenge was for human beings to conform to the external standards. In the modern Copernican world, the epistemological challenge is to identify the internal standards and the practical challenge is to transform the physical world to conform to the internal standards. Conforming to internal standards does not mean adjusting ourselves to the world, rather it means adjusting the world to ourselves.

Two things should be immediately evident. First the technological project, the transformation of the physical world for human benefit, is intelligible only in the light of this philosophical transformation. In retrospect, this is already present in the views of Bacon, Descartes (who spearheaded the modern scientific rejection of the medieval Aristotelian teleological view of the universe) and Locke. The technological project is a state of mind, an attitude, a fundamentally different way of conceiving the relationship of human beings to the physical world.

Second, the transition from classical epistemology to modern epistemology makes possible the transition from a collectivist or communitarian enterprise association to an individualist civil association. The defense of a collectivist enterprise association can never adequately rest simply on the notion that it is a human 'construct', even a universal 'construct'. It is much easier to demand the subordination and allegiance of the individual to an external collective goal if that goal is absolute and independent of human construction. To carry the argument a little bit further, once the social world itself is viewed as a construct, and once the 'imagination' is released from its subordination to 'reason', it is but a short step to the view that all authority is rooted in the 'consent' of the governed. Again, this is already present in Locke. In turn, one might even construe alternative human constructs as an embarrassment of riches rather than a problem to be overcome. It is a short step to conclude that the entire political and legal world should serve the interests of individuals. Given the existence of moral pluralism, it will be asked – what system of law and politics is most consistent with that moral pluralism? – the answer will be civil association that is premised on individual autonomy. The coordination problem is solved by appeal to voluntarily accepted procedural norms rather than agreement on substantive norms.

More importantly, from the perspective of the Copernican Revolution in Philosophy, the very idea of a social technology is bogus and a non-sequitur. Human beings create the epistemological constructs, including science (now viewed as experimental and technological). Physical science is a human construct. It is therefore impossible, and nonsensical, to use physical science to try to describe the structure of the social world or even to explain in physical scientific ways (physics, chemistry, biology, artificial intelligence, and so on) how and why human beings structure the world in the way they do. The tool maker explains the tool; the tool does not explain the maker. In philosophical jargon, the pre-conceptual cannot be conceptualized:

> David Hume and Immanuel Kant ... . It was they who came nearer than anybody has done since to a clear recognition of the status of values as independent and guiding conditions of all rational construction. What I am ultimately concerned with here ... [is the] destruction of values by scientific error ... . The tendency of constructivism to represent those values which it cannot explain as determined by arbitrary human decisions ... rather than as the necessary conditions of facts which are taken for granted by its expounders, has done much to shake the foundations of civilization, and of science itself, which also rests on values which cannot be scientifically proved. (Hayek 1973, *Law, Legislation, and Liberty*, p. 7)

HAYEK: A NEGLECTED ASPECT OF SPONTANEOUS ORDER

Hayek is among the heirs to the Copernican Revolution in Philosophy, a revolution which he carries into the sphere of economics and law. A realist epistemology presupposes that there is a real objective order to the social world, including the economy, and that it is possible to conceptualize that order. Hayek maintains that (a) there is a market order, but (b) the market order is spontaneous (unplanned) – hence has no externally induced overall purpose, and (c) it is not possible to conceptualize that order. It is not possible to conceptualize that order because there is in the market a background of inarticulable knowledge. The market order is an example of spontaneous order, which Hayek describes as a discovery procedure. Competition is a process of creative discovery (Schumpeter's "creative destruction"), the discovery of new products, services, and the creation of new preferences. Entrepreneurship creates new opportunities, new states of affairs. Reading Hayek in light of Oakeshott's first essay of *On Human Conduct* (Oakeshott 1975) helps us to recognize this usually neglected aspect of Hayek's economics. Each action creates a new context within which subsequent understandings will be formed and against which both old and new understandings must be rethought. All conduct both enacts a prior self-understanding, and alters the context within which that understanding is obtained. Thus, all conduct brings about novel contexts and novel understandings. The market is an extended order within which various enterprise associations may exist, but which cannot itself be an enterprise association. Oakeshott would agree that in the end knowledge is not reducible to representation. It also embodies customs, practices, traditions, maxims, rules of thumb, habits, and forms of conduct that cannot be reduced to theory.

Spontaneous orders lack a substantive purpose, but that makes it possible to pursue many such goals within the context of a spontaneous order. That is what Oakeshott calls 'civil association'. Spontaneous orders or structures are arranged according to non-instrumental rules. Because these orders are defined by end-independent or non-instrumental rules, they cannot be said to aim at or achieve any substantive purpose. The ends that spontaneous order serves are the separate ends of those individuals, in all their variety and contrariness. A spontaneous order is not composed of individuals subject to the commands of managers, but of individuals whose actions conform to universally-applied rules of just conduct, which Oakeshott calls "conditions of adverbial desirability" that are immaterial to the object of individual pursuits (Oakeshott 1975, *On Human Conduct*, p. 66). Hayek (and Oakeshott would agree) argues that the substantive arrangement of the components of spontaneous orders cannot rightfully be called just or unjust. This is because they are not intended to fulfill any particular purpose, but only to provide the conditions within which individuals may pursue their own purposes.

Like Oakeshott, Hayek does not deny the value and importance of teleocratic institutions or enterprise associations. He does not advocate the reduction of all substantive, personal relationships – like the family, marriage, friendship, community – to relations according to contract, or non-instrumental rules. "[I]f we were always to apply the rules of the extended order to our more intimate groupings, *we would crush them*" (Hayek 1988, *The Fatal Conceit*, p. 18). Hayek is not a doctrinaire advocate of laissez-faire or of any libertarianism that seeks to reduce all of society to contract relations. He supports the policy of an economic safety net even though he holds that market competition is the best way to organize the economy, and that a safety net can become an impediment to the operation of competition.

Hayek's economic argument applies to the rule by law. The rule of law can exist only within what Oakeshott calls a civil association; law will otherwise degenerate into an enterprise association. The rule of law cannot be salvaged by collectivist politics – this would only be true if all disputes could be resolved in parliamentary discussion because of the alleged prior existence of an ultimate teleology or the General Will. In the *Road to Serfdom* Hayek asserts that free markets and the potential for the rule of law were extinguished in Germany by late nineteenth century positivism.

Hayek has abandoned the notion that there is a substantive common good, even a Smithean invisible hand which tacitly assumes some kind of harmony. What Hayek has done is to collapse the distinction between communitarianism and collectivism. He opposes the notion of planning and how it can be imposed upon us. Let the Socialists have their collectivist conception and the language of the common good as their concept, to be strived-for in an enterprise association; but lovers of liberty should embrace the evolutionary process, so that what emerges is a kind of common good. Hayek does acknowledge the need for government institutions, or what he calls "the rule of law" which is different from the law of rules. To the extent that the rule of law expresses neutral procedural norms within which individuals pursue their private ends, the rule of law is the common good. As in Madison, the rule of law helps to secure the pursuit of happiness.

Contemporary Rousseauean movements in the law like Critical Legal Studies reject the rule of law on the grounds that it is but another mask for economic oppression and exploitation. The planners want a law of rules, administrative law. Without trust you have to have regulations. Supporters of the Rousseauean Narrative have moved away from an understanding of the rule of law as one which emphasizes procedural neutrality to one that focuses on substantive rights, a movement that gives a privileged position to the state over the market.

OAKESHOTT: FREE TO CHOOSE

Michael Oakeshott (1901–90) was a political philosopher, historian and leading intellectual light at the London School of Economics from 1948 to 1969. His major philosophical work was *Experience and Its Modes* (Oakeshott 1933). Operating from within the post-Kantian and post-Hegelian Copernican Revolution, he maintained that what distinguishes us from animals is that we are free to choose how we interpret experience. To be human is to be free; our freedom is employed in our imagination and intelligence; these faculties are used in defining ourselves as individuals and in giving meaning to our experience of the world we inhabit. In philosophy the best way to defend a view is simply to elucidate it; it is futile to attempt to win arguments with other philosophers. "Philosophy consists, not in persuading others, but in making our own minds clear" (Oakeshott 1933, *Experience and Its Modes*, p. 3).

Since we always approach the world with some perspective it is a basic philosophical error to think you can step outside of all perspectives at once. Hence, like Hayek, he identifies epistemological realism as the philosophical origin of all mistaken thought. As a consequence he was an outspoken critic of all forms of utopian thinking, particularly post-World War II British socialism, but also the belief in the existence of social or bureaucratic expertise, all fixed ideologies, and party politics. He laid this out in his 1947 essay "Rationalism in Politics." His epistemology was social: only through interaction with our social inheritance do we become who we are. Our inheritance is a set of cultural achievements and practices, not a doctrine to be learned. The inheritance is not constitutive of, and determinant of, who we are; rather it needs to be re-created through its appropriation. It is not homogeneous, there can be no final or definitive formulation of it, and any explication of it will acknowledge that there are many voices in the 'conversation'. A 'conversation' is an endless, unrehearsed intellectual adventure in which, through imagination, we enter into a variety of modes of understanding both the world and ourselves, and we are not disconcerted by the differences or dismayed by the inconclusiveness of it all. There are limits to discursive reason, and acknowledging those limits is a form of liberation from ideological thinking.

How then is thought related to action? Practice precedes the reflection on practice (in the beginning is the deed and this is the pre-conceptual). We can never fully conceptualize this pre-conceptual, but we can offer a sort of abridged version of it. In practical decision-making we do not infer practical consequences from the conceptualization. Rather we engage in an explication of the norms inherent in the previous practice, or in the words of Oakeshott, we engage in the *pursuit of intimations* of previous practice. Like Hayek's spontaneous order, our inheritance is not a permanently fixed order but a fertile source of adaptation. Arguments constructed out of this material cannot be 'refuted'. They may be resisted by arguments of the same sort which, on balance, are found to be more convincing. Honest and intelligent disagreement is always possible and likely. Oakeshott embraced a non-reductive pluralism which is compatible with liberty. Oakeshott's understanding of his own inheritance was laid out in his 1949 essay "The Political Economy of Freedom":

> The freedom which the English libertarian knows and values lies in a coherence of mutually supporting liberties … the absence from our society of overwhelming concentrations of power … our experience has disclosed to us

a method of government remarkably economical in the use of power and consequently peculiarly fitted to preserve freedom: it is called the rule of law ... . Of the many species of liberty ... we have long recognized the importance of two: the freedom of association, and the freedom enjoyed in the right to own private property. (Oakeshott [1949] 1991, pp. 388, 390, and 391)

What Oakeshott opposed in politics is what we have called the twentieth century Rousseauean administration of things. He identifies this mentality as 'rationalism in politics.' The 'rationalist' is Oakeshott's enemy. "The general character and disposition of the Rationalist" is that "he stands (he always stands) for independence of mind," that is thought "free from obligation to any authority save the authority of reason." The rationalist "is the enemy of authority, of prejudice, of the merely traditional, customary or habitual." "His cast of mind is Gnostic." "[M]uch of his political activity consists in bringing the social, political, legal and institutional inheritance of his society before the tribunal of his intellect." The rationalist searches "for an innocuous power which may safely be made so great as to be able to control all other powers." His disposition is "to believe that political machinery can take the place of moral and political education." All knowledge must be "technical knowledge." The "Rationalist aims to begin by getting rid of inherited nescience and then to fill the blank nothingness of an open mind with the items of certain knowledge which he abstracts from his personal experience, and which he believes to be approved by the common 'reason' of mankind" (Oakeshott [1947] 1991, pp. 5–42; all subsequent quotations from Oakeshott's essays, except for the "Rule of Law" are from this edition).

By contrast, Oakeshott was a self-described conservative, and in his essay "On Being Conservative" (Oakeshott 1956), he explained that "to be conservative ... is to prefer the familiar to the unknown, to prefer the tried to the untried, fact to mystery, the actual to the possible, the limited to the unbounded, the near to the distant, the sufficient to the superabundant, the convenient to the perfect, present laughter to utopian bliss" (Oakeshott [1956] 1991, p. 408). Being conservative is not about being rigidly doctrinaire but about managing inevitable change coherent with past practice through the pursuit of intimations.

Rather than simply dismiss the Rousseau narrative and endorse the Lockean narrative, Oakeshott put them into historical perspective. In *On Human Conduct* (1975) Oakeshott identifies two major views that have developed within the Western Inheritance. The first is "enterprise association" (or *universitas*), which asserts the existence of a collective social goal to which all individual goals are subordinated or within which individuals may pursue fulfillment. This has been the mode of thinking of Rousseau, Marx, and all those who seek to recapture the classical/ medieval sense of community in subscribing to some version of the Rousseau Equality Narrative. In his posthumously published *The Politics of Faith and the Politics of Scepticism* (Oakeshott 1996), those who believe that there is such a universal collective goal see the role of the government (politics of faith) as potentially unlimited in requiring all subjects to work toward that purpose. Curiously the success of what we have called the technological project gives rise to the false hopes of what we have called the Enlightenment Project, specifically the belief that we have the power to achieve some great social project (for example, end world poverty, eradicate all forms of human misery, and so on).

In opposition to enterprise association, Oakeshott posits "civil association" (*societas*) which, by contrast, does not assert the existence of a collective all-encompassing good. Rather, there are only the specific goals of individuals. The role of government is limited to providing the context within which individuals pursue (not necessarily achieve) their specific goals. To the extent that there are rules or laws, such laws specify the conditions of how the pursuit is to take place but not what to pursue. Groups of individuals may choose to form or join sub-enterprise associations (for example, the family, a religion, a sports team) but entry and exit are purely voluntary. Subscribing to civil association reflects a fundamental skepticism about the ability either to apprehend or to achieve a universal good (politics of skepticism). The focus of government should be on preventing evil rather than achieving good.

By identifying the tension between enterprise association and civil association, Oakeshott explicates the ongoing modern tension between equality and liberty. Both are a part of our inheritance. It is primarily a modern tension because the ideal of civil association came into existence only with the Renaissance and Reformation. Modern European states began to take shape in the sixteenth century, and by then they were articulating themselves not only in the new idiom of autonomy but also in the old and inherited idiom of a *universitas*, a teleocratic enterprise in Hayek's words.

In a follow-up essay, "The Masses in Representative Democracy" (1961), Oakeshott introduced another distinction that accounts for the advent of civil association. In contradiction to Ortega's theory, what is new in Western Europe is not the 'masses' but the autonomous individual. This persona arose overtly during the Renaissance, and accounts for all the creativity in Europe in every field:

Almost all modern writing about moral conduct begins with the hypothesis of an individual human being choosing and pursuing his own directions of activity. What appeared to require explanation was not the existence of such individuals, but how they could come to have duties to others of their kind ... . This is unmistakable in Hobbes, the first moralist of the modern world to take candid account of the current experience of individuality ... even where an individualistic conclusion was rejected, this autonomous individual remained as the starting point of ethical reflection. Every moralist in the seventeenth and eighteenth centuries is concerned with the psycho-logical structure of this assumed 'Individual' ... *nowhere is this seen more clearly to be the case than in the writings of Kant. Every human being, in virtue of not being subject to natural necessity, is recognized by Kant to be a Person, an end in himself, absolute and autonomous ... as a rational human being he will recognize in his conduct the universal conditions of autonomous personality; and the chief of these conditions is to use humanity, as well in himself as in others, as an end and never as a means* ... personality is so far sacrosanct that no man has either a right or a duty to promote the moral perfection of another: we may promote the 'happiness' of others, but we cannot promote their 'good' without destroying their 'freedom' which is the condition of moral goodness [*italics* added]. (Oakeshott 1961, in Fuller 1991, pp. 367–68)

Both Hayek and Oakeshott understand human individual freedom in a Kantian sense. The fundamental truth about human beings is their potential for freedom (not to be confused with liberty). We are not simply the product of our heredity or our environment. Neither of these (contra Rawls) fully determines our responses. We are free to choose. Our choices become autonomous when we impose order on them; the choices become heteronomous when we allow others or outside influences to determine or intrinsically modify the choice. Autonomous people do not impose on others because that imposition would be a form of heter-onomy. Autonomous people treat other human beings as ends in them-selves and not merely as means to their own agendas. In an enterprise association, without voluntary entry and exit, however, every human being at best plays a pre-determined role and at worst gets "used" by others. Autonomous people advocate liberty (absence of arbitrary exter-nal constraints) for themselves and others as a means to the expression of their freedom, that is, their capacity for making autonomous choices.

Prior to this period, everyone was part of a community. Some people found the transition from a communal identity to a personal identity challenging and unattractive. The latter define themselves negatively against the autonomous individual. Whereas the autonomous individual wants negative rights and the rule of law, the anti-individual wants the state to become the new community in which they possess positive rights.

The anti-individual is a pathological character, forever parasitic upon the autonomous individual. Oakeshott describes the anti-individual in Rousseauean terms: "the counterpart of the ... *entrepreneur* of the sixteenth century was the displaced laborer." The "anonymity of communal life was replaced by a personal identity which was burdensome" (Oakeshott 1961, in Fuller 1991, p. 371). It "bred envy, jealousy and resentment" (ibid., p. 372). It rejected the morality of 'liberty' and substituted the morality of 'equality', 'solidarity', and 'community' (ibid., p. 375). The anti-individual is a derivative character who survives only by defining itself against individuality. The destructive urge of the anti-individual is inhibited only by the desire to enjoy the fruits of what individuals create. The anti-individual reflects a pathology of someone who has failed to realize freedom and responsibility.

EQUALITY VERSUS LIBERTY REVISITED

The distinction between the autonomous individual and the anti-individual enables Oakeshott to provide a serious response to perhaps the major criticisms that the adherents of the Equality Narrative have of adherents of the Liberty Narrative, namely that the latter cannot (1) establish that the good of individuals is coherent with the social good; nor (2) can they deal adequately with dysfunctional members of the community. To begin with, the assertion of the existence of a collective good is a chimera and throughout human history has been the excuse for the worst crimes committed against humanity. Fanatics not skeptics go on crusades. Like Hayek, Oakeshott denies that we need postulate a Smithean hidden hand. Second, the existence of dysfunctional members of society is not caused by modernity or modern market societies or by the indifference or moral blindness of successful members of society. Social dysfunction reflects the inability of anti-individuals to embrace moral maturity, individual freedom, and responsibility.

Autonomy, or more precisely the lack thereof, explains the existence of dysfunctional people in free societies. The standard Rousseauean diagnosis for the existence of dysfunctional people – and we might add every conceivable social problem – is the lack of resources or the lack of positive rights. The default remedy, given the standard diagnosis, is some form of redistribution. Some proponents of this view are willing to endorse counter-productive public policies (for example, the minimum wage) because of its symbolic reflection of solidarity. As Bertrand de Jouvenel once noted, in the process of redistributing the wealth, the state becomes increasingly powerful. Indeed, "The more one considers the matter, the clearer it becomes that redistribution is in effect far less a redistribution of free income from the richer to the poorer, as we imagined, than a redistribution of power from the individual to the State" (de Jouvenel [1952] 1990, *The Ethics of Redistribution*, p. 72). If Hayek and Oakeshott are right, the existence of these dysfunctional people and a whole host of social problems is the presence of people who have not yet developed a sense of personal autonomy.

Poverty is not the cause of being an anti-individual but the product of being an anti-individual. Many people who are born poor nevertheless pursue autonomy and become economically successful. Many people born into comfort or wealth are nevertheless anti-individuals and sink into the culture of poverty. Being autonomous has nothing to do with intelligence. It is a matter of character. The "leaders" and spokespersons of the anti-individuals exploit their followers. You can become rich and powerful being such a leader. No one objects to your wealth and power, or even your corruption, because you are allegedly helping the "people" (that is, anti-individuals).

Autonomous individuals have a positive narrative and focus on trying to help others to become autonomous. Your success contributes to my success. Anti-individuals find it necessary to have a negative narrative: (a) they are "victims"; (b) they have to demonize or blame somebody else for their problems; and (c) their leaders and spokespersons (including Rousseauean intellectuals) are constantly blaming somebody. The significant difference between criticizing and blaming is that 'criticism' focuses on attacking arguments, whereas 'blaming' focuses on attacking people.

LAW AND THE RULE OF LAW

The distinction between enterprise and civil association (identified and articulated by Hobbes, Spinoza, Locke, Montesquieu, Hume, Kant, Hegel and Mill) allowed Oakeshott to make a further important distinction, namely the difference between law and the rule of law. Law is a social practice. As a practice it is not a place, a building, or a set of people acting in a certain uniform way. It is a practice that emerged in a certain specific historical context. Law – as opposed to merely imposed order – first emerged, according to Oakeshott, with the rise of the modern European state during the sixteenth and seventeenth centuries. What distinguished these states or political entities was not only the imposition of order over an extended and identifiable geographical area but also the additional attributes of (a) not being subject to any external authority (for example, feudal obligations, other states or empires, or the authority of the Papacy) and (b) the custodianship of laws or rules which specified the 'legal' rights and obligations of subjects as well as the procedures for making and amending laws (Oakeshott 1975, pp. 228–29). In this respect, part of the problem with Kelsen's idea of a 'Grundnorm' is that it seems to suggest the idea of a higher legal authority that created or validated positive law, and as such it reflects a residual and dysfunctional idea from the medieval natural law tradition.

The legitimacy of the modern European state as proto-type is not derived from any non-legal substantive norms. The validity of the laws themselves rests solely on the character of their maker and the manner in which they were made, promulgated, and interpreted. What makes someone a subject is not the possession of any 'rights' (metaphysical. natural, human, or otherwise for all of these appeal to some political agenda) and not consent to the rules. Rather a subject is someone who acquiesces in the terms of the relationship. As argued by Hume and Hegel, both the 'state' and 'law' emerged from custom, not contract, hence their validity rests on compliance not consent.

What then constitutes the '*rule of law*'? What distinguishes the rule of law from law in the generic sense is that the rule of law involves categorical prescriptions. To distinguish this kind of law from the heterogeneous collection of rules called laws, Oakeshott introduces the term 'lex'. Lex is "an authoritative system of prescribed conditions to be taken account of in choosing actions" (Oakeshott 1975, p. 139). The expression 'the rule of law', taken precisely, stands for a mode of moral association exclusively in terms of the recognition of the authority of known, non-instrumental rules (that is, laws) which impose obligations to subscribe to adverbial conditions in the "performance of the self-chosen actions of all who fall within their jurisdiction … it is an abstract relationship of *personae*." (Oakeshott [1983] 1999, "Rule of Law," in *On History and Other Essays*, p. 136).

Oakeshott employs the analogy of the *adverb* to describe the kind of restraint law involves. The law that requires us to drive on the right (or the left) does not dictate that I have a car, does not dictate that I must drive, does not dictate my destination if I do drive. What it tells me is *how* to drive, namely, on the same side of the road as everybody else and within certain speed limits. Such rules are not designed to achieve a collective goal but to enable each individual to choose and arrive at his or her destination. This contrasts with the rules of an enterprise association in which specific laws are compulsory, that is they tell us *what* to do.

The rule of law cannot be present when laws are promulgated to achieve targeted results. As Hayek put it, the rule of law gives us the rules of the game but does not determine the outcome. For the same reason, Oakeshott dismisses Rawls' conception of the rule of law because it promulgates "fairness" in the distribution of scarce resources, and "fairness" as what rational competitors, in certain ideal circumstances, must agree is an equitable distribution. This turns law into "regulations understood in terms of the consequences of their operation and as guides to the achievement of a substantive state of affairs" (ibid., p. 170, n13).

Oakeshott has three theses about the rule of law. First, the rule of law is a strictly modern phenomenon. What the classical and medieval world always exhibited was enterprise association. What it had was order and rule *through* law, not the rule *of* law. The development of the rule of law within modern European states reflects several things: the increasing recognition of human autonomy, the gradual articulation of it within the inherited context of Roman private law, and by implication a certain kind of political economy.

Oakeshott's second thesis is that the rule of law can only exist in a civil association. Once you subscribe to an enterprise association, which has a collective goal, you are always able to override the wishes and plans of any individual in the name of the alleged national (common, global, and so on) good.

> As a mode of human intercourse the civil condition is an ideal character glimpsed here or there ... but it nowhere constitutes a premeditated design for human conduct ... . Aristotle discerned some of its important features in the Athenian *polis*, Cicero in the Roman Republic, Hobbes and Montesquieu in the emergent states of modern Europe ... . The most difficult feature of the civil condition to identify and get into place has been law ... . It is made difficult also because the theorists of law have laid so many false trails (for example, misidentifying it as a 'command' and as instrumental to the achievement of substantive satisfactions), and have usually been so much more concerned with the so-called 'sources' of law, with contingent beliefs about its authority, and with its so-called 'purpose' than with what it is. (Oakeshott 1975, *On Human Conduct*, pp. 180–81)

The role of government is to be the guardian of the common good or the conditions. Individuals in a civil association may thus share a common good in the formal conditions to be observed but it is not a substantive collective good in which their interests are subsumed. Within an enterprise association, the law is a set of rules that are instrumental in advancing the collective goal as articulated by the government. The politicized, managerial or totalitarian implications of law within an enterprise association are manifest. Within a civil association, the law is formal, not instrumental, and the rule of law prescribes the conditions within which individuals pursue self-chosen purposes.

What democratic socialist societies lack is the 'rule of law' even though they may have rule through law. Part of the significant difference, as J.S. Mill put it long ago, reflects the placing of the burden of proof in any argument about expanding the role of the state or infringing upon so-called negative liberties. In the presence of the ideal, the *onus* now is on those who wish to violate negative liberties just as it is on the state to prove that I am guilty not on me to prove that I am innocent. Implicit in this, once more, is an underlying tension between Anglo-American ideals (Lockean) and continental ideals (Rousseau).

Oakeshott's third thesis is that every modern state is a historically ambiguous compound of both a civil and an enterprise association. This is not a surprising thesis in view of Oakeshott's other well-known views. In addition to the inherited ambiguity, namely that the modern state is an ambiguous amalgam of civil and enterprise association, there are a number of conditions that reinforce adherence to the idea of the state as an enterprise association: (a) the unending growth of bureaucracy, (b) monarchical lordship, (c) colonial adventures, (d) war, (e) the continuous presence of the anti-individual, and (f) advocacy of world government.

OAKESHOTT'S CORRECTION OF THE LIBERTY NARRATIVE

What Oakeshott achieved is a reorientation of the Liberty Narrative. That narrative encompassed the following elements: Technological Project → Market Economy → Limited Government → Rule of Law → the culture of Personal Autonomy. It is not the technological project (contra Locke and Smith) which is the crucial element. Not only do some people risk turning the technological project into a collective goal (a Tower of Babel) but the technological project has as a serious side effect the growth of the Enlightenment Project and its concomitant faith in social technology.

Nor according to Oakeshott, is the market economy the crucial element in the Liberty Narrative (contra Hayek and Friedman). Free economic activity, effective economic competition and free markets unfettered by monopolies are, in Oakeshott's words, "not something that springs up of its own accord, but are creatures of law" (Oakeshott 1949, in Fuller 1991, p. 395). This is Oakeshott's connection between the rule of law and political economy. Economic competition can only exist, Oakeshott maintains, by virtue of a legal system which promotes it. This underscores the fact that Oakeshott draws a connection between the rule of law and a free society as a whole. This explicit language of promotion, creation, and connection suggests some causal relation between rule of law, economic and general freedom. To say that free market economic objectives are promoted *by* or are the consequence *of* the rule of law is not to say that the objective or purpose of the rule of law is to do so.

From the vantage point of the economist, it could be argued that one direct 'purpose' of the rule of law is to maximize economic utility. However, this directly conflicts with Oakeshott's famous insistence that the rule of law is a mode of ethical association in terms of the recognition of the authority of known, non-instrumental laws. Such ethical association are fundamentally distinguished by Oakeshott from purposive or enterprise associations. As Oakeshott points out in his *"Rule of Law"* essay (Oakeshott 1983), proponents of the rule of law recognize the inconsistency of attributing the virtue of a non-instrumental mode of association to its propensity to produce, promote or encourage a substantive outcome. Peace, order, economic efficiency, or more prominently freedom, are not the consequences of an association of legal persona, but instead are inherent in its character.

Given his view that law must be non-instrumental, all talk about the *purpose* of law is nonsensical and irresolvable metaphysical mischief. The Friedman claim that there is no government that respects individual freedom unless there is first a free market should be rendered as the claim that free markets only exist where there is a government that respects individual freedom. Present day China seems to be a society that is both an enterprise association and has a market economy. Nevertheless, the Chinese market economy is not really 'free'. The notion that authoritarian societies exhibit 'free' markets is a misnomer. Sometimes such societies are characterized by Marxists as capitalist, but no society where one group can arbitrarily and 'legally' exclude others from the market can be said to be a free market society. The overall economy might not be a planned economy, but that does not make it a free economy. From Oakeshott's point of view, a 'free' market economy reflects the existence of the rule of law which in turn reflects the existence of a culture of personal autonomy, namely, civil association.

CONCLUSION: OAKESHOTT AND HAYEK REVISITED

Oakeshott refuses to endorse the idea that free markets trump all other considerations. In a spontaneous order there is no final or definitive ranking of values such that 'a' always trumps 'b'. The ultimate test for Oakeshott on the political level is whether civil association is preserved.

Much to the chagrin of hard-core libertarians, Hayek acknowledged the role of some sort of welfare state. Hayek was not advocating a theory but explicating practice. The world which was the object of his explication was the product of spontaneous order, possessed a market economy, had evolved a notion of the 'rule of law' as a meta-norm, and it was/is a world in which other practices (for example, a welfare state) represented a potential threat to the continuing survival of both a market economy and the 'rule of law'. Neither Hayek nor Oakeshott are, strictly speaking, advocates of a theory, neo-liberal or otherwise. Nor is there or can there be within their framework a contradiction between a market economy or civil association on the one hand and a welfare state on the other. Spontaneous order and evolving historical practices do not eventuate or form a mechanical system that can be deductively ordered or re-ordered. To be sure, there can be tensions, potential conflicts, and even the eventual disappearance of one practice in favor of another. It is these scenarios concerning the tensions that concern both Hayek and Oakeshott.

A similar predicament is present in the work of Michael Oakeshott. The modern (Western European) state is not just a civil association. The modern state is also the product of history and as such has elements of an enterprise association. These elements constitute a distinct threat to the continuing survival of the 'rule of law'. As a consequence, we can expect an indefinite lifespan for the tension between the Liberty Narrative and the Equality Narrative. As long as there is a significant number of anti-individuals it will be necessary to restate (or remind ourselves and others of) the case for liberty.

Autonomous individuals do not need to justify either to others or to themselves why they acquiesce to a system. They do not believe that there is or there has to be a larger metaphysical reason. They do not believe, as Rousseaueans do, that we must commit ourselves to a form of teleology. Autonomous individuals need not conceptualize themselves or others as rational maximizers – there is no sense in providing an argument for why one ultimately chooses what one chooses as long as it does not conflict with one's own autonomy.

This is an enormously practical mode of thinking. There are only ever specific contexts with a history (common law) and we can never move to a general level where the enunciation of principles leads to their own application without context unless we presuppose an enterprise associ-ation. Those who conceive of themselves as libertarian, conservative, liberals, socialists, and so on all fail to perceive the rule of law as a specific alternative form of political organization. Oakeshott is not a classical liberal or libertarian; he is philosophically conservative not understood as membership in a particular party.

One of Oakeshott's major contentions is that we live in a world that is *inherently* morally pluralistic (not relative). There is no rational way to achieve consensus. The rule of law operates within this context, and those who object to Oakeshott's account either (a) have a private political agenda and wish to seize or maintain governmental power in the service of that agenda or (b) hold a *theory* about how the world ought to operate, a theory which has the same logical status as any other metaphysical doctrine on which there can never be consensus or (c) believe that (b) is a rationalization of (a).

The rule of law only exists in civil association and there cannot be even the idea of a civil association until the advent of the autonomous individual. So, the culture of personal autonomy is the key to the logic of modernity. The culture of personal autonomy gives rise to the 'rule of law' which permits the existence of limited government which fosters the market economy and advances the technological project rightly understood. In the context of the twentieth century, Oakeshott reasserted and further elaborated the Kant–Hegel–Mill defense of liberty as opposed to Friedmanesque positivism.

13. Thomas Piketty: the Apotheosis of Rousseau and the French Revolution

Thomas Piketty (born 1971) is a French economist. He published a highly influential book, *Capital in the Twenty-First Century* (Piketty 2014) and a follow-up article "About Capital in the Twenty-First Century," *American Economic Review* (Piketty 2015). He has served as an advisor to the French Socialist Party.

SUMMARY INTRODUCTION: R>G

Inequality is bad and there are no justifiable reasons for it! We need to return to the principles of 1789 France to achieve a just social order. When we do find income equality, it is due to shocks and wars and is not the result of a rational or evolutionary or spontaneous economic process. Although there has been a "compression of inequalities" it is due mainly to "the diffusion of knowledge and investment in training and skills." Nevertheless, "there are a set of divergences associated with the process of accumulation and concentration of wealth when growth is weak and the return on capital is high." This "represents the principal threat to an equal distribution of wealth in the long run" (Piketty 2014, p. 23). Piketty argues that the principal threat is the result of the fact that the annual *rate* of return on capital is greater than the rate of economic *growth*, r>g.

"[I]nherited wealth grows faster than output and income" (Piketty 2014, p. 260). This has nothing to do with market imperfection.

In the first three parts of his book, Piketty analyzes the evolution of the distribution of wealth and the structure of inequality since the eighteenth century. Twentieth century wars wiped out the inequality of the past; but inequality is returning in the twenty-first century.

SUMMARY PART ONE: INCOME AND CAPITAL

Part One reviews the concepts of income and capital and the main stages of their growth.

The first fundamental law of capitalism is:

alpha = (r) x beta
alpha is the share of capital in national income
r is the rate of return on capital
beta is the capital/income ratio.

The second fundamental law of capitalism is:

beta = s/g
s is savings rate
g is the growth rate.

SUMMARY PART TWO: THE DYNAMICS OF THE CAPITAL/INCOME RATIO

Part Two looks at the "main evolution of the capital stock" by way of French and British literature, examining "the dynamics of both the capital/income ratio at the country level and the overall split of national income between capital and labor" (Piketty 2014, p. 237). Modern growth, which is based on the growth of productivity and the difference of knowledge, has made it possible to avoid the apocalypse predicted by Marx and to balance the process of capital accumulation. But it has not altered the deep structure of capital – or at any rate has not truly reduced the macroeconomic importance of capital relative to labor (p. 234).

SUMMARY PART THREE: THE STRUCTURE OF INEQUALITY

Part Three examines changes in the structure of inequality with respect to both labor and capital since the nineteenth century. World War I and World War II and "public policies that followed them played a central role in reducing inequalities in the twentieth century" (Piketty 2014, p. 237). Inequality, he states, has returned since the 1970s. "During the 1980s English speaking countries reduced the top marginal income tax rate." That is a major reason for the increase in income inequality.

The increase in inequality in the United States contributed to the nation's "financial instability" (Piketty 2014, p. 297). The "structural increase in the capital/income ratio" also was a contributing factor (p. 298). Returning to the causes of rising inequality in the United States, Piketty finds that the increase was largely the result of the unprecedented increase in wage inequality and in particular the emergence of "extremely high remunerations at the summit of the wage hierarchy, particularly among top managers at large firms" (p. 298). The US now represents the world of the super manager and a "patrimonial middle class" (p. 304).

SUMMARY PART FOUR: REGULATING CAPITAL IN THE TWENTY-FIRST CENTURY

In Part Four, Piketty argues that capital should be regulated globally in the twenty-first century. "[L]evying confiscatory rates on top incomes is not only possible but also the only way to stem the observed increase in high salaries" (Piketty 2014, p. 512).

THE FRENCH REVOLUTION REVISITED

Right below the Introduction heading, Piketty quotes from *The Declaration of the Rights of Man and the Citizen*, Article 1, 1789: "Social distinctions can be based only on common utility" (Piketty 2014, p. 1). The normative premise of the book is that high degrees of inequality are bad and there are no justifiable reasons for it! The principles are of 1789 France to achieve a just social order (p. 31). He sees John Rawls and his "difference principle" as the modern representative of the French model (p. 480). In footnote 21 on page 631 he cites the following from Rawls' *Theory of Justice*: "Social and economic inequalities … are just only if they result in compensating benefits for everyone, and in particular for the least advantaged members of society." Thus he wants to move beyond the twentieth century European social model and recapture the vitality of the French model of 1789. And his inspiration is the French Declaration as supported by Rawls. The title of the book could easily have been *Rawls for the Twenty-first Century* or the *Twenty-first Century French Declaration of Equality*.

The alleged factual premises are: (1) the long term trend is toward greater inequality; (2) the long term trend of growth is too modest to close the gap, and hence the Lockean Narrative response toward inequality, namely increased growth, is inadequate; (3) in those historical periods where inequality has decreased it has not been because of growth, and it was not a product of deep economic forces (for example, sectoral spillover or the effects of technological progress).

These premises are supported by (a) statistical analysis, (b) historical interpretation or re-interpretation, and (c) economic theory.

The policy prescriptions for overcoming this alarming trend include (a) a greater "diffusion of knowledge and investment in training and skills" (Piketty 2014, pp. 21, 22), to be done by "public policy" rather than "a market mechanism" and (b) a progressive global tax on income. We have vast "global inequality" (p. 64). This can't be overcome simply by free markets but by the diffusion of knowledge, which is "associated with the achievement of legitimate and efficient government" (p. 71). We need to put income distribution back on the agenda and engage in a historically reliable data driven comparison of various countries in order to study "the dynamics of income and wealth distribution over the long run" (p. 19).

Let us turn first to the statistical analysis. It is a huge book, which is impressive in itself, full of data, which is even more impressive in the land of social science; and not only data over ten years in one sector of the economy in one part of a country. We are talking about 250 years of data on all sorts of inequality drawn from public records available in the advanced economies of the capitalistic countries. This is no short-term study that ends with the pathetic plea that more research funds are necessary. We have as close to a definitive study on inequality as we can get on this.

He initially focuses on France. The French Revolution established estate records. And in France the inheritance factor is more important than in the US because of "the demographic growth of the New World" (Piketty 2014, p. 29). The French case of slow population growth "is more typical and more pertinent for understanding the future" (p. 29). Moreover the French Revolution "quickly established an ideal of legal equality in relation to the market," whereas the British retained both royalty and aristocracy, and the American Revolution "allowed slavery to continue for nearly a century and legal discrimination for nearly two centuries ... . In a way, the French Revolution of 1789 was more ambitious. It abolished all legal privileges and sought to create a political and social order based entirely on equal rights and opportunities" (p. 30).

Piketty introduces his notion of "the convergence process" (Piketty 2014, p. 72). Poorer countries are catching up with richer countries by investing in themselves. But catch up is abnormal; slow growth is the norm. "The key point is that there is no historical example of a country at the world technological frontier whose growth in per capita output exceeded 1.5% over a lengthy period of time" (p. 93). "History and logic show" that an expected growth rate of 3 percent to 4 percent is "illusory" (pp. 93–94). He thinks that 1–2 percent is more probable (new normal) (p. 95), "but cannot be achieved, however, unless new sources of energy are developed to replace hydrocarbons, which are rapidly being depleted." It requires a society that embraces "deep and permanent change" (p. 96). "We need to create specific institutions for that purpose and not rely solely on market forces or technological progress" (p. 96). "To recapitulate, global growth over the last three centuries can be pictured as a bell curve with a very high peak" (p. 99).

Moving to the interpretation of the data, in Part Two, The Dynamics of the Capital/Income Ratio, Piketty looks at the "main evolution of the capital stock" by way of French and British literature (Piketty 2014, p. 113). In the nineteenth century, wealth took the form of land or government bonds. And to produce "a reliable and steady income" is the whole point of twenty-first century capital markets. So there is much to learn from the nineteenth century. Unlike the nineteenth century, modern capital has become more "dynamic" and less "rent seeking" (p. 116). Has there been a metamorphosis or decomposition of capital? (p. 118).

The Great Depression "durably discredited" the doctrine of laissez-faire (Piketty 2014, p. 136). Both Schumpeter and Samuelson held the Soviet "statist economic system" in high regard (Piketty 2014, p. 137). "In 1950, the government of France owned 25–30 percent of the nation's wealth, and perhaps even a little more" (p. 137). This mixed economy was "capitalism without capitalists" (p. 138). But this changed after 1980 with the arrival of the deregulation and privatization movement. France "became the promised land of the new private-ownership capitalism of the twenty-first century" (p. 138).

Capital went through metamorphoses but in the end, "its total amount relative to income scarcely changed at all" (Piketty 2014, p. 140). Piketty wants to get to the question: "what fundamentally determines the capital/income ratio in the long run" (p. 149). But to get there he expands his French model to other parts of Europe and the New World.

Piketty examines what he calls "the fairy tale" of Simon Kuznets and Robert Solow in the twentieth century, namely the allegedly mistaken belief in decreasing inequality within advanced capitalism (Piketty 2014, p. 11). Kuznets "noted a sharp reduction in income inequality in the United States between 1913 and 1948" (p. 12). He used "objective data" for the first time (p. 13). But this move toward equality was "accidental" and Kuznets knew that the "Kuznets curve" showing the reduction in inequality had more to do with the shocks of war and depression than "with any natural and automatic process" (p. 13) or of "the inevitability of a balanced growth path" (p. 15). It was also "a product of the Cold War" (pp. 14–15) to believe in and to propose an "optimistic view of the relation between economic development and the distribution of wealth" (p. 16). Following World War II, after initially undergoing a decrease in economic inequality similar to that in continental Europe, English-speaking countries have, over the past thirty years, experienced increasing inequalities. "Since the 1970s, income inequality has increased significantly in the rich countries" (p. 15).

Part Three examines income and wealth inequality at the individual level. The twenty-first century has seen the return of "patrimonial capitalism." This is not something new but a return to the low growth of the nineteenth century. In Part Three, contra Kuznets, he argues that World War I and World War II and "public policies that followed them, played a central role in reducing inequalities in the twentieth century" (Piketty 2014, p. 237). However, inequality, he states, has returned since the 1970s. And he shows the increased importance of inherited wealth over labor from income.

"Many people believe that modern growth naturally favors labor over inheritance and competence over birth. What is the source of this belief, and how sure can we be that it is correct?" (Piketty 2014, p. 237). Will inequality be greater in the twenty-first century than in the nineteenth century? Income from capital is more concentrated than the distribution of income from labor (p. 244).

What is the current structure of inequality at the individual level?

> In every society, whether France in 1789 (when 1–2 percent of the population belonged to the aristocracy) or the United States in 2011 (when the Occupy Wall Street movement aimed its criticism at the richest 1 percent of the population), the top centile is a large enough group to exert a significant influence on both the social landscape and the political and economic order. (Piketty 2014, p. 254)

Inequality from capital is always larger than inequalities from income. "The growth of a true 'patrimonial (or propertied) middle class' was the principal structural transformation of the distribution of wealth in the developed countries in the twentieth century" (Piketty 2014, p. 260). "*I want to insist on this point: the key issue is the justification of inequality rather than the magnitude as such. That is why it is essential to analyze the structure of inequality*" (p. 264). There are two ways of achieving inequality: (1) inheritance, or rentiers, and (2) super managers of merit (see in particular, pp. 276–78).

He now turns to the changed structure of inequality:

> The shocks of the period 1914–45 played an essential role in the compression of inequality, and this compression was in no way a harmonious or spontaneous occurrence. The increase in inequality since 1970 has not been the

same everywhere, which again suggests that institutional and political factors played a key role. (Piketty 2014, p. 271)

He notes the reduction in inequality in France in the twentieth century with the arrival of the managers. "The top docile always encompasses two very different worlds: 'the 9 percent,' in which income from labor clearly predominates, and 'the 1 percent,' in which income from capital becomes progressively more important" (Piketty 2014, p. 280). "The foregoing discussion demonstrates the usefulness of breaking income down by centiles and income source" (p. 286). "In every country the history of inequality is political – and historical" (p. 286).

The transformation of inequality in the United States is more complex than in France. The New Deal and World War II "substantially compressed" income inequality (Piketty 2014, p. 293). But this compression was less than in France. There was an "explosion of US inequality after 1980" (p. 294). The financial crisis of the early 2000s did not alter this structural dynamic; in fact, "there is absolutely no doubt that the increase in inequality in the United States contributed to the nation's financial instability" (p. 297). The "structural increase in the capital/income ratio" also was a contributing factor (p. 298).

> Let me return now to the causes of rising inequality in the United States. The increase was largely the result of the unprecedented increase in wage inequality and in particular the emergence of extremely high remunerations at the summit of the wage hierarchy, particularly among top managers at large firms. (Piketty 2014, p. 298)

The US now represents the world of the super manager.

STATISTICAL AND HISTORICAL INTERPRETATION

Piketty examines the "dynamics of labor income inequality. What caused the explosion of wage inequalities and the rise of the super manager in the United States after 1980?" (Piketty 2014, p. 304). The answer lies in understanding the emergence of a "patrimonial middle class" (p. 304).

Marginal productivity analysis is an inadequate explanation for income distribution. He has a specific section called "The Illusion of Marginal Productivity" (Piketty 2014, pp. 330–33). "Inequalities at the bottom of the US wage distribution have closely followed the evolution of the minimum wage" (p. 310). "Over the long run, minimum wages and wage schedules cannot multiply wages by factors of five or ten: to achieve that level of progress, education and technology are the decisive forces"

(p. 313). But education cannot explain why the top 1 percent "have seen their remuneration take off" (p. 315). What about the invisible hand at work? "In practice, the invisible hand does not exist, any more than 'pure and perfect' competition does, and the market is always embodied in specific institutions such as corporate hierarchies and compensation committees" (p. 332). It is mostly about "social norms of fair remuneration" (p. 333). "During the 1980s (Thatcher and Reagan) English speaking countries reduced the top marginal income tax rate." That is a major reason for the increase in income inequality. The correct explanation lies in the Inequality of Capital Ownership: today, capital ownership is becoming increasingly concentrated and thus may become more problematic than the unequal distribution between super managers and others (p. 336).

> Three questions ... . Why were inequalities of wealth so extreme, and increasing, before World War I? And why, despite the fact that wealth is once again prospering at the beginning of the twenty-first century as it did at the beginning of the twentieth century (as the evolution of the capital/income ratio shows), is the concentration of wealth today significantly below its historical high? Finally, is this state of affairs irreversible? (Piketty 2014, p. 346)

The "major structural transformation was the emergence of a middle group" (p. 347).

Wealth in the US became increasingly concentrated during the nineteenth century. Then came the Progressives. "Perceptions of inequality, redistribution, and national identity changed a great deal over the course of the twentieth century, to put it mildly" (Piketty 2014, p. 349). Inequality dropped between 1910 and 1950. But it is back up again.

So the question Piketty turns to now is will the twenty-first century become eventually even more inegalitarian than the nineteenth century? It is "an illusion" to think "the nature of modern growth or the laws of the market economy ensures that inequality of wealth will decrease and harmonious stability will be achieved" (Piketty 2014, p. 376). It all depends on what happens to governmental tax laws. The form of capital has certainly changed from land to financial, industrial, and real estate. There is now a patrimonial middle class that owns between a quarter to one-third of total wealth. The wealthiest 10 percent now own two-thirds rather than nine-tenths in the nineteenth century. And "it is all but inevitable" (p. 378) that inherited wealth rather than earned wealth will play a larger role. That is the probability of the twenty-first century. The "key question" is the breakdown between wealth created by work and wealth created by inheritance. Inheritance flow in France was 20 percent in the nineteenth century, down to 4 percent by 1950 and is now up to 14 percent. He examines, in turn, three forces that influence the inheritance flow. He is particularly interested in whether the importance of inheritance decreases because people live longer and inheritors inherit later. Part of this interest is to question the Modigliani theory that people (only) save for retirement and the goal is to end up with nothing when you die.

According to Piketty, "the desire to perpetuate the family fortune has always played a central role." Thus the importance of inheritance and gift giving prior to death (Piketty 2014, pp. 391, 393). In this regard, says Piketty, only 15–20 percent of retirements in English speaking countries are funded by annuities. It is only 5 percent in France.

He turns now to the issue of global inequality of wealth in the twenty-first century. *Forbes* claims there were 140 billionaires in 1987 in the world and 1,400 in 2013 (Piketty 2014, p. 433). "Since the 1980s, global wealth has increased on average a little faster than income ... and the largest fortunes grew much more rapidly than average wealth. This is the new fact that *Forbes* rankings help us bring to light, assuming they are reliable" (p. 435). "Global inequality of wealth in the early 2010s appears to be comparable in magnitude to that observed in Europe in 1900–2010" (p. 438). "One of the most striking lessons of the *Forbes* rankings is that, past a certain threshold, all large fortunes, whether inherited or entrepreneurial in origin, grow at extremely high rates, regardless of whether the owner of the fortune works or not" (p. 439). The point? "Capital grows according to a dynamic of its own" (p. 440). He estimates that 60–70 percent of the wealth is inherited rather than earned.

THE 'CORRECTION' OF MARX

Moving beyond statistic and historical interpretation, what is the economic theoretical explanation for all of this?

How does this relate to Marx? (Piketty 2014, p. 227). "Marx usually adopted a fairly anecdotal and unsystematic approach to the available statistics" (p. 229). We have data in the twenty-first century. To sum up: modern growth, which is based on the growth of productivity and the difference of knowledge, has made it possible to avoid the apocalypse predicted by Marx and to balance the process of capital accumulation. But it has not altered the deep structure of capital – or at any rate has not truly reduced the macroeconomic importance of capital relative to labor.

A powerful feature of the book is its sheer length and weight and depth and range of coverage. It is enough to put you at a distance and bow in respect. Like Marx, there are "laws" of capital and predictions. But unlike Marx, there are all sorts of diversions into asterisks and "what ifs" that take up a lot of space without really introducing skepticism into such a vast project. There is sufficient innuendo to suggest that Marx was good for the nineteenth century, but we need a refresher for the twenty-first century.

Capitalism does indeed contain an inherent contradiction: the rate of return on capital in developed countries (r) is greater over time than the rate of economic growth (including wage growth) (g).

$r>g$

This will cause wealth inequality, especially inherited wealth, to increase in the future. In this latest version of capitalism, 'patrimonial capitalism,' the commanding heights of the economy are controlled not by talented individuals but by family dynasties. (R) includes "profits, dividends, interest, rents, and other income from capital." No distinction is made between profits and returns on financial assets (dividends and interest). Another way of putting it is that "*inherited wealth grows faster than output and income*" (Piketty 2014, p. 260). And this has nothing to do with market imperfection. "There are a set of divergences associated with the process of accumulation and concentration of wealth when growth is weak and the return on capital is high." "It no doubt represents the principal threat to an equal distribution of wealth in the long run" (p. 23).

R>g turns entrepreneurs into rentiers. That is why we need a world-wide progressive annual income tax. The argument that there is "a moral hierarchy of wealth" in practice amounts to "an exercise in Western ethnocentrism" (Piketty 2014, p. 445). So much for the slim claim that there is a distinction between inherited and earned wealth. He is impressed by how "we have moved from a society with a small number of very wealthy rentiers to one with a much larger number of less wealthy rentiers: a society of petites rentiers if you will" (p. 420).

HOW ROUSSEAU AND MARX PROVIDE A PEACEFUL SOLUTION

There is an added Rousseau/Marx feature to the contemporary market economy. It is not a necessary feature of the market but an historical appendage. There are still bad guys manipulating the system. The wages of high income earners are "largely arbitrary" and millions of people who live on inherited wealth lack moral legitimacy. In the end the history of distribution boils down to what the "relevant actors" consider to be justice and the influence they have to implement that vision (Piketty 2014, p. 20).

The twentieth century wars wiped out the inequality of the past. Inequality is returning in the twenty-first century. The object is to avoid a global war to end capitalism and find a peaceful way: "can we imagine political institutions that might regulate today's global patrimonial capitalism justly as well as efficiently?" (Piketty 2014, p. 471). The main reason the Great Recession (2007–) did not become the Great Depression was because of government action. But the actions were merely a pragmatic response rather than "the return of the state" response to the first crisis of "globalized patrimonial capitalism" (p. 473).

"The simplest way to measure the change in the government's role in the economy is to look at the total amount of taxes relative to national income" (Piketty 2014, p. 474). Between 1870 and World War I it was 10 percent. Between 1920 and 1980, the amount devoted to social spending rose to 55 percent in Sweden and to 30 percent in the US, Britain and France were in between. Between 1980 and 2010, "the tax share stabilized everywhere" (p. 476). And a second great leap forward by the state is not likely to happen, nor is it likely to decrease. Today about half of government spending goes to health and education and about half goes to replacement incomes and transfer payments (p. 477). This translates as 15–25 percent of national income. "In other words, the growth of the fiscal state over the last century basically reflects the constitution of the social state" (p. 479). So his point is that modern redistribution theory is "built around a logic of rights" to health and education for example. Modern redistribution "does not consist in transferring income from the rich to the poor" (p. 479). This means it should take its bearing from the 1789 French model of social distinctions based only on "common utility." Thus, "equality is the norm" (p. 480). But we are sort of stuck these days with neither going back to the nineteenth century nor going forward beyond pensions, health, and education of the twentieth century to what is needed in the twenty-first century. He would like to entertain the notion of moving from the current level of 50 percent of "public financing" to "two-thirds to three-quarters of national income" (p. 483). Does this presuppose a world of perpetual peace?

The first task is to show how to generate more efficiency in government out of the current 50 percent devoted mainly to pensions, education, and health. Current education policies have neither reduced income inequality nor increased access to education, nor increased social mobility. So much for the theory of merit generated "American exceptionalism" (Piketty 2014, pp. 484–85). There is unequal educational opportunity in the US. Who can afford the high tuition fees? Whatever we do with pension reform, privatization is not the answer. Complexity is the problem and so uniformity is the answer. We need fundamental systemic change.

The two tax innovations in the twentieth century are the progressive income tax and the progressive inheritance tax. (It is unclear from his coverage whether these taxes were the result of accident and force or deliberation and choice.) They were created in wartime and not thought through properly. It is not "the natural offspring of democracy and universal suffrage" (Piketty 2014, p. 498). These two taxes need to be revisited. We need to increase the progressive income tax just to establish and sustain the current global 50 percent level. He mentions in passing that it is ironic that the United States took the lead in taxing "'excessive' incomes and fortunes" (p. 505) at 70 percent. It could not have been for revenue purposes. "The progressive tax ... is thus a relatively liberal method for reducing inequality ... . The progressive tax thus represents an ideal compromise between social justice and individual freedom" (p. 505). "The fear of turning into something resembling Old Europe was no doubt part of the reason for the American interest in progressive taxes" (p. 506). And then there was the Great Depression and World War II.

He wants to show that for most of the twentieth century the US had tax rates that were above the 70 percent threshold that he advocates. The top income tax rate was about 25 percent under "Hoover's disastrous presidency" (Piketty 2014, p. 506). FDR raised it to 63 percent in 1933; 79 percent in 1937; and in the low 90s from 1944 to the mid-1960s. It fell to 70 percent in the 1980s (pp. 506–507). "The top estate tax remained between 70% and 80% from the 1930s to the 1980s" (p. 507). And it was higher on inherited than it was on earned income. But both the UK and US veered away from this "great passion for equality" in the 1970s and 1980s (Thatcher and Reagan) (p. 508). It fell from the 80–90 percent range to 28 percent after the Reagan tax reform of 1986. The countries "with the largest decreases in their top tax rates are also the countries where the top earners' share of national income has increased the most" (p. 509). This totally transformed the determination of executive salaries; the increase in executive pay has nothing to do with the naïve theory of marginal productivity.

Here is his point: "levying confiscatory rates on top incomes is not only possible but also the only way to stem the observed increase in high salaries" (Piketty 2014, p. 512). Eighty percent on incomes over $500,000 or $1m and 50–60 percent on incomes over $200,000 is well within the reach of the United States. "The egalitarian pioneer ideal has faded into oblivion and the New World may be on the verge of becoming the Old Europe of the twenty-first century's global economy" (p. 514).

So how do we "regulate the globalized patrimonial capitalism of the twenty-first century?" (Piketty 2014, p. 515). "Rethinking the twentieth-century fiscal and social model and adapting it to today's world will not be enough" (p. 515). "The ideal tool would be a progressive global tax on capital, coupled with a very high level of international transparency." "The global tax I am proposing is a progressive annual tax on global wealth" (p. 517). "The primary purpose of the capital tax is not to finance the social state but to regulate capitalism" (p. 518). There is a "contributive justification and an incentive justification" (p. 524). And transparency about who owns what assets is vital for this project. We need an automatic global "transmission of banking data" (p. 521). He seeks "a less violent and more efficient response to the eternal problem of private capital and its return" (p. 532). The best response to r>g is a tax on capital. "In this form, the tax on capital is a new idea, designed explicitly for the globalized patrimonial capitalism of the twenty-first century" (p. 532).

In terms of transparency, "justice and efficiency" taxes are better than debt for funding government spending. Besides debt increases inequality. An exceptional tax of 15 percent on private capital is a better way of reducing public debt than inflation or the current austerity measures (Piketty 2014, pp. 540–47). The Central Banks are not the solution; what they do is to "redistribute wealth very quickly" to the rich (p. 551). If we want improvement in the ECB, then we need "the countries of the Eurozone (or at any rate those who are willing) to pool their public debts" (p. 558). And we need European political union (p. 562). This is no more utopian than the attempt "to create a stateless currency" (p. 561).

PIKETTY'S CONCLUSION: THE CONTRADICTION OF PATRIMONIAL CAPITALISM

There is a central contradiction of twenty-first century global patrimonial capitalism: r>g, which is the key measure of inequality. "The right solution is a progressive annual tax on capital" (Piketty 2014, p. 572). The bipolar confrontations between capitalism and communism of 1917–89 are now clearly behind us.

Piketty's argument for equality presupposes a liberty component. "Our democratic societies rest on a meritocratic worldview, or at any rate a meritocratic hope, by which I mean a belief in a society in which inequality is based more on merit and effort than on kinship and rents" (Piketty 2014, p. 422). But inequality should be based on the "common utility" provision of Article 1 of the 1789 French Declaration. So the liberty involved does not stand on its own footing as an individual right; it is contingent on something higher: the common utility or the general welfare (General Will). We have seen this argument earlier in Rawls.

PIKETTY REFASHIONS THE ROUSSEAU NARRATIVE AND THE FRENCH REVOLUTION

Right below the Introduction heading, we get a blurb cited by Piketty from *The Declaration of the Rights of Man and the Citizen*, Article 1, 1789: "Social distinctions can be based only on common utility" (Piketty 2014, p. 1). Perhaps we need go no further than to grasp the philosophical/conceptual and political indebtedness to J.J. Rousseau that runs throughout this book. And, in fact, coming to grips with the common utility declaration is the key to understanding both Piketty's debt to the past and his innovation in the twenty-first century.

Piketty is interested in the same question that Marx and the socialists are interested in and not just because the accumulation and concentration of capital is unfair per se. As important is that it can be shown scientifically to be unfair. In order to show this, however, he has to do what all previous generations of thinkers of both the Liberty and Equality Narratives have had to do, namely, "correct," or update their mentors and teachers from previous generations. So he corrects Marx concerning the accumulation and concentration of capital and applies that to the conditions of the twenty-first century. One of the main influences of Marx on Piketty is his implicit assumption that (g) will be close to zero. Thus the concern of both Marx and Piketty with (r) or the creation and dominance of capital. The claim by both is that there is a central contradiction to capitalism. Piketty, however, does not have the stomach for violence. And he has this wonderful, yet unexplainable, preference for "democratic debate" over "mathematical certainties" (Piketty 2014, p. 571). He wants to move beyond Marx without losing Marx's concern for "questions of capital and class inequality" (p. 655). He also declines to support the notion that the 1 percent is totally responsible for all the ills of the world. And when he suggests that European nations should pool their public debts, that proposal is moderated to "those who are willing" (p. 558).

Piketty has a problem with socialism in the twentieth century. Thus he seeks guidance from the eighteenth century and the nineteenth century. John Maynard Keynes was not a nineteenth century income/wealth inequality sort of socialist. He was primarily interested in unemployment and the role that government should and could play in filling in the gap left by fleeing capitalist investment in the twentieth century. The main aim was to put people to work so that they could consume and get the economy out of crisis. Economic growth, or what Piketty calls (g), was his objective. John Kenneth Galbraith and Michael Harrington are not in the strict Keynes mode of increasing (g). They enter the scene after the Depression and World War II. Galbraith is concerned that most production is unnecessary and most consumption is conspicuous. We need public or environmental socialism, which presumes that we have enough (g) to go around only if we could make it go around more fairly. Harrington is driven with a concern that a Great Society cannot exist unless the public takes care of its other America. He is a social justice Catholic inspired kind of socialist. And thus he would be more open to talking about the issue of (r). But the main problem for Harrington is that the state is not sufficiently involved in housing and education programs.

So the issues that drove nineteenth century socialists were altered by twentieth century America rather than the nineteenth century French Revolution. What drove these three (Keynes, Galbraith, and Harrington) was that the market, laissez-faire, rugged individualism might work for the few but certainly not for the "forgotten man" and the environment. The role of government in the twentieth century was to create and fund programs for those whom the market left behind or issues that the market would not cover. They were socialists in the sense that they saw the market as more of a failure than a success and government as more of a success than a failure.

The privatization and deregulation by Thatcher and Reagan, inspired more by the common sense of the American Revolution/*Constitution* and the commercial solutions of the Scottish Enlightenment, derailed the twentieth century socialist defeat of capitalism according to Piketty. It is time for the left to restate its case. And that case is economic inequality. While it is true that Piketty sees more to economic life than economic science in his appeal to culture, history, and literature – for example see his frequent references to nineteenth century literature and twentieth century movies – he boasts that he is, in effect, the first to ask the right questions, accumulate the correct data, and express the complexity of economic life in easily usable formulas. They are different and more nuanced than earlier formulas and downplay the tendency to inevitability as portrayed by earlier economists. But he still talks about dynamic laws and predicting the future. It is not going too far to say he sees himself as the first great economist of the twenty-first century. "The sources on which this book draws are more extensive than any previous author has assembled" (Piketty 2014, p. 571).

But now we are in the twenty-first century and the French Revolution has much luster for Piketty. Piketty's book arrived at the right time – the twenty-first century – and in the right place – the United States. And it retrieved the core nineteenth century socialist theme of inequality of income and wealth. The real battle is the one fought in the French Revolution, namely, genuine equality. There is also a prognosis: income/wealth inequality is likely to get worse over the coming years. So let the shift from the *Ancien Regime* in France by way of the French Revolution be our guide: get on the right side of history in the twenty-first century.

This sets off the usual panic and excitement among American elites. The French Revolution coming to the shores of America petrifies the Conservatives. So there is a sort of panic over Piketty. The left are ecstatic. Finally we can replace the elitist *Declaration of Independence* and *Constitution* with the egalitarian French Declaration and the democratic concentration of power. For Piketty the enduring battle is not between the rugged individual and the forgotten man; it is between the rugged egalitarian and the greedy 1 percent.

"What is the role of government in the production and distribution of wealth in the twenty-first century, and what kind of social state is most suitable for the age"? (Piketty 2014, p. 471). This is the question to which Piketty keeps returning. It is a vital question because ever since the Great Society programs, the presumption among academics was that public policy was government policy and the presumption was that the federal administration should have all sorts of programs to solve various problems. Piketty raises an important question: how one measures the role of government over time. Why stop with government providing retirement, education and health care? Why not also include "culture, housing, and travel?" (p. 480).

PIKETTY AND THE REAGAN REVOLUTION

What also makes Piketty important is that implicitly at least he recognizes that the Reagan revolution was not simply about cutting deficits, budgets, size and interference. It was the reintroduction of the question: what should government do? Which level of government and which branch of government should do it? Is there a role for intermediary institutions? One might go so far as to say that for Piketty the Reagan revolution from the 1970s to the start of the twenty-first century has been a 'success' in the sense that inequality has returned and the Great

Recession is due to that success. It has, therefore, made "the return of the state" a real possibility. Milton Friedman gets a two page accolade: "The work of Friedman and other Chicago School economists fostered suspicion of the ever-expanding state and created the intellectual climate in which the conservative revolution of 1970–1980 became possible" (Piketty 2014, p. 549). But perhaps this is to give too much credit to the change made by the Reagan revolution. Did the state ever disappear or go into limitation mode in the late twentieth century? Apparently it did not, according to Piketty, because the twentieth century social state hasn't really attacked the problem of (r).

His solution, however, would probably put to rest forever the raising of the question what should government do. We need more than "the return of the state" (Piketty 2014, p. 473). We need "confiscatory rates" on the top incomes (p. 512). But what happens if the electorate doesn't go for it? Does that matter to Piketty? At certain critical moments in his argument, his proposals are tempered by the claim that this can only be done by "collective deliberation" (see for example p. 513). Rousseau ought to trump Locke in theory, but Locke trumps Rousseau in practice. And reforming Locke has produced the dilemma of the current version of the rights generated social state.

What should the level of public debt be in "an ideal society"? "Only democratic deliberation can decide" (Piketty 2014, p. 562). Really? We thought it was r and g. Shouldn't "the golden rule" be that r = g (p. 563)? Isn't the "central contradiction of capitalism" that r>g (p. 571)?

He makes the rather odd value statement that "inequality is not necessarily bad in itself: the key question is to decide whether it is justified, whether there are reasons for it" (Piketty 2014, p. 19). Also (p. 31) he says "I have no interest in denouncing inequality or capitalism per se – especially since social inequalities are not in themselves a problem as long as they are justified", that is, "founded only upon common utility." The "common utility" of the French Revolution (General Will) trumps everything for Piketty.

PIKETTY AND THE PROBLEM OF INHERITANCE

One of Piketty's greatest challenges to those who hold the Liberty Narrative is to explain and defend the liberty position on inheritance. We would reinforce his challenge by emphasizing what he hardly mentions, namely, that the Liberty Narrative, not just the Equality Narrative, is based on a critique of the ancient/feudalism distribution of property that had no link to earning or merit. He is correct to base the Equality

Narrative in that critique, but he does not address the not too subtle differences between the two narratives on inheritance over the last two centuries. In other words, where do the Liberty Narrative and the Equality Narrative part company? It is clear they were allies at a critical moment. He does not help us with this question.

This is the point to recall that J.S. Mill in his *Political Economy* prefers the American model because in America distribution is voluntary rather than forced. Doesn't the liberty principle suggest that I can give my inheritance unequally to family members? Piketty's response is that equal distribution within the family was the norm in the US. He is correct that both the American and French Revolutions were based on the premise that the earth belonged to the living, but surely the attitude toward the past was different in both countries? The French attitude was hostile! And he doesn't raise and answer the question when and why voluntary rather than forced inheritance came to pass in America so that today there is virtually no serious inheritance law at all. We totally agree that inheritance is a major issue for the continued case for both capitalism and socialism and those like Piketty who want to move into new paradigms.

Piketty suggests from time to time that if we let people make their own choices then (growing) inequality will be the outcome in society. This seems to us to be saying that legal and constitutional provisions for equality are insufficient. More than voluntary consent is needed and force is justified to secure equality. Is he going so far as to suggest that people will not live in accordance with certain well laid down principles? Thus we need government to require them to behave in accordance with the vital principle of equality. But why would the people elect officials who pushed equality on them if they were naturally disposed to equality in the first place? Wouldn't such a people punish officials who deviated from equality? So the job of a representative is basically, not just prudentially, to ignore the inclinations of the people toward liberty? Is it ever wrong under the Piketty model for the representatives to inform the people that they are asking for too much equality? What happens if the population doesn't want higher taxation and it takes an emergency like a war or a depression – shocks – to get taxes supported?

Piketty admits that his formula doesn't fully explain the past 100 years. Chris Giles, the economics editor of the *Financial Times*, has argued that wealth inequality has not risen over the past 30 years and that the US does not have a more unequal distribution of wealth than Europe. World poverty, measured absolutely, has fallen, between 1970 and 2006, from 27 percent to 5 percent. Social mobility among members of the children of the bottom 20 percent in the US has increased from 1969 to 2005, so that 82 percent of those children have higher (real) incomes than their parents had in 1969.

There is, if you like, an alternative Lockean Liberty historical narrative. Germany and Japan have become economic powerhouses post World War II because they were lucky enough to be defeated by the US and had market economies, limited governments and the rule of law 'imposed' on them by a Lockean inspired US. Hong Kong was the tail that wagged the Chinese mainland because it was lucky enough to be a Lockean inspired British colony. The same good fortune is to be found in Singapore, and lately India; a similar US inspired good fortune was the lot of South Korea and Taiwan. Former French colonies were not so lucky. The Cold War came to an end when Soviet leaders discovered they could not compete technologically or economically with the US. As Deidre McCloskey put it:

> The original and sustaining causes of the modern world were indeed ethical, not material. They were the widening adoption of two new ideas: the liberal economic idea of liberty for ordinary people and the democratic social idea of dignity for them. This, in turn, released human creativity from its ancient trammels. (McCloskey 2015, p. 8)

THE EQUALITY NARRATIVE REVISITED

What is driving Piketty is the very presence of inequality. He provides an economic interpretation of why there is inequality, but not an explanation, economic or otherwise, of why inequality is bad. He begins with the presumption that the French Declaration and Rawls are correct. Thus inequality is bad.

Inequality would be an economic policy problem if and only if present inequalities prevent individuals from bettering their life. Nowhere does Piketty demonstrate this to be the case. Moreover, many economists indicate in a variety of ways that income inequality does not translate into consumer inequality. The gap between John D. Rockefeller and a public school teacher in the 1930s was less than the present income gap between Bill Gates and a public school teacher now but the quality of life available in consumption has decreased remarkably. Wealth is not a static feature of financial assets; successful corporations come and go; wealthy families come and go; wealth consists of access to goods and services. By any objective measure, 'consumption' equality has increased dramatically.

Inequality is 'the' social problem. How so? Inequality undermines (a) class harmony (Piketty 2014, pp. 3, 30), (b) meritocratic values (pp. 3,

241) and (c) principles of social justice (pp. 26, 287). What exactly is social harmony (what exactly is the General Will)? Is there an empirical correlate to it or is it measured by the dissatisfaction expressed by a number of individuals? Which individuals? How many individuals?

There is in Piketty's mind no basis for claims that high wage inequalities are justified by merit and productivity (Piketty 2014, p. 417), and besides there is the conspiracy of managers who do not peg remuneration to the market. The suggestion that wage differentials reflect a conspiracy on the part of managers to rig the market for CEOs, and so on is a restatement of Rousseau's critique of Locke: the social contract is illegitimate because the powerful "haves" imposed it upon the weak "have-nots." Disproportionately high wages either reflect market forces (supply and demand) which do not reflect merit or they reflect a quasi-conspiracy on the part of managers to bid up their remuneration.

Piketty's objective is *not* to help those at the bottom; his objective is to achieve social harmony by taxing those at the top. There are lots of ways of helping those at the bottom increase their share of financial capital; we can, for example, let everyone invest their social security, or part of it as in Chile, rather than allow governments to spend social security revenues. The nightmare for Piketty is that the improvement of the bottom in absolute terms might only be possible through a market economy whose growth increases relative inequality; in other words, everybody's situation improves but only when the rich get richer than the poor get rich. Presumably this undermines social harmony. This is why there is no focus on increasing (g). This marks a return to the socialism of the nineteenth century.

To put it this way, the Lockean response to inequality is that future growth is what many if not most people want. We are therefore less concerned with our relative position and more concerned with our absolute improvement, and the technological project in conjunction with a market economy, limited government, and so on is how we shall achieve it. Relative inequality or social harmony is a concern if and only if that inequality prevents improvement in absolute growth. Nothing in Piketty's argument shows that to be the case.

Why would anyone think that market forces do not reflect merit? What sort of merit is not compatible with market norms? The only kind we can think of is academic merit. The rules for getting 100 percent on a test are clear and the rules for gaining an academic position, promotion, and tenure are clear (publishing in the "A" journals, and so on). As an academic, Piketty is most likely upset that academic merit is not equivalent to market merit. The theoretical critics of the market are always academics and their journalistic and media allies, even highly paid ones like Paul Krugman. Is this a serious argument or the pathology of envy (Oakeshott's anti-individual)?

Is there a range of inequality that is okay for Piketty? Yes, there is but only that which is consistent with the general welfare. And who decides the general welfare? Social justice accepts meritocracy (Piketty 2014, p. 3) as long as it is consistent with "common utility" and helps the "most disadvantaged social groups" (p. 480 reference to Rawls). This is not equality of opportunity in part because equality of opportunity does not guarantee that the gap between (r) and (g) will close. Piketty explains inequality by r>g. "This is the fundamental force for divergence" (p. 422). Forget market forces or universal suffrage as solutions for inequality. And he would rather not have a violent solution. *Why is it not central to his project that (g) rise?* He says it will be low for generations. He is disturbed that (g) will never rise as fast as (r).

Okay, but what if we tried to push (g) to rise. How would we do it? It won't happen says Piketty. He is not really interested in pushing (g) up because he thinks that (g) is pretty much stable. He is more interested in closing the gap between (r) and (g) by claiming that (g) will never catch up with (r) and thus we must reduce (r). How do we know this? "[T]here is no historical example of a country at the world technological frontier whose growth in per capita output exceeded 1.5% over a lengthy period of time" (Piketty 2014, p. 93). Can there be alternative interpretations for this statistic? After all, Piketty supplements his statistics with historical interpretation. Here is a possible (Oakeshottean) interpretation: Growth eventually slows down in advanced countries because anti-individuals vote for democratic-socialist candidates who promise the redistribution of wealth. Unscrupulous politicians can tap into a residue of resentment on the part of most citizens even in advanced democratic societies because the majority of voters are ignorant of economics (not required even of most college graduates) and still believe that there is a fixed economic pie in which the only way to increase one's share of the pie is to take some from others.

The moral claim to reduce r>g is equality. And the moral source is the French Revolution's embrace of equality and Rawls' theory of justice. And although he often links justice and efficiency, with a touch of transparency and democracy, one suspects that justice trumps if a priority has to be made. Europe he says has never been so rich. "What is true and shameful, on the other hand, is that this vast national wealth is very unequally distributed. Private wealth rests on public poverty" (Piketty 2014, p. 567). But the solution must be made "after democratic debate" (p. 567).

Why should the debate be "democratic"? Or, shouldn't the participants in the debate have some knowledge of economics or the different theories of political economy? Who should provide this knowledge or how should it be acquired? Should it be acquired from private education (a market economy in schooling)? Or government-provided and government-run schooling? Should the debate also be preceded by sensitivity training?

PIKETTY AND ROUSSEAU

Piketty's framework is Rousseauean: poverty replaces profit as the central category of political economic inquiry. What do "we" do with the poor? What do "we" do with the marginalized? Where is "our" social conscience? What is the cause of the poverty of a nation becomes the focus, not what is the cause of the *wealth* of a nation. Piketty also follows the Rousseauean script but with some modifications: (1) although the market economy is not structurally and intentionally "rigged" in favor of the 1 percent there is still an element of villainy in the form of collusion on the part of managers; (2) some degree of inequality is acceptable but how much is never specified except by appeal to another abstraction, namely from Rawls; (3) those that are disadvantaged are somehow always victims; (4) there are no market solutions or legal solutions to public policy issues only political solutions; and (5) the exact institutional structure of the post-Piketty world is never specified except that it will be global.

The *Washington Post* reports, as stated by Andrew Stuttford, December 12, 2015 (retrieved from www.nationalreview.com/corner), Piketty wrote in *Le Monde* that inequality is a major driver of Middle East terrorism and the West have themselves largely to blame. Those who espouse the Equality Narrative attribute the source of the terrorism issue to economic inequality. On the other hand, those who espouse the Liberty Narrative maintain that economic, political, and religious liberty are intimately related. The espousers of the Liberty Narrative would therefore maintain that the lack of religious liberty in the Islamic world is the cultural origin of the problem.

The conversation goes on between the Liberty Narrative and the Equality Narrative.

References

d'Alembert, J.B. (1759) *Melanges de Philosophie*, Volume IV, philosophique, historique et critique. The Hague.

Ashley, A. (1692) *Some considerations of the consequences of the lowering of interest, and raising the value of money. In a letter to a Member of Parliament [i.e. Sir John Somers]*. London, printed for Awnsham and John Churchill.

Bacon, Sir Francis ([1627] 1991) *New Atlantis* and *The Great Instauration*. Oxford: Wiley-Blackwell: 1991 revised edition edited by J. Weinberger.

Beard, C. (1913) *An Economic Interpretation of the US Constitution*. New York: Simon & Schuster.

Becker, C. (1962) *The Heavenly City of the Eighteenth Century Philosophers*. New Haven: Yale University Press.

Bentham, J. (1843) *Manual of Political Economy*. Amazon Kindle.

Capaldi, N. and Lloyd, G. (2011) *The Two Narratives of Political Economy*. Co-published by Hoboken, NJ: John Wiley & Sons, and Salem, MA: Scrivener Publishing.

Carnap, R. (1929) *The Scientific Conception of the World (Manifesto)*. Retrieved on January 6, 2015 from http://againstpolitics.com/the-scientific-conception-of-the-world-the-vienna-circle/.

Carnap, R. (1963) "My philosophical development," in P.A. Schilpp (ed.), *The Philosophy of Rudolf Carnap*. LaSalle, IL: Open Court.

Collingwood, R.G. (1945) *The Idea of Nature*. Oxford: Clarendon Press.

Condorcet ([1795] 1955) *Sketch for a Historical Picture of The Progress of the Human Mind*. New York: Noonday Press.

Constant, B. ([1819] 1988) "The liberty of the ancients compared with that of the moderns" in B. Fontana (ed.), *The Political Writings of Benjamin Constant*. Cambridge: Cambridge University Press, pp. 309–28.

Descartes, R. ([1637] 2014) *Discourse on Method. The Essential Collection*. Copenhagen: Titan Read.

Descartes, R. (1991) *The Philosophical Writings of Descartes Volume III*. Translated by Cottingham, J., Stoothoff, R., Kenny, A., and Murdoch, D. Cambridge: Cambridge University Press, p. 275.

Dicey, A.V. ([1885] 2008) *Lectures on the Relation Between Law and Public Opinion in England during the Nineteenth Century*. Indianapolis: Liberty Fund.

Engels, F. ([1844] 2009) *The Condition of the Working Class in England*. Oxford: Oxford Classics.

Engels, F. ([1880] 1978) *Socialism: Utopian and Scientific. Marx–Engels Reader*. Edited by Richard Tucker. New York: Norton.

Engels, F. ([1887] 1978) *Anti-Dühring. Marx–Engels Reader*. Edited by Richard Tucker. New York: Norton.

France (1789) French *Declaration of the Rights of Man and the Citizen*.

France (1789, 1791, 1793, 1795) Constitution.

Friedman, M. (1962) *Capitalism and Freedom*. Chicago, IL: University of Chicago Press.

Fukuyama, F. (1992) *The End of History and the Last Man*. Glencoe, IL: Free Press.

Fuller, T. (1991) *Rationalism in Politics and Other Essays*. Indianapolis: Liberty Fund.

Galbraith, J.K. (1952) *American Capitalism: The Concept of Countervailing Power*. Boston, MA: Houghton Mifflin Company.

Galbraith, J.K. ([1958] 1998) *The Affluent Society*. New York: Houghton Mifflin.

Galbraith, J.K. (1967) *The New Industrial State*. Princeton, NJ: Princeton University Press.

Galeano, E. (1971) *Open Veins of Latin America; Five Centuries of the Pillage of the Continent*. Uruguay: Monthly Review.

Hamilton, A., Jay, J., and Madison, J. ([1787–88] 2004) *The Federalist Papers* (ed. C. Rossiter). New York: Signet.

Hampshire, S. (1972) "A Special Supplement: A New Philosophy of the Just Society," *New York Review of Books*. February 24.

Harrington, M. (1962) *The Other America*. New York: Macmillan.

Hayek, F. (1937) "Economics and Knowledge," *Economica* (February), I. 3.1.

Hayek, F. (1944) *The Road to Serfdom*. London: Routledge.

Hayek, F. (1945) "The Use of Knowledge in Society," *The American Economic Review*, 35(4): 519–30.

Hayek, F. (1973) *Law, Legislation, and Liberty*. Volume I. Chicago, IL: University of Chicago Press.

Hayek, F. (1976) *Law, Legislation, and Liberty*. Volume II. Chicago, IL: University of Chicago Press.

Hayek, F. (1979) *Law, Legislation, and Liberty*. Volume III. Chicago, IL: University of Chicago Press.

Hayek, F. (1988) *The Fatal Conceit*. Chicago, IL: University of Chicago Press.

Hayek, F. (2010) *Studies on the Abuse and Decline of Reason*. London: Routledge.

Hegel, G.W.F. ([1807] 1977) *Phenomenology of Spirit*. Oxford: Oxford University Press.

Hegel, G.W.F. ([1820] 1991) *Philosophy of Right*. Cambridge: Cambridge University Press.

Hegel, G.W.F. ([1837] 1976) *Lectures on the Philosophy of World History*. Cambridge: Cambridge University Press.

Hoover, H. (1935) Constitution Day speech "Hoover's Warning of the Perils of Liberty" *New York Times*, September 18.

Hume, D. ([1751] 1902) *An Enquiry Concerning the Principles of Morals* (ed. L.A. Selby-Bigge), 2nd edition. Oxford: Clarendon Press.

Hume, D. ([1752] 1987) "On Commerce," in E. Miller (ed.), *Hume: Essays, Moral, Political, and Literary*. Indianapolis, Liberty Fund.

Jevons, W.S. (1862) *A General Mathematical Theory of Political Economy*. Amazon Kindle.

de Jouvenel, B. ([1952] 1990) *The Ethics of Redistribution*. Indianapolis: Liberty Fund.

Kant, I. ([1781] 1999) *Critique of Pure Reason*. Cambridge: Cambridge University Press.

Kant, I. ([1793] 1974) *On the Old Saw: That may be right in theory, but it won't work in practice*. Philadelphia: University of Pennsylvania Press.

Kant, I. ([1793] 1999) *Religion within the Limits of Reason Alone*. Cambridge: Cambridge University Press.

Kant, I. ([1795] 1991) *Perpetual Peace. Political Writings*. Cambridge: Cambridge University Press.

Kant, I. ([1797] 1991) *Metaphysics of Morals*. Cambridge: Cambridge University Press.

Kant, I. (1991) *Collected Works* (ed. H. Reiss). Cambridge: Cambridge University Press.

Kelsen, H. (1934) *Pure Theory of Law*. Leipzig and Vienna: Deuticke.

Keynes, J.M. (1926) *The End of Laissez Faire*. London: Hogarth.

Keynes, J.M. (1931) *Essays in Persuasion*. London: Macmillan.

Keynes, J.M. (1932) *Collected Works*. Cambridge: Cambridge University Press.

Keynes, J.M. ([1936] 2007) *The General Theory of Employment, Interest and Money*. London: Macmillan.

Lloyd, G. (2006) *Two Faces of Liberalism*. Salem, MA: Scrivener.

Locke, J. ([1689] 1960) *Two Treatises of Government* (ed. P. Laslett). Cambridge: Cambridge University Press.

Locke, J. ([1689] 1983) *A Letter Concerning Toleration*. Indianapolis: Hackett.

Locke, J. ([1690] 1979) *An Essay Concerning Human Understanding*. Oxford: Oxford University Press.

Locke, J. (1692) *Some Considerations on the Consequences of the Lowering of Interest and the Raising of the Value of Money*. Retrieved on January 6, 2016 from http://oll.libertyfund.org/titles/763.

Locke, J. ([1695] 2012) *A Vindication of the Reasonableness of Christianity*. Oxford: Oxford University Press.

Lukes, S. (2003) "Epilogue: The grand dichotomy of the twentieth century," in T. Ball and R. Bellamy (eds), *Cambridge History of Twentieth Century Political Thought*. Cambridge: Cambridge University Press, pp. 602–26.

Mao, Z. ([1937] 1967) *Combat Liberalism*. Shanghai: Foreign Language Press.

Mao, Z. (1960) *Long Live Leninism*. Peking: Foreign Language Press.

Marshall, A. (1890) *Principles of Economics*. London: Macmillan.

Marshall, J. Chief Justice (1819) *McCulloch v Maryland*.

Marx, K. ([1844] 1978) *Economic and Philosophic Manuscripts*, in *Marx–Engels Reader* (ed. R. Tucker). New York: Norton.

Marx, K. ([1844] 1978) *On the Jewish Question*, in *Marx–Engels Reader* (ed. R. Tucker). New York: Norton.

Marx, K. ([1845] 1978) *Theses on Feuerbach*, in *Marx–Engels Reader* (ed. R. Tucker). New York: Norton.

Marx, K. ([1847] 1978) *The German Ideology*, in *Marx–Engels Reader* (ed. R. Tucker). New York: Norton.

Marx, K. ([1847] 1978) *The Poverty of Philosophy*, in *Marx–Engels Reader* (ed. R. Tucker). New York: Norton.

Marx, K. ([1848] 1978) *The Communist Manifesto*, in *Marx–Engels Reader* (ed. R. Tucker). New York: Norton (English edition published 1888).

Marx, K. ([1852] 1978) *The Eighteenth Brumaire of Louis Napoleon*, in *Marx–Engels Reader* (ed. R. Tucker). New York: Norton.

Marx, K. ([1859] 1978) *A Contribution to the Critique of Political Economy*, in *Marx–Engels Reader* (ed. R. Tucker). New York: Norton.

Marx, K. ([1863] 1978) *Theories of Surplus Value*, in *Marx–Engels Reader* (ed. R. Tucker). New York: Norton.

Marx, K. ([1867] 1978) *Das Kapital*, Volume I, in *Marx–Engels Reader* (ed. R. Tucker). New York: Norton. Volumes II in 1893 and III in 1894 both published posthumously by Engels.

Marx, K. ([1871] 1978) *The Civil War in France*, in *Marx–Engels Reader* (ed. R. Tucker). New York: Norton.

Marx, K. ([1875] 1978) *Critique of the Gotha Programme*, in *Marx–Engels Reader* (ed. R. Tucker). New York: Norton.

Marx, K. ([1884] 1978) *The Origin of the Family, Private Property and the State*, in *Marx–Engels Reader* (ed. R. Tucker). New York: Norton.

Marx, K. and Engels, F. (1975–2005) *Collected Works*. London: Lawrence and Wishart.

McCloskey, D. (2015) "How Piketty Misses the Point," CATO Policy Report July/August.

Mill, J.S. ([1836] 1977) *Civilization* in *Collected Works* XVIII. Toronto: University of Toronto Press.

Mill, J.S. ([1848] 1965) *Principles of Political Economy* in *Collected Works* II–III. Toronto: University of Toronto Press.

Mill, J.S. ([1859] 1977) *On Liberty* in *Collected Works* XVIII. Toronto: University of Toronto Press.

Mill, J.S. ([1861] 1969) *Utilitarianism* in *Collected Works* X. Toronto: University of Toronto Press.

Mill, J.S. ([1861] 1977) *Considerations on Representative Government* in *Collected Works* XIX. Toronto: University of Toronto Press.

Mill, J.S. ([1865] 1979) *An Examination of the Philosophy of Sir William Hamilton* in *Collected Works* IX. Toronto: University of Toronto Press.

Mill, J.S. ([1867] 1984) *Inaugural Address at Saint Andrews* in *Collected Works* XXI. Toronto: University of Toronto Press.

Mill, J.S. ([1869] 1984) *On the Subjection of Women* in *Collected Works* XXI. Toronto: University of Toronto Press.

Mill, J.S. ([1873] 1980) *Autobiography* in *Collected Works* I. Toronto: University of Toronto Press.

Mill, J.S. ([1874] 1969) *Nature* in *Collected Works* X. Toronto: University of Toronto Press.

Mill, J.S. ([1879] 1967) *Chapters on Socialism* in *Collected Works* V. Toronto: University of Toronto Press.

Needham, J. ([1954] 1984) *Science and Civilization in China, Volume II, History of Scientific Thought*. Cambridge: Cambridge University Press.

Neurath, O. ([1919] 1973) *Through War Economy to Economy in Kind*. Munich: Calwey, reprinted in M. Neurath and R.S. Cohen (eds), *Empiricism and Sociology*. Dordrecht: Reidl.

Oakeshott, M. (1933) *Experience and Its Modes*. Cambridge: Cambridge University Press.

Oakeshott, M. ([1947] 1991) "Rationalism in Politics," in T. Fuller (ed.), *Rationalism in Politics and Other Essays*. Indianapolis: Liberty Fund, pp. 5–42.

Oakeshott, M. ([1949] 1991) "The Political Economy of Freedom," in T. Fuller (ed.), *Rationalism in Politics and Other Essays*. Indianapolis: Liberty Fund, pp. 384–406.

Oakeshott, M. ([1956] 1991) "On Being Conservative," in T. Fuller (ed.), *Rationalism in Politics and Other Essays*. Indianapolis: Liberty Fund, pp. 407–37.

Oakeshott, M. ([1961] 1991) "The Masses in Representative Democracy," in T. Fuller (ed.), *Rationalism in Politics and Other Essays*. Indianapolis: Liberty Fund, pp. 363–83.

Oakeshott, M. (1975) *On Human Conduct*. Oxford: Oxford University Press.

Oakeshott, M. ([1983] 1999) "Rule of Law" in *On History and Other Essays*. Indianapolis: Liberty Fund.

Oakeshott, M. (1996) *The Politics of Faith and the Politics of Scepticism*. New Haven: Yale University Press.

Owen, R. ([1816] 2013) *New View of Society*. CreateSpace Independent Publishing Platform.

Piketty, T. (2014) *Capital in the Twenty-First Century*. Cambridge, MA: Harvard University Press.

Piketty, T. (2015) "About Capital in the Twenty-First Century," *American Economic Review*, 105(5): 48–53.

Popper, K. (1963) *Conjectures and Refutations*. London: Routledge.

Proudhon, P.J. ([1840] 1994) *What is Property? Or an Inquiry into the Principle of Right and of Government* (also called his *First Memoir*). Cambridge: Cambridge University Press.

Proudhon, P.J. ([1847] 2011) *The Philosophy of Poverty*. Calgary: Theophania Publishing.

Rawls, J. (1971) *A Theory of Justice*. Cambridge, MA: Harvard University Press.

Rawls, J. (1993) *Political Liberalism*. Cambridge, MA: Harvard University Press.

Rawls, J. (2001) *Justice as Fairness: A Restatement*. Cambridge, MA: Harvard University Press.

Robbins, L. (1935) *An Essay on the Nature and Significance of Economic Science*. London: MacMillan and Co.

Robespierre, M. (1794) "On the Principles of Political Morality." Retrieved on January 6, 2016 from http://legacy.fordham.edu/halsall/mod/1794robespierre.asp.

Rousseau, J.J. ([1750] 2014) *Discourse on the Arts and Sciences* in *The Major Political Writings of Jean Jacques Rousseau*. Chicago: University of Chicago Press.

Rousseau, J.J. ([1754] 2014) *Discourse on Inequality* in *The Major Political Writings of Jean Jacques Rousseau*. Chicago: University of Chicago Press.

Rousseau, J.J. ([1755] 2009) *Economie Politique*, also known as *Discourse on Political Economy*. Oxford: Oxford University Press.

Rousseau, J.J. ([1762] 2014) *The Social Contract* in *The Major Political Writings of Jean Jacques Rousseau*. Chicago: University of Chicago Press.

Rousseau, J.J. ([1762] 2015) *Le bonheur public*. Political Writings. Volume 1. Oxford: Facsimile Publisher.

Rousseau, J.J. ([1762] 1979) *Emile*, or *On Education*. New York: Basic Books.

Rousseau, J.J. ([1772] 2008) *Considerations on the Government of Poland*. New York: Evergreen Review.

Rousseau, J.J. ([1782] 2011) *Reveries of a Solitary Walker*. Oxford: Oxford University Press.

Rousseau, J.J. (1986) *The First and Second Discourses*. New York: Harper & Row.

Saint-Simon, H. (1803) *Geneva Letters*. Retrieved on January 6, 2016 from www.marxists.org/reference/subject/philosophy/works/fr/st-simon.htm.

Saint-Simon, H. (1825) *Nouveau Christianisme*. Paris: Bossange Pere.

Smith, A. ([1759] 1978) *Theory of Moral Sentiments* in *The Glasgow Edition of the Works and Correspondence of Adam Smith*. Oxford: Oxford University Press.

Smith, A. ([1762–63] 1978) *Lectures on Jurisprudence* (A) in *The Glasgow Edition of the Works and Correspondence of Adam Smith*, Volume V. Oxford: Oxford University Press.

Smith, A. ([1763–64] 1978) *Lectures on Jurisprudence* (B) in *The Glasgow Edition of the Works and Correspondence of Adam Smith*, Volume V. Oxford: Oxford University Press.

Smith, A. ([1776] 1978) *Wealth of Nations* in *The Glasgow Edition of the Works and Correspondence of Adam Smith*, Volume II. Oxford: Oxford University Press.

Smith, A. (1982) "History of Astronomy," II, 12 in *Essays on Philosophical Subjects*. Indianapolis: Liberty Fund.

de Soto, H. (2000) *The Mystery of Capital: Why Capitalism Succeeds in the West and Fails Everywhere Else*. New York: Basic Books.

Tocqueville, A. de ([1835] 2006) *Memoir on Pauperism: Does Public Charity Produce an Idle and Dependent Class of Society?* New York: Cosimo Classics.

Tocqueville, A. de ([1835] 2010) *Democracy in America*. Volume I. Indianapolis: Liberty Fund.

Tocqueville, A. de ([1840] 2010) *Democracy in America*. Volume II. Indianapolis: Liberty Fund.

Tucker, R. (1978) *The Marx–Engels Reader* (2nd edition). New York: Norton.

US (1776) *Declaration of Independence.*
US (1789) *Constitution.*
US (1791) Bill of Rights.

Index

'This book is a timely and very scholarly reminder that we must not trade liberty for equality. To begin with, liberty is valuable for its own sake – not everything can be valued in terms of dollars and cents. Furthermore, it is the poor who will suffer in the long run if the West begins to trade more equality for less liberty. This book is a very welcome corrective to current debates which could lead to the enslavement of free peoples.'

Philip Booth, St. Mary's University, UK

'Read this articulate adventure in Liberty, from John Locke through Adam Smith to Thomas Piketty.'

Vernon Smith, Chapman University, USA and 2002 Nobel Laureate in Economics